CW00552945

SOUND FELLOWS

The Story of York Philharmonic Male Voice Choir

Colin Hockridge

Colin Hockridge 2016

© Colin Hockridge 2016
Published by Colin Hockridge

ISBN 978-1-5262-0363-2

Colin Hockridge hereby asserts and gives notice of his right under Section 77 of the Copyright, Designs and Patents Act 1988 to be identified as the author of this work. No part of this publication may be reproduced, stored in a retrieval system or transmitted in any form or by any means without prior written permission from the publisher.

Cover design by Linda Rodgers

Typeset, produced and printed by
Inc Dot Design & Print, Inc Dot House, Seafire Close
Clifton Moor York YO30 4UU Tel: 01904 477944 www.inc-dot.com

Contents

Introduction

York Philharmonic Male Voice Choir – known as the Phil – is a healthy, active choir singing up to 30 concerts a year in and around York. Since its modest beginnings in 1925, through national and international acclaim in the 1970s, and to the high reputation held today, the choir has always sought to entertain and to support local charities. It is then an ongoing story of which this book is an account of the first 90 years.

Unfortunately there are few formal philharmonic archives available as most were lost in the 1990s. So this history is unable, for example, to list all the officials and members throughout the years. However, the story can be told using as sources: an incomplete collection of choir magazines, known as *Philharmonic News* [PN] covering the years 1933-1938 and 1965-1974; the collection of York Old Priory Magazines known as *Notes and Views* [N&V] covering the period 1914-1939 held in the York Explore Archives; choir member scrapbooks and personal recollections; the published autobiography of Archie Sargent – *Voices Pipes and Pedals* [VPP]; and extracts from the diaries of his wife Janet, and the unpublished memoirs of William H Birch. The story of twinning with the male voice choir in Münster has been helped by a German publication *40 Jahre Partnerschaft 1968-2008* written by their member Ludger Voss. Information on Leeman Road Adult School and the Quaker Meeting sourced from records held at the Brotherton Library Leeds, with background material from 'The History of the Adult School Movement' (Rowntree and Binns: Headley 1903).

This has been written by a chorister so the language used does become more personal as the narrative progresses; for example 'the choir' in a sentence set in 1935 is more likely to be 'our choir' when describing 2005.

The book is divided around the three generations of music leaders. The first takes the story from 1925-1962, describing the high points of the 1930s, the extreme lows of the 1940s and the slow post war rebuild. This section also includes a chapter on the York Male Voice Choir, an older successful society which impacted on the Phil, not least in its choice of name. The second generation takes the story from 1962 to 1994 describing national and international acclaim. This is followed by extended chapters on 'Carols in Kirkgate' a series of Christmas concerts begun in 1962, televised in the 1970s and still as popular today; and the twinning with the Münsterscher Männergesangverein [MM] begun in 1968 and still a key part of choir life. The third and current generation brings the story up to date describing the continual refreshing of performances and ambition needed to keep standards high, audiences happy and a steady stream of new members.

Part One
The First Generation
1925-1962

As a white candle in a holy place,
So is the beauty of an aged face.
As the spent radiance of the winter sun,
So is a woman with her travail done...
The Old Woman: Campbell/Roberton – a 1930s 'hit'

Chapter 1
Cecil H. Fletcher

The early years (1925-29)

Setting the Scene

The York Philharmonic Male Voice Choir – the Phil – began life in 1925 as the Leeman Road Adult School Male Voice Choir (LRAS). It was formed by a handful of men in the front room of a small terraced house, whose only resource was their shared intention to become better singers.

Before 1900 there were few opportunities [other than churches for men and boys but with chapels including women] for most people to join a choir. However, from the turn of the century up to the Second World War, music societies formed and thrived in all manner of communities and settings.

This was made possible by both education and opportunity. By 1900 standards of education for the majority of the population, both by the state and through adult schools had greatly improved; and work-based neighbourhoods, such as Leeman Road, which had grown so much during the century, were maturing. Churches, social institutions, and major employers, were ready to support the forming of choirs and bands. So by 1900 these developing communities had a basic education and sufficient free time and disposable income to allow for joining societies. For musical groups, the mass printing of sheet music and ability to hire brass band instruments made it even more affordable – fuelling the growth. Three other choirs relevant to the history of the Phil formed at this time: York Male Voice in 1899, seemingly strong enough to maintain its independence; York Old Priory in 1898, linked to both the Wesleyan Chapel and the adult school; and Burton Stone Lane Male Voice in 1900, linked to the local working men's club. Other choirs of the period included the York Co-operative Choral Society and the Rowntree Choral Society. Monkgate Methodist Circuit also had a male voice choir (MVC) and most of the adult schools in the city had some form of musical society. A number of these ceased during the 1939-45 war. Only one society relevant to this story was formed after the war – the York St Lawrence MVC in 1947 – and today only two remain: York Old Priory, now known as York Priory Choir; and the York Phil.

As so many of the good choirs at this time were either church based or sponsored in some way, they could be described, in modern language, as being 'top down'. The Leeman Road choir was the opposite being 'bottom up'. A comparison with the Rowntree Choral Society illustrates this point. In 1932 the factory management invited Archie Sargent to set up and lead a factory choir: rehearsal facilities; a music budget; and one of the best choral conductors in the city were all in place before the first rehearsal. Compare that with the birth of the Phil, seven years earlier, a handful of men in the front room of a small terraced house in Leeman Road whose only resource was their mutual desire to be better singers.

The Leeman Road district of York was built to support the success and growth of the Victorian railway network. Sited between the river and the railway and close to the station and carriage works, it provided housing primarily for the many families linked to the industry. Locally it was often referred to as 'railway city'. There were no tree lined avenues of grand villas, and the lower parts of the district were always under threat of flooding from a swollen River Ouse. As will be noted a number of times in this narrative, during the years 1925-1935 the Phil grew from an enthusiastic group of four men to become one of the most significant male choirs in the region. It attracted new members from other musical societies in the city, singers who lived in other parts of town and newcomers. It is reasonable to assume that these men joined for the quality of the music, the culture and the comradeship and not for the quality of its rehearsal and local performing facilities.

Leeman Road Adult School

The Quaker sponsored Adult School opened in 1891. It was the first such branch in York, in that it was an offshoot of the central school in Lady Peckitt's Yard, and not part of an existing Quaker Meeting. The social club was developed between 1896 and 1898. York Quakers, in particular the Rowntree family, were deeply committed to the adult school movement, with individual members giving not just financial assistance, but also their time as administrators and teachers. Arnold Rowntree, nephew to Joseph and the youngest son of John Stephenson Rowntree, was committed to the school in Leeman Road. Before his marriage he lived in the district to better understand the people and the way in which the school might serve them. He remained steadfast in this support and was an invaluable help to the male voice choir, acting as its first President.

The early purpose of the adult school movement was to provide scriptural teaching and elementary education, meeting a need for the three Rs not then met by the state system. This requirement had passed its peaked around 1880 as state provision improved, and so social clubs and interest groups became the main focus of activity. The range of these was considerable including, for example, the provision of allotments. The Leeman Road School, as a teaching organisation, closed around 1928 but the social clubs continued.

A Quaker meeting was established at the school, but not until 1904 when it was felt that: *there was a considerable nucleus of thoughtful men and women who were connected with a large and vigorous adult school;* sufficient to make the venture viable. The society did not flourish and, with membership declining, closed in 1925. In the Meeting minutes of the time one reason given for the decline was 'upward mobility'; members were moving away from Leeman Road to the newer estates being developed within the city.

Leeman Road Adult School Male Voice Choir

The choir began when four men met in a modest terraced house in Leeman Road. They were: Tom Clark, in whose house they met; William Payne; Alf Boston and Harry Tallantyre. They were not young men. We know that Payne was 48 and was the longest living of the group, being photographed with the choir in 1967 at the age of 90. Tom was 41. He was, or had been, a member of York Old Priory Choir, and Harry Tallantyre may have been 44. They did not have a vision of a full sized choir but wanted to be a better group than they were.

One Sunday morning in April 1925 Alf Boston, who we know from a later reference had sung for Cecil Fletcher years earlier, Payne and Tallantyre took the ferry to Clifton to seek Cecil's help.

This picture shows the ferry crossing. The road bridge, which now stands alongside (to the right of this photo) was not opened until 1963

The three set out on a journey, a new adventure and what a success it turned out to be. It is not known how they made the inspired decision to invite Cecil Fletcher to be their leader. He was, without doubt, the perfect choice, and even 90 years later the Phil still feeds from the legacy of those early years. Described by one early chorister as being a '*genial man, who knew how to handle men and music,*' Cecil shaped and nurtured a choir which by 1939 had become one of the most significant in the region. Success in competition and concerts was enhanced by a culture of commitment to serve both its members and the wider community.

It would seem that Cecil, in agreeing to their request, had a greater vision and immediately set to work. Henry Brough recalled that in April 1925 Cecil was a member of a well known York concert party called 'The Follies', but Henry does not tell of any leadership role, if any, that he took in that group. Cecil immediately invited his fellow members to join the new venture. Three took up the offer: Jim Hardisty aged 20yrs; Harry Payne; and Henry Brough then only 17 yrs old. This was perhaps a measure of Cecil the leader as in this, his first decision, taken between his invitation and the first rehearsal he effectively doubled the size of the group, greatly reduced the average age, and introduced singers with talent and performing experience. Jim Hardisty became one of the best of the pre-war soloists. Henry, a bass soloist, sang with the choir for a total of 65 years. The expanded group was too large to fit Tom's front room so the embryonic choir immediately transferred to the welcoming and supportive Adult School. In 1977 Henry recalled that many of the early younger members came from the Boys Club at the School, but there was a range of ages within the choir. This was commented on in a PN article in February 1933 referring to inter-choir competitions: *Our 'Veteran Quartet' – the average age being somewhere about 63 – put up a remarkable performance in their try out the other night. They are entered in the quartet class at the Inter-Choir Choral contest and youngsters will have to look to their guns if they wish to lower the colours of the old stalwarts.*

At first, a member of the adult school played the piano for the choir, but within a few months Jane Brough, Henry's older sister, became the accompanist assisted by Kathleen, the younger sister.

The founding members were serious in their intent and immediately set up the society and established a management system. With the choir only three months old, records were already being maintained and practical issues addressed: *12th July 1925: Proposed that the conductor be allowed 6d per week for ferry fares. The secretary was asked to see the ferryman re. Cheap rates for members.*

The first archived photograph is a York Evening Press (YEP) cutting dated 1926-27. There are 27 choristers in this photo.

ALL OUR YESTERDAYS: The choir in 1926-27. Mr Brough is on the back row, third from the right, with the open-neck shirt. His sisters are on the front row. Jane, left, was accompanist and Kathleen was her assistant. They are sitting on either side of the then conductor, Mr Cecil Fletcher.

Jane Brough stayed as accompanist until the war, was a regular contributor to the choir magazine, and was also active in social events. Her contribution was acknowledged when she became the first of only four female Honorary Life Members of the Choir.

Although the school gave the choir a name the building was not able to meet its needs and a transfer to the Methodist Chapel in Albany Street soon followed. Nevertheless the school facilitated the fledgling group in many ways. The support of Arnold Rowntree as the first choir President was invaluable, and ensured that the structure of this new choral society was properly formed and managed. The network of adult schools also gave the new group immediate access to other interested parties. For example, a lasting friendship grew with James Street School as well as Old Priory and others.

This enthusiasm and support of all the people involved was needed to compensate for the poor quality of rehearsal premises. The facilities provided were much less than would have been available to many city-centred based societies.

Jane Brough described the difficulties faced during its first year:

THEN & NOW

Sitting at the piano last Monday evening whilst the choir were practising 'Hymn before Action', I had a sudden mind's eye picture of the then Leeman Road Adult School Male Voice Choir practising the same composition for their first appearance on the choral competition platform at the Yorkshire Choral Competition in 1926.

This particular piece has always been a favourite with us, perhaps because it brings back to the older members such happy memories of our intense delight and excitement when we were so successful as to be chosen to sing in the final evening session. We came away from that first competition feeling that we had indeed done well, not only in beating ten other choirs, but in being second to the York Old Priory Male Voice Choir who had beaten us by 20 marks.

The Class 'B' Male Voice for which we had entered was a decent sized class in those days, and we felt it was indeed a fine achievement for a choir of about 20 or so voices, most of them very inexperienced to have done so well at a first attempt.

Mr Fletcher had two pet phrases in this particular piece in those days. One was 'ere yet we draw the blade', and the other was 'Lord grant us strength to die' and I think members will agree with me that he has been most consistent in his concentration on these two phrases especially the latter one which is really the most important in the whole piece.

Looking back on those first few months of struggling against all manner of obstacles, including the fact that only two or three members knew anything at all about music or singing, that our practice room was far too small, and that we had to use a piano that was terribly out of tune,(a number of notes absolutely refused to play at all) it really does seem – when one looks round at the present choir of 40 men singing the piece with tunefulness and interpretation – that the Conductor, and the few faithful pioneers are reaping the reward of their hard work, and in these days of disillusionment it is cheering to have some of our ideals turning into actual realities. PN May 1934.

Cecil Harold Fletcher

Cecil Fletcher in 1935

In March 1946 Cecil Harold Fletcher, the founder conductor, died at the age of 51. The impact on the society was such that an extraordinary meeting was called and the choir adopted the additional title of 'The C.H. Fletcher Memorial Choir'. This designation, which still applies, was important to choir members at that time and remained in general use until the 1980s. Cecil Fletcher must have been greatly respected as a musician and loved as a person for such an honour to be bestowed. Yet in the oral and written records of the choir little is known about him, nor about his reputation or experience as a musician. He was not a professional musician, as were some of the conductors of York Male Voice choir; he is recorded as being an apprentice grocer, then a traveller (salesman) and latterly a civil servant. We have no idea why, as a young man of 31, he was asked to lead the fledgling choir, and what, if any, were his musical links to the Leeman Road district. In a later chapter, using extracts from the articles in the collection of

PN and N&V magazines from the 1930s, and also from the autobiography of Archie Sargent, we will get an understanding of Cecil both as conductor and friend; but what experience and qualities did he already have in 1925?

A search of the 1911 census shows Cecil Harold Fletcher aged 17, an apprenticed grocer, living at 31, Garfield Terrace, Leeman Road with his parents Thomas, a bricklayer; mother Dorothy; and his two younger sisters Doris and Gladys. Other families who were key to the success of the choir lived nearby: the Broughs in Hanover Street; the Hardisty family in Albany Street and Tom Clark in Roseberry Street; all three heads of these families worked for the railway. So Cecil was a local man and must have been known to many in the area. It is also difficult to imagine that these families did not have some contact with each other through the social groups in the adult school. We know, from descriptions of Christmas Eve Carol singing in the district, that Cecil played the violin, so can assume that he had displayed his musical talents whilst still a boy and young man.

In 1917 he married Alice Moss, a shop assistant, who in 1911 lived with her family at 10 Lavender Grove, about a mile away on the other side of the railway. Alice's father was a joiner at the carriage works. When called up to serve in the Durham Light infantry in 1916 Cecil gave his occupation as traveller. After the war Cecil and Alice moved across the river to live in Burton Stone Lane and raised two children, Harold – who later joined the choir – and Joyce. It seems that in 1927 Cecil's sister – Doris – married Alice's brother – Thomas – so a brother and sister married a sister and brother. There are references to choir members called Moss in the magazine collection.

First Concerts and Competitions

The first performing opportunities came with leading the singing at Sunday services at the adult school. The first competition entered was in May 1926 at the Yorkshire Choral Competition held in the Festival Concert Rooms – Male Voice Choir 'B' Class for smaller choirs. LRAS came second to York Old Priory. This was an excellent result, but there was still much improvement to be made as can be seen in this report from N&V July 1926:

In the MVC B class eleven choirs competed and Old Priory men retained possession of the W.H.Birch Shield. In so doing they recorded their third consecutive victory in this particular class. Although their competitors were not of such class as in the case of the Ladies class there is no doubt that our male section sang as they have never sung before and as a consequence their victory was of a runaway order.

B Class marks:

Old Priory	*93 + 93 total 186*
Leeman Road AS	*83 + 83 total 166*
Doncaster	*82 + 83 total 165*

York Old Priory Choir was a remarkable body formed by Jack Forster in 1897. It was an extremely successful society able to work as a mixed voice, female, or male choir. Tom Clark, a founder member of LRAS, had been an Old Priory member, and this coming together in competition in 1926, was the start of a close friendship between the two groups.

The following year, in the same competition, the Leeman Road choir, by a margin of two points, won its first award – The W.H. Birch Shield. This new choir was able to celebrate success in a very public way as recorded in N&V June 1927.

The exhibit of 8 Shields a Rose Bowl and a Silver Cup – the ten trophies at present held by York Choirs in Messrs. Oliver's window makes one wonder whether any city or town of the same size can boast such a record. Old Priory holds 4, York Male Voice Choir 3, Queen Anne's, James Street United and Leeman Road Adult School 1 each.

In October of 1927 Leeman Road Adult School Choir took second place in the B class at Scarborough Festival, losing out to the Hull Gleemen.

When, in the 1970s, Henry Brough recalled these early days, he had fond memories of the regular contests with Hull Gleeman at Scarborough. It was at one of these that an enthusiastic conductor, a blacksmith by trade, swiped his music stand with one hand, caught it with the other, and didn't miss a beat.

At this time competitions comprised two performances. There were two set test pieces. A good result in the early session with the first test piece meant your choir was invited to sing the second in the evening session, at which time the cups and prizes could be won. There was also a means by which adjudicators could speed up the event by ringing a bell and stopping a poor performance. The test pieces had to be dissimilar. For example, in the competition of 1926 LRAS sang *Hymn before Action* in the afternoon and the madrigal *How merrily we live* in the evening. Competition success could also boost a choir's finances. In the York Choral Festival of 1926 the prize money for success in the Yorkshire Challenge Cup (A class competition for larger choirs) was considerable; 12 guineas for first place, eight for second and four for third. To put that into context the members' subscriptions for singing with the LRAS was 3d per rehearsal attended; so a first prize A Class win would yield the same income as 1008 weekly subs.

The choir also enjoyed 'outings' which were subsidised by the money raised by Christmas Eve Carol singing. It could be that they did this in their own style as in June 1927 N&V noted that: *LRAS mixed business with pleasure on Whit Monday by visiting Scarborough and by giving a performance in Peasholme Park.* This was thought to be *'a great idea'*.

What's in a name?

The growing choir identified itself with its location as, indeed, did almost all such groups. The Leeman Road Adult School Male Voice Choir was neither the shortest nor easiest title to advertise or report and so the name evolved. Concerts at this time would not have merited much press interest, but competitions were covered. In such reports the 'Male Voice' part of the name was superfluous and so the name shortened to Leeman Road Adult School Choir. This was the title used by the Yorkshire Herald in May 1927. With limited space and single column reports this was often abbreviated to LRAS. We don't know what the choir called itself in those days, but it may have been comfortable with this designation. It is not difficult to imagine steam engine driver and bass singer Henry Brough declaring that he worked for the LNER and sang with the LRAS. Although LRAS was suitable for use in York it was not accurate enough when the choir competed elsewhere. So York was added as a prefix, the choir being reported as York LRAS.

We have no record of the debate that must have taken place over the ambitious and significant next change of name, but the critical date is known. The choir had moved out of the adult school to better facilities at Albany Street Chapel, and was growing in size, quality, confidence and ambition. A culture had been established in which it strove to succeed both in competition, and in serving the community by performing as many concerts as feasible. The choir, whilst representing the city in competitions across Yorkshire would also, for example, give concerts to the inmates of the York Institution (the Workhouse). Most of the choirs close to LRAS had titles linked either to a chapel or an adult school e.g. Victoria Bar or Old Priory.

But there was also York Male Voice Choir, a prestigious and very ambitious competition choir. Although it is thought that its origins lay in the Melbourne Terrace Methodist Chapel, it adopted a name to suit its ambitions and identified itself immediately with the city. For the LRAS to change its name to the York Philharmonic Male Voice Choir was a bold move but one which proved its worth. The inclusion of the word 'philharmonic' not only delineated the two male choirs by name but also by culture. The sense of the inclusive nature and passion of 'philharmonic' matched the culture of LRAS.

With the term philharmonic often being used in the title of many prestigious orchestras and choirs, its inclusion in a choir still only five years old also reflected the confidence of Cecil and his team. In a meeting held on 2nd November 1929 the new name was adopted; Henry Brough was elected to the committee and subscriptions were raised from 1d to 3d per week. *Notes and Views* used the new title first in February 1930.

It appeared in the local press in March, when the re-titled choir gained its first competition success: the Wilson Shield at the Barnsley Music Festival. In May YPMVC won the Rose Bowl and £8 at the Scarborough Festival. Between these two dates on the 6th May in the York Choral Competitions, the York Philharmonic Male Voice Choir took second place to the Hull Gleemen in the W.H. Birch Challenge Shield; Hull scored 88 & 86; YPMVC 85 & 85.

There is a chorister's report of other parts of that day in Scarborough not covered by the press:

After travelling by train to Scarborough the next rendezvous was to be the Roscoe Rooms for a final try out, this was anything but promising. However, like at Barnsley in March, we had something up our sleeves beating the redoubtable Hull Gleemen by 2 points and securing the rosebowl for York. Celebrated in the Spa buffet. The bowl was then filled with wine and the members gathered round the conductor congratulating him.

There was an unexpected bonus in adopting the new name, one still enjoyed today. Almost immediately the choir became known as 'the philharmonic' or, more often, the Phil, a short familiar title which has always evoked a feeling of friendship and closeness with the society.

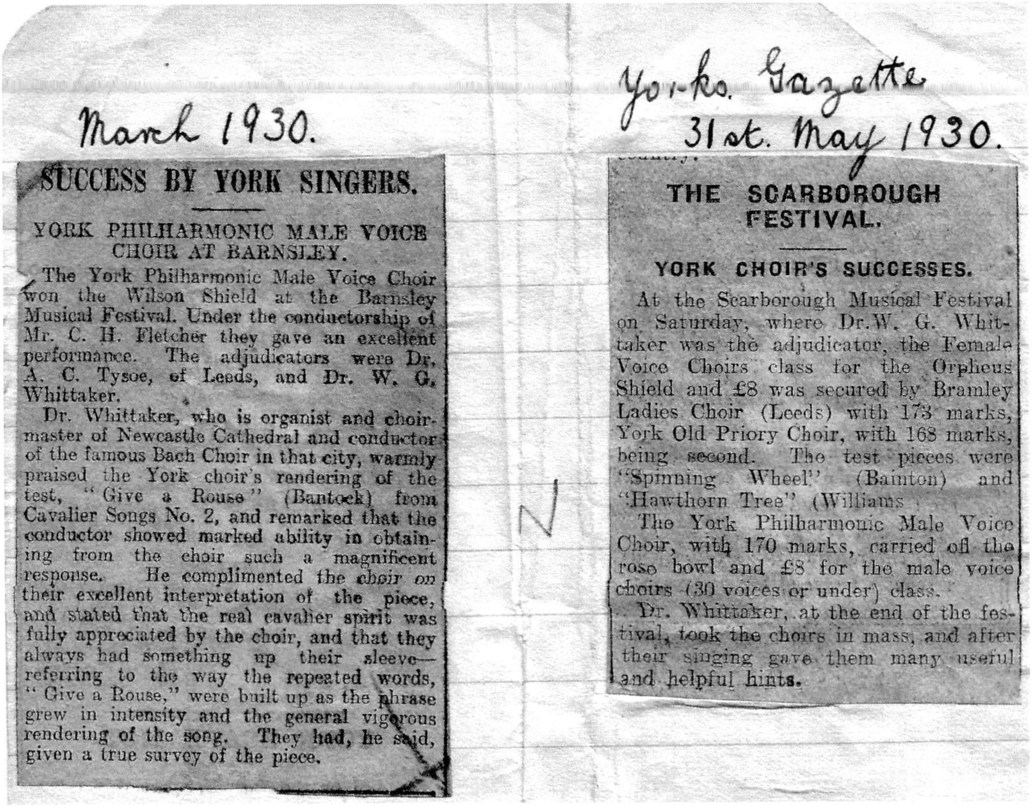

March 1930.

SUCCESS BY YORK SINGERS.

YORK PHILHARMONIC MALE VOICE CHOIR AT BARNSLEY.

The York Philharmonic Male Voice Choir won the Wilson Shield at the Barnsley Musical Festival. Under the conductorship of Mr. C. H. Fletcher they gave an excellent performance. The adjudicators were Dr. A. C. Tysoe, of Leeds, and Dr. W. G. Whittaker.

Dr. Whittaker, who is organist and choirmaster of Newcastle Cathedral and conductor of the famous Bach Choir in that city, warmly praised the York choir's rendering of the test, "Give a Rouse" (Bantock) from Cavalier Songs No. 2, and remarked that the conductor showed marked ability in obtaining from the choir such a magnificent response. He complimented the choir on their excellent interpretation of the piece, and stated that the real cavalier spirit was fully appreciated by the choir, and that they always had something up their sleeve—referring to the way the repeated words, "Give a Rouse," were built up as the phrase grew in intensity and the general vigorous rendering of the song. They had, he said, given a true survey of the piece.

Yorks. Gazette 31st. May 1930.

THE SCARBOROUGH FESTIVAL.

YORK CHOIR'S SUCCESSES.

At the Scarborough Musical Festival on Saturday, where Dr. W. G. Whittaker was the adjudicator, the Female Voice Choirs class for the Orpheus Shield and £8 was secured by Bramley Ladies Choir (Leeds) with 173 marks, York Old Priory Choir, with 168 marks, being second. The test pieces were "Spinning Wheel" (Bainton) and "Hawthorn Tree" (Williams.

The York Philharmonic Male Voice Choir, with 170 marks, carried off the rose bowl and £8 for the male voice choirs (30 voices or under) class.

Dr. Whittaker, at the end of the festival, took the choirs in mass, and after their singing gave them many useful and helpful hints.

1930-1939 – a remarkable decade

A review of the 1930s cannot be made without reference to two other choirs and two other conductors: York Old Priory led by Jack Forster; and Monkgate Methodist Choir led by Archie Sargent. The impact that Cecil, Jack and Archie and their three choirs had on the musical life of the city was so significant it was acknowledged by Arnold Rowntree in a speech reported in the Easter 1938 edition of CWM – the Cocoa Works Magazine.

Just as Vienna was a city of music so York was known all over for its music. He thought the city was favoured in having in its midst three men who had brought choral music to a very high standard. There was Jack Forster, Mr. Sargent and Mr. Fletcher; he liked to think of the value and the service to the city that they had rendered.

Some biographical details of Cecil Fletcher have already been given. He was the only York born one of the three and was 36 years old in 1930. There is one written record of Cecil describing his conducting style, and this appeared in *Notes and Views* February 1937. By this time the Phil was a mature choir needing to adjust to its increasing status. This led to the introduction of contracts for singers, detailing what the choir could offer the members, and what the choir expected in return – a move designed to encourage the 'part attendees'. The decade saw the introduction of a choir badge, and the first entry into a class A large choir competition. Not surprisingly, Cecil's article reflected this as he talked about work-load and rehearsal schedules. It is, perhaps, a different piece to one he may have written ten years earlier, but the essence of his style emerged. *I like to allow them to have a good sing and not to constantly stop for corrections.* The choir was allowed to enjoy a song and then a discussion could be had to discuss improvements. The article ended with the plea to all who take up a conductor's baton to remember and practise the three essentials – *music first, choir second, himself [the conductor] a humble third.*

J.H. [Jack] Forster J.P. [aged 62 in 1930] was the eldest of the three. Born in Scotland he had lived most of his life in York where he owned a successful mineral water business – Forster and Coverdale. In 1897 he founded the York Old Priory Choir. This was also born from an adult school class and started with a modest 13 members. At first it was known as the 'Priory Street Class Choir' or informally as 'Jack Forster's Choir'. In 1908 it adopted the title Old Priory Choir and in 1926 added the prefix York. Its aim was to *give its services to worthy causes and to compete in occasional competitions.* Jack led it with great success for more than 40 years. Other members of the family were also involved. Duncan, his only son, became the accompanist in 1914 at the tender age of 14. Later, as his voice developed, he also sang bass, and additionally served the choir as Concert Secretary. His sister, Eve, served the choir as librarian. Duncan met and married soprano Renee Skinner in the choir; and, apart from war service, rarely missed a rehearsal or a concert. Sadly, in December 1935, after only two years of marriage, he was diagnosed with tuberculosis and spent many months in a sanatorium. PN magazines often carried reports on his health but he never recovered and died in 1942.

York Old Priory was a remarkable group being three choirs in one. It gave concerts, and entered competitions, as a mixed, ladies or male voice ensemble. In April 1937 the choir held its 40th anniversary. The York Evening Press wrote:

The choir's beginning in 1897 was a humble one. There were then 13 members. During those 40 years the choir has gained success in many Yorkshire festivals, but its main purpose remains what it has always been, the helping of worthy causes.

In support of this aim it has given more than 800 concerts in more than 50 towns and villages, including York, Hull, Leeds, Scarborough, Thirsk, Ripon, Darlington, Starbeck, Goole, Selby, Pocklington, Malton and Market Weighton. Its busiest season was when it included 49 rehearsals, 44 concerts and 5 competitions.

In addition the choir has entertained various national conferences and among them was the British Association. On three occasions the choir has been invited to broadcast, and in recent years at its annual concerts has introduced to the York public such well known figures in the musical world as Heddle Nash [tenor] and Roy Henderson [baritone].

It was a highly successful competition choir. In reporting on the May 1927 York Choral Competition, the Yorkshire Herald noted that Old Priory had won again, the fifth time in the last seven years, but expressed concerns at rumours that it did not intend to enter again for some time. The choir was so confident that, in 1928, it offered its services to a 'Conductor's Class' in the York Choral Festival. For this the choir learnt a piece of music without any interpretation. The class was judged by how different conductors could then, without any rehearsal, get the choir to perform to their wishes.

Jack Forster was a life-long friend of W.H. Birch. They sang together both in small groups and in the successful York Male Voice Choir. Both also served on the committee of the York Choral Competitions. In addition there are references to Jack conducting other choirs; including Ouseburn and District, and the Argossy Sea Rangers. It is WHB who noted that Jack Forster never considered himself to be a professional musician, and indeed learned [and presumably taught] all his music by the tonic sol-fa system. This was a form of musical education particularly aimed at choral singing, indeed the Revd John Curwen, the Yorkshireman who devised the technique, did so as a means to improve hymn singing in Sunday schools. It was at its most popular in the late 19th century. Unless Jack Forster thought this the most efficient way in which to teach music, we might assume that he had not received a traditional formal musical education himself.

York Old Priory c 1926 with 5 trophies: Jack Forster is in the middle of the 2nd line

Archie W. Sargent was the youngest being 33 years old in 1930. He was also the most accomplished musician of the three. We know much more of Archie's successful and active musical life as he published his memoirs (Voices, Pipes and Pedals A.W.Sargent Mitre press 1971). Born and bred in Kent, he grew up in a musical household centred on a Primitive Methodist Chapel, and was influenced by the adult school movement. Archie's father played in an orchestra at the local adult school, and his mother, an accomplished singer, was also organist at a small chapel. Although he wasn't specific on dates it would seem that he both accompanied his mother's singing, and played at afternoon services from the age of 10-12 years. At 15 he was invited to be the deputy choirmaster and organist at *the most vigorous chapel on the circuit, well known for its singing and choral performances.* He served as a naval radio officer in WW1 and was lucky to survive a mid-Atlantic collision. After the war he joined the Inland Revenue. In March 1921 he became engaged to Janet, the youngest daughter of a Methodist minister. As a young girl she was training to be both a singer and pianist. Archie wrote:

...when unfortunately a serious illness of her father caused the latter to be abandoned. Her voice, mezzo-soprano, had a most beautiful quality, and would fill a large hall without efforts. Indeed had she yielded to competent advice, and taken up singing professionally, she would have gone a long way. The pleasure of listening to her, and from time to time accompanying, has been a great joy to me through the years.

Janet, as will be described later, was the second woman to be granted honorary membership of the York Philharmonic Male Voice Choir.

In November 1921, Archie transferred with the Inland Revenue to York, one incentive being that Janet was then living with her family in Leeds. This was a fortunate turn of events with Archie now able to be near Janet. However, Brian Sargent, their son, believes the move to Yorkshire fulfilled an ambition his father had held since childhood. As a young boy, Archie took a passionate interest in choral music and vowed that he would live where he could find the best choirs; and at an early age had decided that these were all in Yorkshire. As a civil servant with the Inland Revenue it was most unusual that he was able to fulfil this ambition, and to spend almost all of his working life in one city.

Archie was soon invited to be choirmaster at Victoria Bar Chapel where he built up the choir from 12 to 60, and achieved success in the York Choral Competitions. His attitude to competitions was one which resonated with what we know of both Jack Forster and Cecil Fletcher:

As regards choral competitions generally, my own policy throughout the years has been that an occasional entry can be immensely helpful in the development of a choir's technical equipment, platform poise, and general experience of singing before a large audience. It has seemed to me; however, that a more extensive excursion into competitive festivals can lead to what has been called 'pothunting' particularly if a choir meets with conspicuous and continued success.

In 1928 he conducted his first *Messiah,* when the Victoria Bar Choir performed and Old Priory provided the soloists. Showing an early determination to achieve the highest standards, this presentation did not take place at Victoria Bar but across the city in the Monkgate Chapel, which had a better organ. This was such a success it became an annual event. Archie went on to conduct 43 of these performances before retiring from York. In 1930 Archie, as organist and choirmaster, transferred from Victoria Bar to Monkgate and the bonds between the three conductors and choirs strengthened.

Photographs of Archie Sargent copied from Voices Pipes and Pedals

The Author at 23 . . .

and 73

So in 1930 Jack Forster, as the elder mentor with 33 years experience, was conducting a very successful choir; Cecil Fletcher was confident enough to take the renamed York Phil onto a bigger stage; and Archie Sargent, now well known and established in his adopted city, was taking on the challenge of rebuilding another depleted chapel choir at Monkgate. Although the three men from different backgrounds had different standards of musical ability each shared a vision of what a good choir should be, and what it should do; and each had the gift of being able to get the very best from a collection of amateur singers.

There was an active and well-received choral life in the city at this time with male voice choirs other than YMVC and YPMVC. Burton Stone Lane MVC had been formed in 1900 and was still listed in city directories in 1955. This was a choir capable of winning Class B competitions, yet is not often referred to in our choir magazines. Also the Monkgate Methodist Circuit had a male choir of some 30/40 voices. There was also a greater variety of performing venues than is available today. The Phil sang mostly in chapels and halls. In the 1920s many major events such as the York Choral Competitions had been held in the Festival Concert rooms, a building lost to the city, just at the time when the Phil was ready for the 'big' stage. In his memoirs WHB wrote: *The Festival Concert Rooms demolished in 1929 played an important part in the musical life of York at this time. Built for the York Festival of 1825 they were at the rear of the Assembly Rooms having a frontage on Museum Street. Also used at this time was the Exhibition Buildings (Art Gallery).*

The Exhibition buildings were refurbished in 1931 and were regularly used by many musical societies. Another feature of the 1930s – no longer available – was the number of large well equipped cinemas. The Rialto, privately owned by Jack Prendergast, with an excellent cinema organ, was a particularly successful live performance venue. An illustration of the use of these venues for choral music was given by Archie Sargent:

In 1932 the three sections of Methodism Wesleyan, Primitive and United were combined and became the Methodist Church. It was arranged that, on a particular Sunday evening throughout the country, thanksgiving services should be held after the normal worship. In York the building chosen was the Tower Picture House......I had asked my old friend Harold Fredericks to play the cinema organ and a choir of 200 assembled. When the time came to commence we found that in a building with an accommodation of 1100 there were roughly 1400 people.....Outside the building was a crowd stretching across the street and they too were singing.

What of the music being sung? Looking back from today it is not difficult to imagine that most of the music – the part songs – being sung by the Phil was 'Victorian' in date or in style; to which the answer must be yes and no. Works by Sir Arthur Sullivan, who died in 1900, were popular – in particular *The Lost Chord*, a favourite of both audiences and choristers. In April 1935 founder member of the Phil, William Payne wrote: *...Then latterly our concert at Monkgate Wesley Chapel. I might say that never in my life have I enjoyed singing as much as I did in Arthur Sullivan's 'The Lost Chord'.* This piece is still part of the choir's repertoire and is still popular with audiences. Other popular pieces of the time were by contemporary composers. These included *The Old Woman* by Sir Hugh Roberton, conductor of the famous Glasgow Orpheus Choir. He was a friend of Jack Forster's, and kept in close contact with York choirs; indeed he dedicated a composition *O Brother Man* to Archie Sargent and the Monkgate Choir. *Music when soft Voices die* by Sir Edward Bairstow – organist and choirmaster of York Minster until 1946 – became, and remained, popular; as did *Feasting I Watch* by Elgar (1857-1934); both pieces being suitable for concerts and competitions. *The Tide Rises, The Tide Falls* – a setting of a Longfellow poem by Adam Carse (1878-1958) – was also a pre-war favourite. In a recent review of the Phil's music library, the Bairstow and the Elgar pieces were kept, but *The Old Woman* and *The Tide Rises* were discarded, being thought unattractive to a modern audience. The copies discarded were not 1930s originals but were dated 1977 and 1950 respectively, so the pieces clearly remained popular for some time. The cost of music is always a consideration for choirs and it is good to note that the Phil – in its early years with its modest resources – invested in contemporary pieces.

The Philharmonic News

The source material for describing choir life in the 1930s comes from copies of *Philharmonic News* held in the archive. Unfortunately this is not a complete set. The magazine was first published in October 1932 and we have issues ranging in date from January 1933 to May 1938. Although not a full record the collection does give much valuable information and paints a portrait of life at the time. One copy missing, which would have been extremely useful in compiling this history, is that of May 1935. Issue no 24 – April 1935 – is titled 'Tenth Anniversary'. A small diary entry in this issue states: *The choir was formed in April 1925. Next month we will publish a 'year by year' progress report.* There were eight issues per choir year from October through to May. It was a subscription magazine with an annual fee of 2/6d including postage, a price which didn't increase. It was not an original idea, as a magazine (*Notes and Views*) of the same size and make up and with a very similar editorial style was already being produced by Jack Forster for the Old Priory Choir. Archie Sargent also adopted the idea and produced, from 1939, an annual journal for the Monkgate Methodist Choir called *The Carillon*. Such magazines were very unusual and received much praise. Perhaps, in a York context, with the influence of the adult schools and with Rowntree, for example, as a major employer publishing its CWM (*Cocoa Works Magazine*), we should not be too surprised at the quality, value and success of such in-house publications. The introduction of PN was also helped by the deepening relationship between the York Phil and Old Priory Choirs. As editor Cecil Fletcher wrote in issue 8 June 1933:

We now come to the last issue of the Philharmonic News for the season 1932-33. Considering that the journal is in its first year, it is pleasing to state that it has been more or less a success. It has been a success in so much that it has further strengthened that fine team spirit of which we are so proud in the choir. It has kept the choir in closer touch with its friends, and has, we think, proved interesting reading. It has not been quite a financial success, but one could not reasonably expect this in its first year. We have not yet secured a sufficient sale, but believe this will increase next season. The warmest thanks are expressed to all those who have sent matter for publication, to those who have contributed financially; and to Mr. J.H.Forster the Editor of the 'Old Priory Choir's' journal 'Notes and Views' for his great assistance in ordering paper, stencils etc. through his account, thus reducing our expenditure considerably and relieving the editor of that worry.

Cecil must have given a great deal of time to make this journal a success, and also demonstrated skills as editor and graphic artist. As over the years the choir became more successful and busier, the time given to the magazine both by Cecil and some contributors seems to diminish. Reproduced below are the front covers of four editions from March 1933, December 1934, April 1937 and May 1938 showing the shift from individual hand drawn early copies to the standardised simplicity of the typed final copy. It is in the May 1938 issue that Cecil wrote:

This is the last issue of the Phil News for this season, and also the last of the monthly issues. It has been decided to publish four quarterly ones instead of the eight monthly. October, December, March and June will be the months of publication (spring, summer, autumn and winter as a reader suggests) and each number will contain approximately twenty pages.

PN included all that might be expected of a club newsletter: concert reports and letters of thanks; diary notes; details of new members and sickness; plus key family events etc. But it was much more than a newsletter; it was a humorous, informative magazine

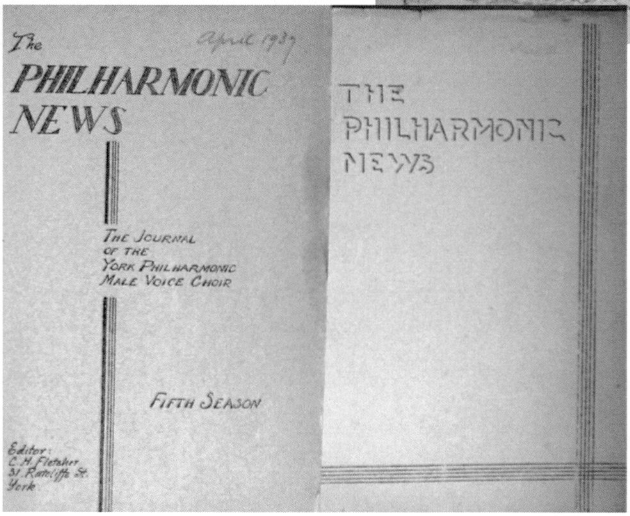

with contributions from choir members and their families on a range of subjects. It also gave members of the James Street Adult School, led by their President A.E. Burgess, an outlet for their articles. It compiled and printed crosswords and other puzzles, jokes; and occasionally held essay writing competitions for the children. Awards were offered for the first correct entry opened for the crossword puzzle. The prizes were not described and given the financial fragility of this publication could not have been extravagant. The magazines describe a choir at ease with itself, yet one very much aware, and in touch with the wider world: both with the economic difficulties at home in the 1930s; and the concern over new political tensions in Europe. As a consequence of its conversational, familiar style the collection gives an insight into choir and family life at this time. Reading back from a distance of 80 plus years, one striking aspect is the awareness of mortality and the uncertainty that accompanied illness. In the 'members news' section there were frequent references to ill-health and infection. Very rarely does the editor give specific details, but often described a situation as 'serious', in a style of writing which suggested a hope of recovery, rather than the expectation that might be expressed in 2015. Allied to this are references to members being injured at work, many more than would be expected nowadays. Rose coloured spectacles should also be set aside in the reminders of winter fogs – especially during Christmas Eve Carolling.

Not only was the choir fortunate in the calibre of the magazine's editor, there were also within its ranks good writers, both male and female. First and foremost was an accomplished and energetic poet and bass solo singer Albert Snowden. His verses appeared on a number of subjects and often included references to the difficult economic times of the 1930s, as well as rising fear of Nazi Germany. Two ladies who made regular contributions were Ada Cade, wife of Bill Cade, a top tenor, and accompanist, Jane Brough. Ada wrote pieces of interest, including a lengthy article on Edward Grieg published in January 1936, but was at her best when making observations as a choir wife, and Jane published descriptive pieces of her summer holidays.

Here are two of Ada Cade's contributions. The first was published in January 1933, when she and Bill had been married for eight years. The second from June 1934 described a visit to a rehearsal before a competition:

A woman once asked me if I didn't object to my husband belonging to a choir. "It must take him away from home quite a lot and leave you lonely" she said. "I wouldn't like mine to belong to anything like that". I replied "look here, I think a choir is one of the finest organizations a man can belong to. Daily he is bending over his work, cramping his chest and then once or twice a week he goes to choir practice, takes deep breaths, fills his lungs with God's glorious oxygen and sings beautiful poems; instead of which he could sit in 'The Widows Arms' every night take deep draughts straight from the wood, inhale smoke polluted air while he is moaning 'She was only a baker's daughter' or some such piffle.

Furthermore by his singing such songs as 'There is a Lady sweet and kind' and 'The Old Woman' he is learning to place womankind in her proper sphere and I like to think – I may be deluding myself – that he sometimes thinks of me whilst voicing these clean beautiful thoughts. A singer may have feet of clay, but his heart must be in the right place to enable him to interpret the meaning of the words. He must feel what he sings therefore he is an artist painting delightful mind pictures for us, of windswept shores, heroic deeds, tender lovers or nestling babes and we are uplifted.

I shall never forget hearing Old Priory Choir sing 'The Eriskay Love Lilt' at one of their annual concerts eight or nine years ago. Nothing has ever affected me like that rendering, it must have stirred some dormant emotion as I was entranced and the memory of it is very real to me. If a song can do that to a listener, what cannot it do for a singer?

No, I am glad that my husband is privileged to belong to a choir, and one cannot be lonely when one can switch on to companionable things as 'The Glasgow Orpheus Choir' or a reading from Charlotte Bronte "Times change and we with time but may choral singing go on forever." A Cade

The Glasgow Orpheus toured, broadcast and recorded, so was well known. Bill had been a member of York Old Priory Choir, and in the late 1920s a large crowd had heard the Glasgow Orpheus Choir, directed by Sir Hugh Roberton, in the York Festival Concert Rooms [a concert arranged by Jack Forster and for which Archie Sargent block booked 60 tickets so that all his Victoria Bar choir could attend]. These references by Ada would have been understood and appreciated by her readers.

She later attended a rehearsal:

***Rehearsal:** May 18th, a cold, sad, weepy day. Why had I promised to trail from Huntington leaving a nice cosy fire to enter the desolate district of Leeman Road to hear the rehearsal for the Sheffield Festival?*

"Oh there'll be a lot of women there and you'll enjoy it" my husband said. Well there wasn't a lot of women there but I did enjoy it, and oh, what an eye opener I got. I just wish some of you wives, mothers or sweethearts had been there. You think you have got a caveman don't you? Well you ought to see them quail when Mr. Fletcher puts them through their paces – and they answer not a word.

In the first place he had them stood for a solid hour. I'm sure their feet must have ached after being at work all day. (No chairs available on the evening in question. Ed.) Now had we asked them to stand for ten minutes only at a sink washing up on a Friday night, would they have remained mute???

Again, they would be putting their heart and soul into a line when, – a loud clap; you could hear a pin drop. Good! I thought, Cecil's pleased and clapping his hands – was he – don't you believe it. He got on to those poor baritones something awful; even sang it for them, then off again; another clap – a silence that could be felt. The tenors this time, then, while I was wondering what could be wrong, I heard a voice soft and caressing floating on the air like a gentle Zephyr.

I thought someone had switched on to the 'Epilogue' and the Reverend So and So was reading a psalm, or a notable poet reading his lines, but it was only the conductor reciting the song and emphasising the meaning thereof. What a versatile man!

Then, a "Come on, try it again" until at the last attempt even he couldn't find fault.

"It was Pan who counselled you." A God like being who could stand there facing our forty cave-men and say his say, and, no back answers. No wonder they sang so prayerfully 'God grant us strength to die' when his eagle eye held sway.

Well I'm ever so pleased they won but between you and me, they daren't have done otherwise.

I'm entering on a correspondence course with Cecil on 'How to control the mighty atom-man and bring him to subjection – no result – no pay'.

Is it reasonable to suggest that all choristers of today stand at the sink and wash up without complaint?

In the same June edition, poet Albert Snowden described the competition day as follows:

We've won the Cup!

We've won the cup and now it's up to us to try and hold it.
We sang real well from Bell to Bell and jolly well we told it.
Our Battle line was really fine and well portrayed the story
And now it's done and we have won the honour and the glory.
The second piece will never cease to charm the music lover.
The rhythm fine and every line leaves beauties to discover.
And Cecil says he's nought but praise our rendering was topping.
One felt the breeze blow through the trees and set the grasshoppers hopping
I've cause to think we made them blink, we made a real good showing,
At any rate we cleaned the slate, and it was well worth going.
The only thing that's bothering is, If we left behind us,
Two of the boys who in the noise somehow quite failed to find us,
For half-way back we found alack! that two had missed their places.
Let's hope the twain came back by train If not they'd show their paces,
Sheffield to York is not a joke, twould take them all day Sunday,
And they'd be glad that someone had provided Whitsun Monday.
Oh what a tramp with clothes all damp, and feet all on the tickle
Mitchell is out, there's not a doubt and Lazenby's in pickle
Now I must go and leave you so 'good luck' and no back pedal.
We won the test, and what is best our Cecil's got a medal.

The two missing choristers are assumed to be Messrs. Mitchell and Lazenby.

The Australian Cricket team was in England for an Ashes series and there was an English cricketer named Mitchell; and Lazenbys (part of Crosse & Blackwell) made preserves and sauces, which could have influenced our poet's style. There was a Lazenby who only joined the choir two months before this incident, so this could have been his introduction to choral competitions.

Albert Snowden had another poem in the same edition, which also had a diary entry congratulating Bill and Ada on the birth of a son – Brian.

Bill Cade also contributed concert reports to the magazine, and Mr and Mrs Varley – Ada's mother and father – were regular contributors; her father with reflective pieces; her mother having the same light hearted style as Ada. Here is an excerpt from May 1937 when Mrs Varley described moving house from Bolton Percy to Huntington, to be close to Bill and Ada.

... so we decided to take off at dawn. Luckily the lorry arrived just then and loading up commenced. We had a spot of bother with Granddad who would insist on taking his armchair, fishing tackle and garden tools first. I thought that if we could only take the peggy tub, pans and straw mattresses (useful if we had cattle later) while no one was about, during the second load the neighbours would be getting up and notice what a nice sideboard we had etc. which would create a good impression. I must record that we nearly came to grief with this flitting. The driver going at 50 miles per hour, lost control and we nearly lost granddad who had insisted that he accompanied every load to see that nothing fell off.

The magazines recorded events in member's lives. For example we learn that Bill and Ada lived in Huntington; Bill worked at Rowntrees and was not known for his skills as a gardener.

Loud cheering was recently heard in a Huntington garden. It was eventually discovered that Bill Cade was celebrating the blooming of a spring flower that bore a distinct resemblance to its picture on the seed packet. June 1933

We also know that he was taken ill suddenly in January 1933:

It came as a shock to learn that Bill Cade had been suddenly struck down with illness. He was down at the Editorial office just a few hours before it started. We wish him a speedy recovery and hope to see him at the rehearsals erelong. Bill is one of our most enthusiastic members and what is more his enthusiasm is shared by Mrs. Cade and his little son Brian.

We learn that he recovered a month later. We also know he had a significant visit to the dentist in 1934:

It seems very strange to see Bill Cade standing at the back of the first tenors, especially as he was always a front ranker. On enquiring at the dentist's we are informed that it will be at least three months before he will be able to crack a nut.

We also know that in June 1934 their young son Brian was better again after having been ill for some time. Young Brian, aged eight, took second prize in a children's essay writing competition following a choir outing by river boat to Nun Monkton. His prize was some sheet music, and he sent a letter of thanks to the choir. We also know that he passed exams to enter the Minster Song School, and later gained a scholarship to Archbishop Holgate's Grammar, where he immediately joined the orchestra.

References are also made to the occupations of choir members and to their other achievements. Tom Clark was a key figure in the life of the choir. He had provided the very first rehearsal facilities, and had also been a member of York Old Priory.

In April 1933 another aspect to his life was described:

We regret that space cannot be found to publish the glowing account of Tom Clark's fine record as a 'Harrier' which appeared in a recent issue of The York Football Press. It would take a full page to record the prizes he has won. Tom has been a member of our choir since its inception.

We also learn that the choir had in its ranks five cobblers:

"Can Cobblers sing?" we have been asked. Judging by the number we have in the choir we would say they sure can. There is Mr. W.Payne, Mr. H.Payne, Mr. M.Neal, Mr. J.Bond, and, of course, Mr. J.Hardisty who has recently taken over the business of Williams and Sons. Readers who are down on their uppers, or who contemplate hiking this summer would do well to consult the 'St. Crispens Quintet'. They're sure good at a Sole-O..... May 1933

Founder member Jim Hardisty was a real asset to the choir, being one of its most popular soloists. His value increased in October 1934 when he introduced a new member to the choir.

Now that Morris Cowley – not a singing member, at least not vocal – has joined the choir we can get things done. Morris and his owner Jim Hardisty, have given much assistance to the conductor in making arrangements for concerts, trips etc. Morris let me explain is a motor car pictured herewith:

It is true that we have had many stops on the road to blow down some tube or other to coax him to go. It is true that we have occasionally been startled by a shrill whistle, which upon investigation has proved to be only something unstuck at the back. We are optimistic to believe that this rattling 'good member' will train on. The reports that Morris has put two lamp standards out of action, and that the wheels won't go round owing to excessive pressure from the mudguards, have not been confirmed at the time of going to press. May Morris have a long and 'happy' stay with us.

The illustration of the car being chased by a tram is by Cecil; there were no reports of the conductor ever failing to arrive at a concert due to mechanical failure.

A considerable amount of information was given on members and their families, yet Cecil, as editor, made only rare references to himself or his own family:

A hearty welcome to the Bass line is extended to our Conductor's son Harold Fletcher. May 1934

Congratulations to Harold Fletcher on passing the second year Technical Grouped Course Examination 1934. June 1934

In March 1934, in a lengthy piece appealing for better attendances at rehearsal, Cecil did allow himself a personal reference:

.....One ambitious member was overheard asking this question the other evening. "Do you think that a 100% attendance could ever be arranged?" Well why not? What have other members got to say? It would certainly be great to have all those 48 voices singing 'O Mariners out of sunlight' or some such piece. Our conductor has had dreams of those 100% dos. By the way! He has only missed one rehearsal in nine years and he was then half dead but would have crawled down had not his wife intervened.......

Another personal and intriguing reference was made in February 1937:

Mr. Alf Boston has, through prolonged indisposition, been compelled to resign from the choir. We are very sorry to lose him. He was an enthusiastic member and an asset to the first tenors. He has sung for C.H.F. since 1913.

Alf (one of the original four in Tom's front room) *has sung for*, not with, C.H.F. since 1913(?) We know so little about Cecil's life before 1925 that this is a revealing and intriguing statement. In 1913 Cecil was only 19 years old. What choir or musical group was he leading at such a young age?

We also learn little of two other key characters – the piano playing sisters Jane and Kathleen Brough. Jane joined the choir in its first few months, and it seems she was also known as Jinny or Jenny. Her contributions, as a pianist, were often acknowledged, and Albert Snowden in a poem did once describe her as a vision in blue. As well as playing the piano she wrote articles for the magazine including descriptions of holidays taken in the Yorkshire Dales and the Lake District. Both sisters played a key part in providing rabbit suppers on Christmas Eve.

There is even less detail given of her younger sister Kathleen, but the choir did offer congratulations on her marriage:

Heartiest congratulations to Kathleen Brough on the occasion of her marriage to Mr. Cyril Atkinson on November 28th. 1936. Kathleen has been the assistant accompanist to the choir for a number of years.

The wedding took place at Victoria Bar Methodist Church following which a reception was held at the De-Grey Rooms – the bride and bridegroom leaving later for London where the honeymoon is being spent.

To Kathleen and Cyril we wish many, many years of good health and happiness.

As resident poet, Albert Snowden tended to write about current events, or about individuals or sections within the choir. These were often playful yet respectful and often quite lengthy. Typical of his work is this 'shorter' one in praise of William Payne – the eldest in the choir, a founder member and one of the five shoe repairers:

This time I think I'll spill some ink in praise of an old member,
To William Payne, long may he reign, I sing this cold December.
He smacks his lips at songs of ships, of fishermen or sailors
Or Vikings bold in days of old, or songs of deep sea whalers.
He once told me, his family, had followed the sea for ages,
And when at home from o'er the foam, brought parrots home in cages.
He plays his part, with all his heart and would do if on a stretcher.
And he'll tell you, his talent's due to Mr. C.H. Fletcher.
Sing on old man you do and can, you never were a wobbler,
You can't be all upon the sea and so you are a cobble [r]. January 1933

But there were times when there was more of an edge to his work. With references to the economic difficulties of the time and to rising political tensions this offering is from November 1933:

Keep Smiling

The summer's gone, ah lack-a-day, my heart is sad and dreary. The days are getting shorter and the sun is getting weary. He just can't last the day out and his gleams are getting wan, the men have lost their sunburn and the girls have lost their tan. The rain begins to patter as we sit around the fire, the Irish sweep is over and I haven't had a wire. In fact there's lots and lots of things to make a man feel glum, the apple tree is empty and the pear tree and the plum. The cellar too is empty where we used to keep the coal, and my Auntie's on the Parish and my Uncle's on the dole. Disarmament has broken down and

Armament is rife. The rich have all the money and the poor have all the strife. The USA have all the gold, the Japs have all the trade. The Germans have got Hitler and they say their debt is paid. The French have got the wind up because Berlin's on the Spree. The Russians have their five year plan the Dutch their Zuider See. We have our politicians and our minsters of state. But we haven't any money and we cannot pay the rate. But still there is a brighter side at least there ought to be. So let us look around awhile and see what we can see. I still have got a bob or two of which to make some use and its nearing Christmas, well the wife will want a goose. It may run to a turkey and won't we give it socks. Then the butcher and the bakers' boys will want their Xmas box. And the chilly little snowflakes will be gently falling down, turning the earth a lovely white instead of beastly brown. There'll be lots of berries holly and mistletoe of course, then a taste of Christmas pudding and a little bit of sauce. There's sure to be some skating and some sleighing down the hills and let's hope there'll be some money with which to pay the bills. So let us sing a carol, and a jolly roundelay to greet our old friend winter who has started on his way.

Occasionally others would also write in verse as did W. Bolton, known within the choir as 'Porky the Treasurer'. When, in February 1933, he needed to encourage members to pay their subscriptions he did so in rhyme:

An "owed" to the Philharmonic

Oh to be in England, Now that winter's here
To listen to the Philharmonic, Their singing brings good cheer.
The first tenors' tone is always good, Their comradeship is true,
It also is when pay they should, Their "subs" are overdue:
The second tenors a motley lot, Some small, some tall some new,
They tone into the upper lot Their "subs" are overdue.
The first bass of the Philharmonic, Gives you a feeling too,
Some notes are good and some are chronic, For their "subs" are overdue.
The Bottom bass, they sound like thunder, Some are shy, maybe one or two,
But they tone in, and I shouldn't wonder. Their "subs "are overdue.
If only members would pay their subs, Of three pence per one week,
You've no idea what extra good The "Outing" would be, so to speak.
Now all true members Don't get surly, Forget all cares that make you blue,
Get up to practice and pay up early, The "sub" that's overdue.

Re-union Smoking Concert

Another successful social event was held by the choir on Saturday September 26th. This was in the form of a Smoking Concert and was arranged for the purpose of; members past and present, uniting to enjoy a 'free and easy' prior to the commencement of the heavy concert season which is before us. Considering that it was Saturday evening – a night on which most men like to be shopping or visiting some of the local entertainments – a fair number of members attended. The party was excellently entertained by Mr. Martin Boggan (tenor) and Mr. Harry Shipman (humorist). Both artistes put themselves fully into their work, and, from the beginning everybody settled down to a jolly evening. Mr. Boggan delighted with several songs, each admirably treated, and the writer was pleased to note that his voice is as charming as ever. Mr. Shipman has a style that always appeals, and of his several humorous items it is hard to say which was liked most. Mr. Boggan and Mr. Shipman also sang duets which were well received. Others who entertained were Mr. E.Jubb – an ex member who had come from Malton to be with us – Mr. W.Hodgson and

Mr. J.Hardisty. The duties of accompanist were in the capable hands of Mr. L.W.Wreghitt. During the evening the conductor addressed the company. A great night! enjoyed by all.
CHP October 1936

The period of 1925-35 saw the advent of talking pictures, the growth of radios and gramophones, and new musical styles – jazz. As happens in every age, new ideas take a time to be accepted by different generations. In May 1933 one writer [Maurice Bradley] described syncopation as *'the sincerest form of clattery'*, and it seems that this American music took time to be accepted. On the other hand the radio was welcomed, yet contributors reminded readers that this could not surpass or replace a live performance. But by 1935, with other York choirs being broadcast on the BBC Radio Northern Network, Ada Cade was looking forward with great ambition: *Before your coming of age, people the world over may have heard your message of song by wireless and seen you on television*

In May 1936 appeared an article which reflected Cecil's growing reputation. He had been invited to be a regional adjudicator within a nation-wide competition.

Golden Voiced Singing Girl Competition

The Golden-Voiced Singing Girl of Great Britain competition organized by the Gaumont British Picture Corporation and the News Chronicle attracted our interest when Mr. Edward Prangnell and Mr. C.H.Fletcher were appointed adjudicators for the York and district area. After two strenuous evenings at the elimination tests, the adjudicators commenced their task at the contest proper which was held at the Picture House Coney Street during the week commencing May 6th last. Similar contests were taking place in all the principal towns of Great Britain during that week.

From the eight competitors who had survived the elimination test and thus qualified to sing in the competition proper, the adjudicators were confronted with the task of finding the golden voice that would proceed to the next stage. Their final selection was Miss Mary Leak of Hull who proved to be a singer of fine dramatic sense, with voice, diction and techniques almost perfect. Miss Leak sang an aria from Cavelleria Rusticana [Mascagni].

From York Miss Leak qualified to sing in the circuit final at Doncaster which she won, and again in the divisional finals at Doncaster which she also won. By this feat she earned the title of 'Miss North England' and proceeded to London to compete in the semi-final along with Miss London, Miss Scotland, Ireland, Wales etc. – fifteen in all. She succeeded in the semi-final along with five others and in the final narrowly missed the premier award. Here is the result. Section A (operatic, concert and ballad)

First Prize: £250 and one year's free training at a first class college of music

1st. Miss Marjorie Savage London

2nd Prize £50 Miss Mary Leak Hull

3rd Prize Miss L McCardle Ireland.

The adjudicators in London were, among other notable musicians, Mr Plunket Green, Mr Eric Coates and Mr Norman Allin. As Miss Leak passed through York, we are naturally proud of her performance and we sincerely congratulate her. She has promised to sing at one of our concerts in the near future. Mr L.W.Wreghitt (York Minster) was the official accompanist at York and also accompanied Miss Leak at Doncaster.

Cecil had picked another winner!

This miscellany of extracts has been chosen to illustrate choir life at this time. It seems to have been a welcoming society, wanting to work with and encourage others, particularly the womenfolk, to share in choir life and in the production of this excellent magazine – *Philharmonic News*. It also suggests a society dedicated to its own improvement, and keen to serve the community in which it was based. It is, however, just a rough sketch rather than a painting, but does serve as an introduction to more specific aspects of choir life.

Before considering the specific topics of Inter-Choral Competitions, Concerts, Competitions and Carol singing, it is interesting to note what the magazines wrote about management structure and tensions in the choir as it grew in size and success. The February 1933 issue has an illustration on the front cover and contains the poetic appeal for subs to be paid. The February 1937 issue, with a simplified formal cover, contains an AGM report. It is as though the comic frivolity of youth has been subdued by the responsibilities of maturity. The magazines allow today's reader to see some of the steps along this road, and to get a sense of the growth both in maturity and ambition of the choir. The December 1933 issue published an extract, by Alderman W.H. Birch, from the 'The Yorkshire Gazette' under the title of 'Music in York': *The York Philharmonic Male Voice Choir came into being in 1925, under the leadership of Mr. C.H.Fletcher, having its inception in the Leeman Road Adult School. For a recently formed Society their record is a good one, having won five first prizes, seven second prizes and two fourth prizes in 14 festivals besides giving a number of concerts to charities. The membership of this choir is 43, and it is in vigorous condition.*

This shows just how much had been achieved in only eight years. The choir was fortunate in the support it received from talented individuals – apart from the singers – committed both to choral singing and the Adult School movement. Arnold Rowntree was the President, Alderman W.H. Birch, a successful businessman and local politician, became a Vice President, as did W.H. Sessions who, with his wife Edith another supporter, ran the successful Sessions print and publishing firm. Within the ranks, competent secretaries and treasurers came to the fore, not the least of whom was S.P. Wilson, the first choir secretary. He ran a clothing outfitters business on Clifton Green, and when ill health forced his retirement from singing, became a Vice President. As secretary he was the subject of a poem of praise by Albert Snowden in which he was described as being *'Not very tall, in fact quite small.'* In the same March 1933 issue SPW himself issued this amusing plea:

Being of the unfortunate shall I say singers in the middle section, I usually get pushed well under the conductor's baton. When singing at Monkgate, CHF stood on something very high, and I, being somewhat short – his boot was on a line with my mouth, and I was frightened to death of singing a wrong note being so near the boot. Please Mr. Conductor don't get so elevated in future and allow me to sing in comfort.

Sadly, S.P. Wilson died in 1936 but was remembered by means of a Rose Bowl awarded annually as part of the Inter-Choral Competitions.

The change of name in 1929 reflected the growing confidence which also saw, in October 1934, Cecil launch a long term campaign to grow the membership to 70 in order to compete at the highest level in 'A' class competitions.

In 1935, 10th Anniversary year, there were 21 concerts given, 60 rehearsals, the inter-choral competition, and a garden party in the local vicarage gardens. The celebratory year began with an invitation to tea with the President:

On Monday April 29th next we have the honour to be entertained to tea by our President Mr. Arnold S. Rowntree and Mrs. Rowntree in commemoration of our tenth birthday. We all look forward with pleasure to this happy occasion. The year ended with an anniversary dinner on March 21st 1936 in honour of the ladies. The 10th Anniversary issue – April 1935– published letters of congratulations from: Arnold Rowntree President; Archie Sargent organist and choirmaster at Monkgate Methodist; Harold Fredericks organist and choirmaster at Victoria Bar Methodist; Edward Prangnell conductor and member of York Co-operative Choir; Jack Forster conductor of York Old Priory; and Wm. H. Birch. Here are the letters sent by Archie Sargent and Jack Forster:

Greetings to the gentlemen of the York Philharmonic Male Voice Choir from York Monkgate Methodist Choir and congratulations on the achievements of the past ten years culminating in a virile membership of 51, a high standard of choral excellence and a splendid spirit of camaraderie.

You are most fortunate in possessing a Conductor of Mr. Fletcher's calibre. He has ability, enthusiasm, tact and personal charm and with him you will achieve great things in the future.

We offer you very sincerely all good wishes for success in every sense of the word during the days that are to come.

Please accept our sincere thanks for all your help at concerts and services in which the choir has functioned from time to time at Monkgate.

May good fortune attend you Philharmonic!

Archie Sargent.

To my friend Cecil Fletcher and the members of the Philharmonic Male Voice Choir!

It is a very great pleasure to me to offer my sincere congratulations to you and your men on the tenth birthday of the York Philharmonic Male Voice Choir.

By painstaking and genial leadership on the part of the conductor, by unswerving loyalty on the part of the members, and by hard work, good fellowship and untiring devotion to the cause of choral singing, together you have built up a choir from a very small beginning, which now ranks as one of the musical institutions of the city.

During the last ten years I have watched your progress with keen and kindly interest.

You have achieved successes in the competitive field of which you have every reason to be proud, but to me, of far greater importance and more worthy of commendation is your service to the community. Your willingness to help any good cause, and your desire to give pleasure to your fellows is more to be admired than prizes won.

That you may continue to find joy in such service that the spirit of comradeship which is manifest among you may deepen and increase and that success – success in the highest sense – may be yours in greater measure as the years go by is the sincere wish of Jack Forster.

To be described as *'one of the musical institutions of the city'* by one with the reputation of Jack Forster was praise indeed.

In the same issue the following entries from an established and a new member appear next to each other:

Dear Mr. Fletcher,

This year the Philharmonic celebrates the tenth anniversary of its formation. Commencing with half a dozen members the choir has now a membership of over 50 – a splendid tribute to your skill and efforts as conductor. As a Vice President I should like to convey to you and the choir my congratulations on this notable ***'Landmark'*** *in the choir's history.*

My eight years association with the choir is crowded with happy memories, Contests at Scarborough, York, Pontefract, Barnsley, Elsecar, Sheffield etc. Concerts, outings, rehearsals – what a jolly friendly crowd our member are and how they sing. They often give me a thrill on practice nights.

In conclusion, let us keep on with the good work. 'Let gladness dance and weave in joyous years.'

S.P. Wilson Vice President.

As a new member I should like to say how much I appreciate Mr. Fletcher and the York Philharmonic Male Voice Choir. Snobbishness is unknown to them, they are keen and attentive, genuine music lovers and what some of them lack in musical knowledge they redeem by their keenness. In fact from Mr. Fletcher (our good friend and conductor) downwards to every member of the choir (not forgetting Miss Brough) they're real good fellows.

I have spent some happy hours in their company and hope to spend many happy years with them. I consider it an honour to have been admitted as a friend and I hope a good average singer.

Here's to us on our tenth anniversary. 'The York Philharmonic Male Voice choir' may we go on for years doing our best for Mr. Fletcher and the choir and strengthening our comradeship wherever we go.

W.J. Moss.

These are clear indications that the sense of pride shown by those outside of the choir was matched by those within.

Here is a photograph of the choir taken in 1935 at the tea hosted by Arnold Rowntree to celebrate the tenth anniversary.

The best attempt at naming these choristers suggests:

Back row: Messrs. Harbour, Pickering, Boston, Colley, Colley, Dorrington, Hodgson, Dutton, Hardisty, Snowden, Stead, Taylor, Thornton, (?).

Third row: Messrs.Cade, Berkley, Colley, Fletcher, Clark, Calam, Marsden, Calvert, Colley, Hodgson, Mitchell, (?), Shawn

Second row: Messrs. Neale, Webster,(?),(?), Harrison, Payne, Arnold Rowntree, Lord Mayor Herbert Harrowell, Cecil Fletcher, Miss Jane Brough, Bolton, Jackson, Moss, Wilson

Front row: Messrs. Wrigley, (?), Busby, Poole, Murray, Richardson, Green, Thornton, Lazenby, Dixon, Henry Brough

This photograph appears to have been taken on the same occasion and shows guests.

The gentleman in the chain of office, next to Arnold Rowntree, is the Lord Mayor Herbert Harrowell. Jack Forster is in the centre with his arms folded. On the same

row to the left, as viewed, are Archie and Janet Sargent, with W.H. Birch the fifth person in from the left.

A minute dated 7th May 1935 gave this instruction: *For the Garden Party on the 29th May – for liquid refreshment Mr. Colley was authorised to obtain 1 bottle each of lime juice, lemon squash and grapefruit.*

In 1935 there was much public praise and affirmation of all that had been achieved and all that might yet be achieved. The year saw an increase in membership, particularly of quality singers (thought to have transferred across from the York Male Voice Choir). But in 1936 there was intimation that the choir was experiencing some growing pains, with tensions coming to the surface. This was first noted in the February issue. The choir sang at Clifton Methodist Church in support of the fund to pay for fitting an electric blower to the organ. The magazine published a letter of thanks from the church; and then, on the back page, this entry from a clearly upset conductor:

C.H.F. refuses to believe that it was the 'wet night' which prevented eleven top tenors from attending the Clifton concert. There is also no truth in the rumour that the four tenors who so successfully carried the top line are to receive a special reward. We often wonder whether tenors fully realise the 'importance' of their line in choral singing

In the spring it was proposed that the choir continued to meet throughout the summer. In keeping with similar groups the choir season, started in September and ran till May. It was the custom to take a three month break in the summer. However, such a long gap gave little rehearsal time before the busy autumn schedule began. At the same time demand for concerts was so great that a number were being refused. Here, for example, is the list of immediate engagements as published in October 1936.

Monday October 5th. St George's Methodist Church Hull Road
Monday October 12th. Acomb (Sanctuary) Methodist Church
Sunday October 25th. Albany Street Methodist Church
Saturday October 31st. York Co-operative Wholesale Society
Wednesday November 4th. Burton Stone Lane Methodist Church
Thursday November 19th. Massed Choirs (Exhibition Buildings)
Sunday 6th December. Melbourne Terrace Methodist Church.

In the May 1936 issue the secretary announced the intention to continue with one rehearsal a week all through the summer:

Summertime

Now that Summer-time is here and most of our members are likely to be mapping out their summer programme of Swimming, Tennis, Cricket etc I would like to appeal to them not to omit the choir from their timetable. As you are aware, it is the intention to continue practices throughout the summer, just once per week, and not too much to expect if you are only a little bit keen, but I think I can assure you that apart from enjoying it just as much as you will your tennis or cricket, you will be agreeably surprised how much that weekly practice will help you in taking up choral work seriously when the dark nights come round again. This last two or three weeks we have had a little insight of the fine stuff we are preparing for next year's concert programme. We have no bookings as yet for summer concerts but it is essential that we are in a position to make a flying start next season and, therefore, I ask you , when booking up your summer sports you will keep 'Monday night – practice night' first on your list. It is not much to expect but it will help us all to keep in touch and make the final polishing up of the new programme considerably easier.

May you all enjoy your summer sports and return ready and keen for another successful concert period. We have had a wonderful and busy time and I hope you are all looking forward to a better one in the season to come.

No doubt someone else better able than I will explain to you the disadvantages of having long breaks from singing, but this I will say, and I think you will all agree that it is easier to lose touch by long absence than it is to take up the threads again. Secten (F. Colley)

It must have been difficult to prepare a programme in September for such a list of engagements as shown above, particularly as two of the listed concerts were on Mondays – rehearsal night – so the request for summer rehearsals is understandable. We are not told how successful they were. However in the October 1936 issue Cecil wrote:

It is not often that we have to commence a new season with a list of resignations but two have recently been received and two others are anticipated.

F. Colley, as secretary, made this appeal:

I would therefore just like to take this opportunity of making an appeal through the mag. To all those members who have not yet started practice to show up, so that we can make a good start with our winter programme. If you are missing a pal out of your own line look him up, it's probably just what he is wanting.

Then in the November issue:

What has happened to our second tenors lately? Only one turned up to rehearsal recently. This was one of our best lines once upon a time. The register records nine names, and unless we have at least 50% at rehearsals progress is hampered. What about it? Second tenors!

In November, S. P. Wilson, long term member and secretary died, another blow to choir morale. A warm tribute was paid to him in the December issue, which also carried the news that there would be no Christmas Eve Carol singing in the district:

For the first time in eleven years the Philharmonic will not go carolling. Weather conditions have been very trying during recent years and the fact that we have tacked on that eleven years to our ages, well, it makes one think. We shall miss that good old Christmas supper though.

All of this suggests a choir struggling to adapt to its success, but the issues were resolved and the choir thrived.

January 1937 brought complaints from the residents of Leeman Road at the lack of 'Carolling' (reinstated in 1937), and this letter of encouragement from Jack Forster:

My message for the New Year to the Philharmonic Male Voice Choir is 'Carry On' no matter what happens. From long experience I have most intimate knowledge of the discouragements, disappointments and disagreements which come to hamper and hinder the work which a conductor and his choir are trying to do. It is possible that the Philharmonic has its troubles and trials, though judging from the enthusiasm in and enjoyment of their work which are so evident when they are on a platform, and from what I know personally of your merry men, such things must be few and far between. Even if they do come your way, I would impress upon the members (and conductor too) not to be disheartened by small disturbances – for after all such things are usually very small but rather to ignore them and renew their allegiance to the great cause of choral singing of which the Philharmonic Choir is one of the live exponents in our city.

You are doing a fine service not only to your fellowmen by your singing but to yourselves; you are finding expression for your talents, are enjoying a happy fellowship one with another, and cultivating and increasing a knowledge of and a love for fine words and good music.

I am proud to know you and to have been associated with you on so many occasions.

So I say 'Carry On' giving pleasure to any and all who seek your service and may 1937 be the best year you have yet known.

In the same issue Cecil wrote a review of 1936 including:

....Recording a choir's activities has the possible tendency of leading the outside world to believe that things are 100% with the choir when actually there is some need for improvement. In reviewing 1936 then I have asked myself whether I am satisfied with the year. My answer was yes and no. Yes to the social activities and no the serious side - work. Attendances at rehearsals have not been all they might have been. It is true that overtime, awkward shifts etc have been the main cause of non-attendance which cannot be avoided. It is not however the non-attendance that has caused the grouse, it is the lateness in commencing a rehearsal. THE LOSS OF PRECIOUS MINUTES (5,10,15, and so on). To many such a complaint may seem trivial but to a choir which has such activities as the Philharmonic such a loss is detrimental.....

In the same month:

A form of contract for membership with the choir has been prepared and is in process of being signed by present members. The contract clearly informs the member what is required of him and also what will be guaranteed him in return for services.

In February 1937 a membership badge was introduced bringing in to being the choir logo still used today.

YP
M.V.C.
A freehand sketch of the York Philharmonic Choir's Membership Badge

In March the Seventh Annual Inter-Choral Choir Competition was described as "An outstanding Success" and in May the number of Vice Presidents was increased to give a truly substantial musical and managerial support structure to Cecil and the choir committee. There were six extremely competent and committed Vice Presidents; Ald. W.H. Birch JP, J. H. Forster JP, Harold Fredericks, H. Marchant Haigh LRAM, A.W. Sargent, and W.H. Sessions JP. An apparently happier Cecil, as editor of the magazine, was able to write:

The Philharmonic has completed its concert season but work will be strenuously carried on up to June 26th the date of the Cleethorpes Musical Festival for which we have entered [winning a creditable third place with a choir of only 33 competing against those with over 50 singers], and to add: *All invalids of the choir are now reported better. We have visions of that 100% attendance.*

Any difficulties of 1936 seem to have been resolved and with a stronger management team, contracts for members and membership badges, the Philharmonic had clearly come of age.

Concerts in and around York

York Male Voice Choir [see later chapter] had been set up as a competition choir giving in addition *one grand concert a year.* The York Old Priory Choir had been set up at the same time with the intention of singing *in support of good causes.* Established some 25 years later, the York Philharmonic held the same view as York Old Priory. The list, in the previous chapter, of engagements for two months in 1936 showed that much work both supported and entertained Methodist churches in the city. These were often in aid of Chapel Anniversaries or Choir Sundays but were also held as midweek entertainments. No reference is made in the magazines to the 'Entertainment tax' which was in force till the 1950s. This tax included concerts given in churches, which may help explain why many of such concerts were called 'Musical Services'. It is difficult to know how this tax was levied, particularly as entry was normally free with the hope that a successful concert with a good audience would generate income by means of a silver collection. It was also the custom in those days for audiences to request 'encores' throughout the performance so a number of items were often sung more than once. Many of these concerts became annual fixtures, and the choir accepted invitations from chapels large and small. For example in December 1933 came this review from the Wesley Chapel in Priory Street:

The Lecture Hall in Wesley Chapel has for many years been the venue of concerts of high excellence but the writer does not remember a more pleasing programme than that given by the York Philharmonic Male Voice Choir recently. There was a tone about the choir which could only be the result of sound training coupled with a keen enthusiasm on the part of all the members.

In March 1936 a reviewer of a concert in Haughton Road Chapel, Burton Stone Lane wrote:

...I have no thought of passing comment on any single item excepting 'The Lost Chord'. I am afraid our small organ did not lend any colour to the rendering, but our poor old instrument was on its best behaviour that night because there are one or two notes that

stick and refuse to rise – with of course disastrous results.

Despite the organ the choir still gave an annual concert.

Regular concerts were also given in the Adult Schools of James Street, Priory Street and Acomb. In November 1933 the choir sang at the opening of the St Barnabas (Anglican) Church Hall in Leeman Road, a local event of significance.

...This concert will be remembered by all whom attended because in addition to a fine and varied programme the event was part of the 'opening ceremony'. We were the first choir to sing in that hall and showed our appreciation of that honour by displaying real good form, and testing to the full the acoustic properties of this new concert hall........After about 45 minutes singing which constituted the first half we were invited to adjourn to a room below to partake of refreshment. This gave the choir a break and incidentally allowed the audience to have a free and easy chat and perhaps discuss the singing.

On our return we received a fine ovation – an indication that they had talked things over and had decided that they liked us. The second half was even better than the first and one felt sorry when the concert was over......

The day before this 'prestigious' local event the choir had given a concert in The York Institution (The Workhouse):

Although we could not field a full side for our concert on November 22nd last at the York Institution we nevertheless were able to provide an interesting and amusing entertainment. Part songs, solos, and humorous duets constituted the programme and many were the encores. Space won't permit a report in detail. We were the means of making our less fortunate friends happy.

These two concert reports appear next to each other in the January 1934 issue under the heading – *Other Concerts*. The choir also gave concerts for the York Companions Club:

Our concert given in the St. Thomas's Parish Hall to the members of the Companions' Club – most of whom are unemployed – was indeed a huge success. It had been the custom to provide refreshment for the members of the club, but on this occasion none was served. A large number of those present seemed rather sore at this neglect. It was therefore left to us to get the men in a good humour. A well balanced choir together with a good room for singing enabled us to put over an exceptional good show. We soon won over the audience, and a right joyous evening resulted. Encores were numerous – in fact we had difficulty in getting away after the last item. They certainly would have liked another hour of it. March 1934

These were not one off events; support for the men in the York Companions' Club became a regular engagement.

The November 1934 issue printed a thank you letter for a concert given to an audience which would have been predominantly female:

At the last committee meeting of the Acomb branch of the BWTA I was asked to write you a letter expressing their thanks and appreciation for the very excellent concert the York Philharmonic gave at the Adult School Acomb on their behalf.

What a delightful evening it was. I am sure everyone in the audience enjoyed every item.

The choir, who sang their pieces almost exclusively without copies, made them wonderfully effective and deserve the greatest praise. Mrs Adamson, our President, who is a lady of good taste in music, remarked how well rendered they were, as were also the solos, humorous items and violin solos.......

BWTA (?) – The British Women's Temperance Association.

Another regular event was the York Chrysanthemum Show. Here is the report from December 1935:

The concert given by the choir at the Chrysanthemum show of Saturday 23rd. November was very successful. A varied programme lasting two hours was given and although the large crowds moved about slowly inspecting the flowers, it was creditable that no serious noise interference resulted. On a few occasions, when apparently the piece being sung was particularly to the liking of the crowd, there was perfect quiet. Everyone seemed to enjoy the show which, we think, was the best for many a year.

That December 1935 issue also carried a report of another occasional social/ musical evening spent with the Rowntree Sales Office staff. These took the form of a dinner and concert held at the City Arms.

In the majority of events someone would be elected to 'take the chair' to act as a master of ceremonies and to offer a vote of thanks. One of the most successful, and entertaining chairs was Mr. W.H. Sessions. Amongst his many achievements he wrote and published two books on Quaker humour. Mr. Sessions regularly 'took the chair', in particular when the choir sang at James Street Adult School. Here are extracts from three years as published in March 1933, March 1934 and April 1936:

It is strange how the treatment by an audience can linger in one's memory and when memories are pleasant, future visits are eagerly anticipated. When we were invited to James St. Adult School 1933 Anniversary there was a unanimous "Aye" for we all remembered a right pleasant evening in 1932, but surely it could not be that 12 months had passed by. 12 whole months, yet on taking our places on the platform it seemed that we were just returning after the interval, so fresh in our minds was the memory of our previous visit.

*The same thoughts must have been in Mr. Sessions mind, for he opened the concert with the remark. "It hardly seems a year ago since we were here and the ladies in the back row misbehaved themselves". But the ladies in the back row were not so much in evidence this night. Had they forgotten a year ago, or perhaps – well anything might have happened.......*1933

The Philharmonic Male Voice Choir is certainly in great demand just now – four engagements in seven days – commencing with our annual visit to James Street. We are, of course, expected to maintain the standard we have already set at the school, and right well did we do it..........

A visit to James Street would not be complete without some reference to 'the ladies in the back row' but the originals of two years ago seem to have given way to a new and younger generation who, we hope, will give good service to James St. for many years to come. 1934

....Mr. W.H. Sessions our Vice-President, occupied the chair and his quotations from the 'Book of Low Comedy' as he terms it had the audience, including the famous 'back row' in merry mood throughout the evening. The people of James Street have come to look upon us as annual visitors and we hope that circumstances will allow us to entertain them for many years to come. 1936

No details of the 'misbehaviour' of 1932 were ever published.

During this decade, invitations were also accepted to sing outside York, at churches in Malton, Scarborough, Pickering, and Selby; and in April 1934 the Tower Theatre Goole, at the request of the National Union of Railwaymen, on behalf of Union's Local Widows and Orphans Christmas Cheer Fund. These out of town concerts were almost always well received. Here, for example, is an extract following the third visit to Wheelgate Methodist Church in Malton:

....The people of Malton gave us a wonderful welcome, and the tea and supper they provided for us was a feast for the gods. It was a sincere welcome – one which we appreciate and will always remember. Thanks to all at Wheelgate, we look forward to our next visit. The following letter has been received:-

'That the YPMVC are popular in Malton was quite evident on Sunday April 10th when on their third return visit to Wheelgate Methodist Church they drew large audiences to hear them both in the afternoon and evening. Their visit was eagerly looked forward to, for the choir has many friends in Malton.

The programmes were delightfully rendered and the audiences were not slow to voice their appreciation......' PN May 1938

On that occasion the choir sang at a musical service at 2.30pm and then again in the evening service:

*....A fairly large number of members and their friends left York by bus and car at 1.30pm and arrived in time to commence a Musical service at 2.30pm. The church was full, and we found a very appreciative congregation. The afternoon's programme lasted ninety minutes, and after tea we gave musical items at the evening service which was again well attended. The singing we felt was even better in the evening...*PN May 1938

The choir gave many concerts on midweek nights, but these Sunday events seemed popular with both choir and audiences. Sundays in the 1930s would be 'quiet,' even 'dull' days with no shops open, no cinemas, no plays in theatres, and probably few if any places to find anything to eat. It could be that in a small market town like Malton a hungry traveller passing through on a Sunday evening might find a pub open offering a menu choice ranging from pickled eggs to pickled onions. So a Sunday afternoon musical would have been an excellent way of providing a concert for the town. The choir would have a large and enthusiastic audience, the church could receive a reasonable collection and the town officials could rest easy knowing no laws were being infringed. An extract from April 1936 (a reprint of a Yorkshire Herald report) describing an earlier Malton concert stated:

Considerable interest was taken in the visit of the York Philharmonic Male Voice Choir to the Malton, Saville Street Methodist Church, on Sunday afternoon, and it was appropriate that the chair should be taken by the Lord Mayor of York (Councillor W.H.Shaw) who has such close associations with the Malton district.

The Lord Mayor took the occasion to impress upon the large company present the importance of attending a place of worship at least once each Sunday.

The visit of the choir, which was a real treat for music lovers, was in the nature of a return event. They were at Malton Wheelgate Methodist Church last September when they made a most favourable impression..... PN April 1936

Following a concert in Selby, one choir member made these thoughtful and frustrated comments.

I didn't feel at all like doing a concert the night we went to Selby, but how pleased I was that I did go. The response to every item was quite refreshing which prompts me to ask. "Do we do too many concerts in York?"

Selby was new ground to us and I should imagine that concerts such as we gave that night are few and far between.

Certainly I am not out 'applause hunting' for silence can be just as eloquent, but one could feel that we had those Selbyites in the hollow of our hands and, I have felt the same with concerts at Malton, Pickering etc. There is an entirely different atmosphere.

Just consider that from early January into April the choir is engaged practically each week; this is a serious call on members time and in some cases their pockets as I have known members break working hours to help the choir at more important engagements.

Is it likely that the people in York will put themselves out to hear us when we can be heard so regularly?

I know it is our rule that these appeals shall, as far as possible be given consideration, but is it right that all the work should be given to the Philharmonic?

There are other and similar choirs in the city who could and should take a more active part in helping to raise funds for these various organisations.

I feel we should all reap some benefit from the arrangement. F. Colley PN March 1938.

However working in York could still bring new experiences as noted in November 1937:

A very large audience attended the variety concert on Tuesday November 2nd in the Rowntree Theatre which had been arranged by Industrial Orthopaedic Society in aid of funds for the building of a new wing to the Manor House Hospital Leeds. The artistes who took part have gratuitously given their services and were Don Scales (boy accordionist), Shah Din Sufis (monarch of mystery), The Harmony Four (vocal quartette), Kathleen and her Millionaires Accordion Band, Cliffe Riche (comedian), Arthur C. Taylor (tenor), York Harmonica band and the Philharmonic Choir.

The Choir opened the concert with five varied pieces and we were well received. It was our first appearance in the splendid theatre and we hope it will not be our last. The programme was non-stop and a thoroughly enjoyable two and a half hours were spent. One could scarcely realise that it was carried out without rehearsal, so successful was the timing.

We were extremely pleased to help towards such a deserving cause which, we understand, benefitted considerably. PN November 1937.

The article carried this footnote:

It was pleasing to see Harry Pickering (one time choir member and now stage manager at the Rowntree theatre) at the variety concert the other evening. We could not resist asking him to join the tenors and have a sing. He enjoyed it too!

Monkgate Three Choirs Festival

Without doubt the most successful concert series of the decade was the one performed with Old Priory and Monkgate choirs. In 1930 Archie Sargent began the rebuild of the choir at Monkgate Methodist Church. The first mention of the choirs coming together is from March 1933:

In connection with the Anniversary Services of the Monkgate Methodist Church our members took part in a musical service on Sunday afternoon February 12th. During the service I could not help thinking how fortunate the Monkgate Methodists were in possessing such a beautiful building to meet in.

Mr. Fletcher conducted the Philharmonic Choir in eight part songs and Mr. Sargent directed the Church choir in four chorals all delightfully rendered.

It was very interesting to note the pronounced difference evinced in the singing of the part songs and the choral items – so different in sentiment and composition but both beautiful and pleasing.

Mr. A.W.Sargent delighted the congregation with two organ solos, the 'Handel Fantasy' particularly appealed to our members with whom it is very familiar. Mr. Albert Snowden sang two solos 'O Love Divine' and 'River of Years' in his usual finished manner. A long and interesting programme terminated with the singing of 'Jerusalem' (Parry) by the combined choirs. S.P. Wilson.

In 1934 following a mid week concert at Monkgate, Archie Sargent wrote of the Philharmonic:

'The occasions on which I have listened to the choir have been comparatively rare and yet I feel a sense of kinship and understanding when I hear them and see them in action. This is probably because I feel that they have the right spirit – magnificent camaraderie, enthusiasm and an ever present anxiety to know more and to do better'. PN March 1934.

It is at this time that these three conductors and choirs came together in a way which enhanced the reputation of each. The Three Choirs festival held as a Sunday afternoon concert in Monkgate to celebrate Choir Sunday soon attracted audiences of up to 1000. In his memoirs Archie Sargent wrote:

I was thinking one day of the famous Three Choirs Festival in which Gloucester, Hereford and Worcester Cathedral choirs combine in a great festival, and the idea came to me that it might be possible to arrange a festival of Three Choirs in York – in our Methodist Church. Accordingly I spoke to my friends Jack Forster and Cecil Fletcher who responded at once. Jack would bring the Old Priory Ladies, and Cecil, The York Philharmonic Male Voice Choir. Monkgate choir, which of course, was a mixed voice combination, would complete the trio, and we commenced the Three Choirs Festival in the afternoon of our Choir Sunday each year. In arranging something new of this kind, it is quite impossible to forecast public reaction, but in this case, after the introduction of the series, there was no room for doubt, and the congregations assembled for this event almost as large as for 'Messiah'. ....I recall some thrilling experiences during those programmes and one comes to mind at the moment. Cecil Fletcher and his Philharmonic men had decided to include in their programme 'The Lost Chord' (Sullivan) and I was asked to play. The men sang magnificently, and at the conclusion, there was one tremendous burst of applause which continued without the slightest sign of any diminution, Cecil acknowledged this several times, and still it persisted. Finally, he decided to repeat the last section. He told me afterwards that after the men had given this item the performance of their lives, he felt it was expecting too much to ask them to sing it again from the beginning...

That performance was in March 1935 and William Payne, a founder member of the Philharmonic, in a piece reflecting on the first ten years of the choir wrote: *'Then latterly our concert in Monkgate Wesley Chapel. I might say that never in all my life have I enjoyed singing as much as I did in Arthur Sullivan's 'the Lost Chord'.* PN April 1935.

It was at this time that Archie recalled the following suggestion by Cecil:

... the possibility of the Monkgate Choir entering a competitive festival next emerged as a result of a chat with the genial founder conductor of the York Philharmonic Male Voice Choir – Cecil H. Fletcher. He had been in Sheffield and said, in the course of our conversation that there was an excellent class for Church and Chapel choirs.

Monkgate entered, and won, for the next two years when the class was disbanded (apparently through lack of entries). Archie then expressed the frustration of many choirs at festival organisers:

My personal impression at the time was that a dramatic diminution in the number of entries had been caused by the difficulty of the test pieces chosen. For example, it was not to be expected that the average church or chapel choir could undertake Elgar's 'Light of the World' much of which is written in seven parts.

Archie was not new to competitive work as he had led the Victoria Bar choir to repeated success in the York Choral Festivals. It is interesting to note that he recorded this reference to Cecil influencing the decision for Monkgate to compete; perhaps it was affirmation that the Monkgate choir had now reached the necessary standard.

Archie does, however, give more information about Jack Forster, who as the eldest of the three seems to have been admired as a mentor by both Archie and Cecil:

One of my happiest recollections of this period is a warm friendship I enjoyed with the founder-conductor of the York Old Priory Choir, whom was affectionately known everywhere in the area as 'Jack Forster'. He was a Scot, direct, outspoken, generous to a degree, and a most loyal friend. He lived for his choir, and, under his skilful direction, the choir became one of the finest mixed voice choirs in the North of England. I say mixed voice but actually it was so well balanced, that there was a Ladies section and a Male Voice section acting independently of the full choir. Their successes in Choral Competitions were legion......I shall never forget Jack's encouragement to me when our work in York commenced, and this continued until his retirement – and after. For a number of years he sang, with a contingent of his choir, in our performances of Messiah.........He was a great fellow and friendship with him was indeed a privilege.

The Three Choirs Festival was instrumental in bringing the Monkgate Choir to the attention of the BBC – with astonishing consequences. There may have been some sadness within the ranks of the Phil as all choirs aspired to broadcast, at least on regional radio; York Old Priory had given three broadcasts and York Male Voice Choir at least one. Monkgate was now to embark on a radio career surpassing all the others; yet the Philharmonic was not able to achieve the same accolade. Reproduced below is an extended extract taken from *Voices Pipes and Pedals*. This was reported by YEP:

Audition for Broadcast

Choral Concert in York Monkgate Methodist Church

A representative of the BBC attended a choral concert in York yesterday to hear the Monkgate Methodist Choir, who achieved fame in 1935 by winning the Fulwood Wesley Trophy for open church and chapel choirs at the Sheffield Music Festival. This success was repeated last year. The audition was for broadcast.

In the group of three items given for auditory purposes was 'Save us O Lord' composed by Sir Edward Bairstow organist of York Minster. The other two were 'O Most Merciful' (Bullock) and 'The Crucifixion' (arr. Hugh Roberton). The last one was a very exacting piece, but was rendered with masterly effect.

The three choirs who contributed to the programme at the Monkgate Methodist church toward an effort in aid of the choir funds were, Monkgate, the York Old Ladies Priory Choir, and the York Philharmonic Male Voice Choir.

'A choral Sunday with different choirs is an idea I introduced three years ago and which has made a tremendous appeal to the public' said Mr. A.W.Sargent (organist and choirmaster) to a representative of the Yorkshire Evening Press. How great this appeal is with lovers of music in York was shown by the large audience. Despite the fact that it rained heavily all afternoon, the church, which accommodates about 1000 people, was filled. Chairs had to be used by a number of people, and the audience in the gallery extended into the choir seats.

After groups of church sings by the three choirs mentioned, the programme concluded with a fine effort by the massed choirs, augmented by members of James Street United Choir, Rowntrees Choral Society and the Male members of the York Old Priory Choir. They sang the wonderful Hebrew hymn 'On Jordan's Banks' (arr. M. Bruch). Altogether there were about 150 voices, and with organ effect. The inexplicable beauty and power of the song were brought out excellently. The massed choirs were conducted by Mr. J.H.Forster, and the organ was played by Mr. Sargent. The Monkgate choir, conducted by Mr. Sargent, also sang 'Crimond' and 'Nobody knows the trouble' (arr. H. Roberton) and 'Light of the World' (Elgar). The Old Priory Ladies' Choir was conducted by Mr. Forster. They sang some beautiful selections, such as 'The Mother's Song' (Schubert/Bairstow). 'How far is it to Bethlehem' (Geoffrey Shaw),'A Grecian Landscape' (Cyril Jenkins), and 'The Snow' (Elgar). 'Feasting I watch', 'It's oh to be a wild wind', 'The Wanderer' (Elgar) and 'The Lost Chord' (Sullivan), with Mr. Sargent at the organ, were some noteworthy items by the Philharmonic Choir. The concert was an outstanding success. With a programme so varied, a contrast between a women's' choir and a men's' choir, and the music moving to the ultimate triumph by five choirs, this was, perhaps expected. But the audience found the character of the music highly satisfying and imaginative, and they displayed their appreciation by great applause.........

Within a few days we learned that the audition had been successful, and that the BBC would call for us when required. Very shortly afterwards, the first call came. It seemed that requests had been received by the BBC from various parts of Yorkshire, for a recital of revival hymns, and the BBC wanted a Methodist Choir for the purpose. We had just been accepted, and so they asked whether we would take this engagement. This, our first experience at the microphone and on radio, took place on 16th June 1937.

Three months later came the second broadcast, prompting this entry in the Radio Times:

The first broadcast by this choir on 16th June was followed by an unusually large number of appreciative letters from listeners in many part of the country. The many who asked for more are likely to be well pleased if they listen to this York recital. The success of the choir at the Monkgate Methodist Church is to a considerable extent a credit to the enthusiasm and initiative of the organist-choirmaster, A.W.Sargent, who is in charge this evening.

Four months later, broadcast number three led to this entry in the York Evening Press:

This will mean the choir will have done three broadcast in seven months, which creates something of a record, I think for a York choir, if we except the Minster Choir which is heard every Tuesday on the Evening broadcast.

The choir made a total of 22 broadcasts.

The Three Choirs Festival was the most successful series of joint concerts in which the Philharmonic, under the leadership of Cecil Fletcher, was able to take part.

Competitions

All choirs of any merit do, at some time, enter a choral competition. In this pre-war period there were a number of comprehensive festivals in the region, including the York Choral Festival, which offered classes for all types of choir. We know that the LRAS competed first in May 1926 only 12 months from inception. We also know that by the end of 1933 the Phil had competed in 14 festivals. Throughout its 90 year life the Philharmonic, as a competition choir, has had one disadvantage. In Male Voice competition size matters and it is difficult to achieve success with a choir of say 36-40 when up against 60-70 singers. In October 1934, Cecil launched a recruitment campaign to raise membership to 70.

An effort is to be made to reach a membership of seventy voices and in the next month's and subsequent issues of the journal a clock will appear showing by a pointer the monthly progress made in the effort. We have forty members to date but past experience has proved that when concerts of music festivals have to be attended many members have been unable to attend on account of their work, the balance, in consequence, has upon many occasions suffered thereby. With a membership of seventy we could almost guarantee 48 voices (a number necessary to do justice to the majority of male voice pieces) and should the whole seventy voice be on duty, well!

Cecil must have been encouraged as membership reached 58 by April 1935, but the target of 70 was never reached, and the clock made few appearances in the magazine.

In an earlier chapter we read the amusing account by Ada Cade of the rehearsal that preceded competing in the 'First Annual Competitive Festival in Sheffield' which the choir won. Cecil later recommended this festival to Archie Sargent. It seems that the competition was organised not to showcase the city centre or civic pride, but to help build a community spirit on the recently built Manor estate. So the classes, other than the finals, were held there and the Manor Community Association took an active role in the organising. It seems it was a success in that it led to the formation of a Manor choir. It is likely that this community based approach appealed both to Cecil Fletcher and Archie Sargent. After the first win on Whit Saturday 1934 Cecil was enthusiastic in writing:

This festival was the outcome of activities by a number of ambitious musical people, and we don't hesitate to say that it was a huge success; it would be even safe to predict that Sheffield will eventually produce one of the finest Musical Festivals in the country. One pleasing feature of the festival was that every test piece, whether for solo, choir or instrument, was an ideal concert piece and competitors, even if they did not win, had the satisfaction of knowing that the time spent in preparation had been well spent for they could add one or two jolly good items to their concert repertoire. PN June 1934

Sadly, music festivals have a life cycle of their own and as noted in the comments by Archie Sargent earlier, the test pieces became too difficult for the majority of choirs in his chosen class of church and chapel choirs. This view of festival choices was echoed in a piece published in N&V 1928, following poor turn outs at both York and Scarborough festivals:

It seems a disease that Festival Committees suffer from, this choice of difficult, intricate, acrobatic and oft times unmusical test pieces. Test pieces which are absolutely no use to a choir afterwards for concert purposes and very often they cost 6d or 8d a copy.

The enthusiasm shown by Cecil and many others did not, however, help with the financial aspects of running festivals. In the April 1937 issue of PN is the following brief entry:

Sheffield claims to be a musical centre but music festivals are 'bad business' there. Forty people who guaranteed a £200 total towards the last festival expenses will have to pay up: £316 was lost. There were 10,000 entries, but audiences often numbered only a few score.

Financial considerations were also a key factor in the Yorkshire Choral Competitions. One money-raising initiative was a bi-annual Massed Choirs concert in which the Philharmonic took part and was probably the only occasion when the Phil shared a concert platform with York Male Voice Choir.

Here is the advert for the 1934 concert as it appeared on the back page of PN:

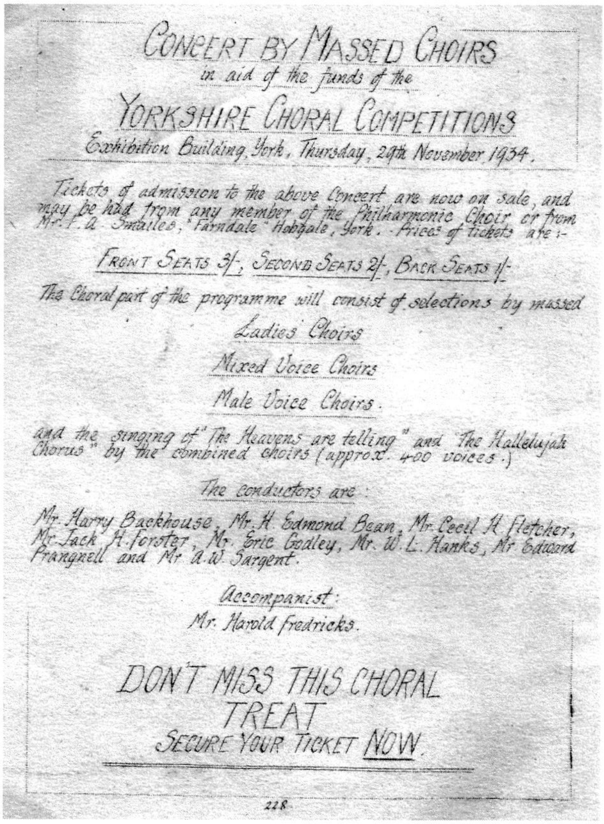

It is clear that the many choirs in York were willing to come together for concerts of this type. In the December 1934 issue the editor commented that:

... it is doubtful whether the concert by combined choirs in aid of the Yorkshire Choral Competitions was the financial success anticipated as the Exhibition Hall was far from crowded.

There was another massed concert in November 1936, which presumably also failed to meet financial expectations, and the Choral Competition ceased soon after.

York as a city struggled to put together any large competition choirs, a situation which helps explain the single-minded determination of the successful York Male Voice Choir to recruit and select a choir of 50 with the specific ambition of winning competitions. The culture and geography of the city did not seem to lend itself to the formation of large choirs based on a single industry or district as could be found elsewhere in Yorkshire. This frustration was eloquently expressed by S.P.Wilson, the secretary of the Phil, in an article in June 1933:

York on a night in June!

Having finished work for the day I reach for my hat and stick (two relics of Victorian days alas) and take a walk down Bootham into the fairest and most historical town in England. Walking along under the trees Bootham Bar and the City walls come into view. Passing through the Bar we see the Minster in all its matchless beauty – then on to Lendal Bridge. Looking towards Ouse Bridge we have a wonderful view of the river described as

'Venice in England'; Hill's boatyard with its splendid trees, and then the Guildhall with its ancient Watergate.

Passing under the bridge we suddenly receive a thrill, for in addition to the glorious view that meets the eye, the sound of music reaches us. A party of young men are singing an old melody that is popular on the wireless. Their voices, perfectly blended, sound very sweet coming up from the river, and I could not help thinking what a pity it seemed that we could not rope these singers into our depleted choirs. They are material we are so much in need of. They evidently know it is good to sing, or they would have been content with shouting. How is it that a city like York with a population of 90,000 has only one or two choirs of 30 to 40 voices or so when a small place like West Melton at Rotherham can put a choir of 70 or 80 voices on a platform? How often one hears people talking of the magnificence of York Minster but never a word about the wonderful singing to be heard within. Here we have one of the finest, if not the finest, Church choir in England singing every day and it is all taken as a matter of course. Most towns would go into raptures if they possessed such a choir. Is it that York people fail to realize the joy to be had in singing, and the pleasure it affords the listener? Or is it true what has been said, that York is a sleepy old place noted for its parsons and pubs, who knows!

Mr. Wilson's views are in some way supported by an entry in PN two months earlier in April 1933:

We could not contest the male voice class at Pontefract this year. The class was on Saturday afternoon March 25th and many of our members could not get off work. Shipley Musical Union won the class. This is not surprising because they sang wonderfully well at York last May – only beaten by a point by Burton Stone Lane Choir.

Looking back from 2015, it seems remarkable that Leeman Road and Burton Stone Lane (in which Cecil Fletcher lived) could both have male voice choirs capable of winning competitions. The two districts are either side of the river but still only a short bicycle ride apart. If they had worked together maybe they could have had a winning choir at that Pontefract festival.

In most of the reports on competitions there is a reference to the size of choirs competing. For example: The South Yorkshire (27th Annual) Music Festival July 1933:

.....Ten choirs had entered this class and all turned out to show their abilities. We had a feeling that we would have to pull all out, as we only had 34 voices against 48-50 voices of each of the other choirs. It certainly was a handicap, but it made us more determined than disheartened.

Our turn came at last and it is pleasing to report that we put up a splendid show. "We must have qualified for the final and have to sing again this evening!" said someone but, no, we just failed.

Sir Hugh Roberton, the adjudicator, was warm in his praise of our effort, but apparently something went wrong with our pianissimos; they were a little too delicate or something like that – and did not carry very well.

If only we had had ten more voices we – but never mind, it was a wonderful achievement to secure 5th place in 'Class A' and so close in marks to the winners too. Those 'West Riding' choirs can sing, but we hope to lower their colours ere long. PN Oct 1933. Only four marks separated first place from fifth.

Four years later small numbers were still a competitive handicap. Cleethorpes Musical Festival 26th June 1937:

"Choir number one will sing again!" That was Dr. C.Armstrong Gibb's opening remark when making his comments on the afternoon session of the Male Voice Contest at Cleethorpes Musical Festival on Saturday June 26th last, and most worthily had the choir earned the right to sing in the final for the prize of £10 and Challenge Cup presented by the Cleethorpes Chamber of Trade.

It was a great thrill to those 33 members who left York by bus that Saturday to test their skill against Class A choirs of fifty strong all well known and successful choirs such as Thurnscoe, Scunthorpe, The Moorland Gleemen etc..........

..refreshed and in fighting trim for the final we made our way again to the Pier Pavilion when, on account of the rapid progress of the preceding classes we had to marshal our forces rather hurriedly to again take first turn. Every man was fully aware of the task before us if we were to be successful in this round, and right well did they respond but no matter how we tried we had to take third place. It was a real fighting finish but it was a case of numbers being able to give that little extra quality the pieces required. It was a case of 33 against 50. PN October 1937

Cleethorpes was a Class A competition, so a third place with a small choir was a good result. Four months later in October in another A class the Phil learned another fundamental truth about choral competitions; that it is just not possible to please all adjudicators all of the time:

The Philharmonic took the count at Armthorpe. Yes! We bit the dust for the first time, for we were placed seventh out of seven choirs.

Saturday October 16th saw us journey to that outlandish spot – Armthorpe – about four miles from Doncaster – to contest the open male voice class. The test pieces were 'Sound an Alarm' (Handel) and 'I dare not ask a kiss' (Bairstow) and the choirs who took part were Sheffield Orpheus, Edwinstowe, The Moorland Gleemen, Armthorpe, Rossington, Thurnscoe and the Philharmonic. The adjudicators were Cyril Wynn Esq. HM Inspector of Public Schools and Dr. Hutchinson.

Having whacked five of these choirs at Cleethorpes, and with 'Sound an Alarm' too we fancied our chances for at least a place. The adjudicators didn't however and there we are. We are not advancing any theories or offering any excuses for the defeat for the Philharmonics are sportsmen and can take it. We prefer to look on the humorous side of Oct.16th 1937. We know now what it feels like to go in like a lion and come out like a lamb.

Well never mind, Philharmonics, there's plenty of festivals and, after all, seven's a lucky number. Keep plodding, we'll win the next. PN Nov.1937

The Inter-Choral Competition

Without a doubt the most successful competitions the Choir ever took part in were those organised by itself. In 1930 Cecil introduced an Inter-Choral Competition, an inspired idea which so grew and expanded as to be as significant in its own sphere as Archie Sargent's introduction of the Three Choirs Festival.

In summary the competitions can be described as follows:

The object of these competitions is to encourage the members of the Choir to gain confidence in themselves; to overcome "stage fright" and to develop their musical talent by giving individual expression in song.

There were solo classes for each section, a class for quartets, and then four soloists were selected for the Finalist Class. Apparently a duet class was offered but did not prove popular. The contest was held in an evening at the City Arms

Hotel in Fawcett Street and proved immensely successful. Within three years, with competitions going on till almost midnight, the programme became too long. The time was then extended to an afternoon and evening. In later years it outgrew the City Arms and, due to demand, added two open classes inviting male singers from other choirs to take part. In 1937 this was extended further by adding open female classes – soprano and alto. The intention for 1938 was to add open choral classes for small choirs of up to 20 singers. It was on the verge of becoming a city-wide Music Festival organised and run by the choir when the war intervened.

Henry Brough, a founder member of the choir and a regular competitor had won the 1936 bass class with a rendition of 'The Floral Dance'. He shared some memories in a hand written note in 1979, a significant year given that after a 30 year gap, the contest had been revived – for one year only:

In Retrospect

In my past article for 'Contact' [the choir magazine of 1979] I made reference to the 'Inter– Choir Choral Competition' so I should like to enlarge on this subject.

This competition was instituted many years ago when 'Ces' Fletcher was conductor, the idea being to encourage members of the choir to "try their arm" at solo singing. The first contest took place in the now defunct City Arms Hotel, a goodly number of members and friends attended and the event was a pronounced success.

The programme was made up of two tenor solos, two bass-baritone solos and a quartet class. I think every choir member took part and really enjoyed it.

The winners of the four classes 'sang off' at the end of the contest and the winner became choir Champion and was awarded a gold medal the other three being awarded silver medals.

The winning group in the quartet class was awarded a silver rose bowl to be held for one year. This trophy was presented to the choir by Mr. 'Snigger' Wilson one of our second tenors.

The winner of the gold medal was barred from the ordinary solo classes for a period of three years, at the end of this time there being more gold medallists a 'gold medal' class was formed for which Mr. Fletcher provided a challenge cup to be held for one year. An attempt was made to start a duet class but for some reason this did not find favour.

There were various incidents at times which seemed amusing viz. when a certain bass soloist was singing the test piece 'The Lute Player' his dentures were slack fitting and the first word of the piece was 'The'. He put so much emphasis on this word that he blew his teeth out but managed to catch them on his copy. Another incident was when the aforementioned 'Snigger' Wilson was singing 'To Daisies' and had his words typed out on pieces of paper which he discarded one after another until when he was finished he was surrounded by sheets of paper.

The competition became so well known that eventually we opened it out to other choirs in York and district with the addition of other classes, there was a faint hope that this might lead to reviving the York Musical Festival but the outbreak of war put an end to this.

Additional rehearsals were made available to assist choir members who could not practice at home, so no one was precluded from taking part.

The competitions predate the introduction of *Philharmonic News* so the first to be reported was the third:

On Wednesday March 1st 1933 the Third Annual Inter– Choral Competitions of the York Philharmonic Male Voice Choir were held in the City Arms Hotel in the presence of the Vice President Mr. C. Martin, Mrs Martin and about forty friends and supporters; and was without doubt one of the most enjoyable events in the history of the choir. The scene of the contest was the large dining room of the hotel kindly placed at our disposal by the landlord Mr. Handsley. A lofty spacious room, beautifully arranged and decorated, and with excellent acoustic properties made conditions just ideal for an event of this nature.

The object of these competitions is to encourage the members of the choir to gain confidence in themselves; to overcome "stage fright" and to develop their musical talent by giving individual expression in song, and it must have been very gratifying to the Choirmaster of these men to hear such a high standard of singing, and to note the vast improvement on previous competitions.

In choosing the test pieces Mr. C.H.Fletcher had very carefully selected songs suitable in range and with abundant scope for expression, yet with such an appeal in them to attract a record number of entries. Mr. Edward Prangnell the conductor of the York Co-operative choral Society adjudicated all the classes. He handled the many delicate situations with the masterly manner of an expert musician, his decisions were popular, his criticisms helpful and enlightening to the competitors witty and entertaining to the audience........

The 'Quartet Class' had reluctantly to be postponed as the time had reached 11.30pm, and so arrangements were made to hold this class at the next choir rehearsal when Mr. Prangnell promised to be present in the same capacity....... And so after four solid hours, hard work – excitement – thrills – nerve attacks – disappointments – congratulations – regrets – resolutions – ends the third choir contest, still improving that much envied team spirit in our great little choir, always believing that the chap who beat you probably practiced more than you. Roll on the next contest! J. Hardisty Contest Secretary

PN March 1933

City Arms Hotel, Fawcett Street, 1919

The City Arms was also the venue for the 10th Anniversary Dinner held in March 1936.

The fourth Competition was reported in March 1934:

...Immediately a start was made with the contest proper, and it was soon evident that

the quality of this year's singing would be an improvement on previous contests. Midway through the programme there was a pleasing break. For sometime past it has been felt that the services of our secretary Mr. S Parker Wilson, and our treasurer Mr. W.Bolton should be acknowledged in a manner more tangible than a 'vote of thanks' at an annual meeting, and to my idea it was a fine gesture indeed to ask Mr. Tom Clark, who is one of the original members of the choir to make a presentation of an inscribed silver cigarette casket on behalf of the choir, to these officials in recognition of their valuable services.

At the same time Mr. Fletcher presented to Miss J. Brough (accompanist) a box of chocolates with the best thanks of the choir. Mr. Fletcher remarked that, to play fifty five solos in the course of a few hours needed not only ability but stamina. No-one he added would envy Miss Brough on this night.

The second half of the programme was then commenced, but owing to the large number of entries, and the fact that time was getting short, it was decided not to read the adjudicators remarks but just to announce the marks awarded. J. Hardisty PN March 1934.

The adjudicator on this occasion was Mr R.Marchant-Haigh LRAM later to become a choir Vice President.

By the sixth occasion in 1936, the contest had so increased in size as to require two adjudicators, Mr. Edward Prangnell – conductor of the York Co-operative Choral Society – and Cecil Fletcher. Jane Brough's marathon as accompanist was now shared with her younger sister, Kathleen, and Mr. L. Wreghitt of York Minster. It was recognised, at this time, that the contest would in future require an afternoon and evening, and that open classes would be allowed so that members of other choirs could take part. The City Arms would not be able to host for an afternoon and evening and so a change of venue would also be required. PN March 1936 magazine carried a report on the contest from one of the regular contributors who signed off as B.Flat but who was most probably choir wife and ardent fan – Ada Cade:

AN INTERESTING EXPERIENCE by the Musical Critic to the Sporting Wink

An Inter-Choir contest resembles on some respects a public execution. The victims are volunteers, and very courageous they are as they ascend the scaffold and do their stuff in more or less heroic attitudes. Afterwards having imbibed a variety of corpse-revivers they are thoughtfully dissected by a couple of kindly vivisectors, who do their job in such a happy way that nobody feels cut up about their decisions. I thought as an outsider that to hear the same song sung umpteen times would be a little boring – but no – you never knew what would happen in those sombre woods, or what sort of partner you might get in the next Floral Dance. In an aside I heard one chorister say that he had sung the 'Floral Dance' all the way from Scarboro to York on some trip or other; the flowers must have been a bit faded by the time the Bar walls came into sight.....

Some of the volunteers went up in fours. Health bubbled out of them and Edward V111 should live to be 200 and brewery shares rocket to the moon after all the healths that were drank. It struck me, whilst the execution was in progress, of the heroic unseen part women had played in bringing their men-folk up to concert pitch. Weeks of rehearsals at home – "I shouldn't sing anymore tonight love – you'll strain your throat." "Yes! you're word perfect and the tune's not too bad." "You ought to be with Caruso."

One word more: – "Your adjudicators are wonderful" (what small glasses they drink out of!) It borders on the miraculous to be able to write a running commentary whilst the singing is in progress and to note when and why a fellow hits the wrong trail in a sombre wood, or why he has nothing left so pants after hopping around too vigorously in the Floral Dance. Sorry I had to go half way through the programme – I enjoyed it! B. Flat

'Same song sung umpteen times!'
Sombre Woods: Bass solo with nine entries
Floral Dance: Bass solo with eight entries
Here's a Health: Quartet with eight entries

In 1937, the expanded contest transferred to the St. Lawrence Hall, with nine classes including two open for Tenor and Bass solo. This contest also included a duet class which attracted five entries. This one did not reappear in the next contest, bearing out Henry Brough's recollection that it was not popular. Much better accepted was the Open Bass solo class, which attracted a remarkable 16 entries. Archie Sargent and Jack Forster adjudicated and Harold Fredericks (organist and choirmaster of Victoria Bar Chapel) was the official accompanist. The competition was now reaching out beyond the Phil.

The timing of the contest varied through the years: for example in 1933 it was held on March 1st; in 1934 in February; and two were held in 1937, the seventh annual on March 6th, and the eighth annual brought forward to December 11th. The date of the ninth (of which we have no record) was published with the report of the eighth, and was set for December 3rd 1938, with a promise to have the syllabus available by March 1st – excellent organisation indeed. The shift in date from March to December is not explained and cannot be linked to any ambition to replace the Yorkshire Choral Festival, which had always been held in May. It is more likely that it was brought forward to balance the workload given the remarkable success of the Three Choirs Concerts at Monkgate which were held in March and which attracted audiences of up to 1000.

The growing success of the competition brought with it the challenges of organising a suitable venue and managing both the day and the finances. The competition secretary Jim Hardisty wrote this in PN November 1937:

We are not begging for money but for support, so pardon me if I mention funds. This competition yearly costs the YPMVC a large sum of money, it is our offspring and we gladly contribute, earn and save all we can to develop it to the best of our ability. By the generosity of the Educational Committee of the York Co-operative Society we have a large and beautiful hall at our disposal; three experienced musical judges are gratuitously giving their services, and our organizing committee is sound. So all we beg for is a large entry supported on the day by friends and admirers to ensure the biggest day in the history of the choir. But we would like a trophy for the open octet class. If any reader has an old shield, cup or rose bowl that has become his own after three years of ownership, and he has no further use for it, we would be glad of it. PN Nov.1937

Two more open solo classes were added: Soprano and Contralto. The record is not clear as to whether there were any entries for the octet class referred to by Jim Hardisty. There were three adjudicators: Jack Forster; Archie Sargent and Luther Greenwood, the conductor of the Colne Orpheus Glee Union and a man described by Archie Sargent in a later obituary as:

...without doubt, one of the finest choral conductors in this country, and, before, "the ills that flesh is heir to" began to assail his physical body, the Colne Orpheus Glee Union was one of the finest male voice choirs in Europe.

Harold Fredericks was once again the accompanist. With nine classes, an afternoon and evening available, and the introduction of an additional first class adjudicator from outside of the city, time still ran out and the quartet class was deferred to a later date.

The contest report included the following:

Thanks are also due to Mrs C.Fletcher for her work as accompanist at the Thursday evening competition rehearsals. PN Jan.1938.

This is one of only two references made to Alice – Cecil's wife – in any issue of PN in our possession. It shows that she too was an accomplished musician.

In the same issue Jack Forster wrote:

I was particularly pleased that the efforts of the enterprising Philharmonic choir met with such magnificent response, not only in the classes confined to their own members but also in the open classes, and I hope that the competition will expand more and more, introducing quartet and choral classes, and, who knows it may eventually replace the loss that the city and district has suffered by the relinquishing of the Yorkshire Choral Competitions.

Will H. Birch commenting on the eighth contest wrote:

The competition had the result of showing that York possesses some very fine talent and so long as we can produce singers in every class able to sing and interpret songs with such a degree of tone and finish we need not despair for the future. PN January 1938.

The list of Challenge Cup winners over these eight years reads:

1931: E. Jubb
1932: A. Snowden
1933: J. Hardisty
1934: A.Richardson
1935: W. Hodgson
1936: J. Hardisty
1937: E. Kneeshaw
1938: G. McQuattie

George McQuattie was a new recruit to the choir as recorded in March 1938:

We welcome Mr. George McQuattie, a baritone, to the choir. George took the part of Jehan Le Loup in the recent performance of the Vagabond King. He has also sung in choirs conducted by Sir Hugh Roberton.

There is no winner shown for 1939, but it is known that a competition was planned. The competition was 'on the brink' of becoming a music festival and this was clearly influencing the thoughts of some, although not all the membership. A minute of 19th January 1939 reported:

Inter-Choral Contest for 1939. Proposed by the secretary and one other "that we add an elocution class to the Philharmonic Contest", but this was laughed down.

Sadly the future brought despair as with the outbreak of war all hope of a revived York music festival came to an end. The competition was not revived until 1949.

Christmas Eve Carolling

There are many accounts of the tradition of singing carols in the district on Christmas Eve. This was one time in the year when the choir sang to raise money for itself rather than others. The proceeds went towards the summer outings. Canvassers would visit all the houses in the area to get support and financial commitment from residents. Then at midnight on Christmas Eve, the choir would set out led by Cecil Fletcher and his violin. At 2.30 am they would return to the Mission Hall for rabbit pie then go back out till approx 4.30 am. After Christmas, the canvassers would go back out to collect the money, known as Dibs, pledged by the residents. This could raise as much as £25, a significant sum at a time when choir subs were 3d for each rehearsal attended. The Carol singing started in 1925, the first year of the choir, and was an annual event till 1935. In 1936 a decision was taken to stay at home. As the magazine noted, the weather in previous years had been awful and they were now all 11 years older than when they started. However in January 1937 the choir received so many complaints from residents that at the AGM of 1937 the decision was taken to start again that year.

The singing of Christmas carols in the streets is an ancient tradition dating back to medieval times. It seems that as Victorian cities expanded with new districts such as Leeman Road so the new residents brought the tradition with them. This extract from PN Dec.1935 shows how long well established the tradition was and what the perils of late night carolling might be:

Several years ago – perhaps thirty – the writer was carolling with a party in a well known district in York. Things went well for a time, when, unfortunately, a man who had imbibed too freely joined us. Our only objection to this was that his harmony was not exactly what is written on the stave. "Let's tell him off" suggested someone, but our conductor, not wishing to invite trouble advised that we move away into another street in the hope of losing him. Imagine our surprise when on resuming our singing, a window suddenly went up, and a bag of bones 'plus etc' came tumbling down upon us. We were actually singing at the home of our intruder. I can only think that he had gone in the back way, seized the bag of bones which had probably been bought for the dog, and took his revenge for our unfriendliness towards him.

This story was illustrated by Mr. Walter Varley.

The way in which the carolling was organised was described in an article entitled 'The Waits' published in January 1933:

Canvasser: "Good Evening madam, would you like the MVC Carol Singers on Xmas Eve?"

For seven years now our canvassers have put this question to all the residents in our district until I think, it must by now be regarded by everybody that it is 'our Pitch' and so through our canvassers we take on one of our biggest and most remunerative engagements of the whole year.

Xmas Eve. Midnight approaches and one feels, probably with some regret, that he must break away from his own family party or from the family reunion and turn out to do his best to make this one engagement as successful as possible.

It is no dicky bow and starched shirt front engagement this but one where we might be called upon to brave the worst of which the elements are capable, and therefore the order is to be well shod, plenty of warm clothing with mufflers and gloves complete regardless of whether we look like singers or not. Comfort and safety are the first consideration. And so, off we go, the familiar rat-tat and call of 'Singers' is heard up and down the streets and as we group up round our conductor we feel that we are hailing Christmas in the right spirit. Sometimes we are joined by merry revellers who have imbibed well if not wisely but this is rare nowadays, things are not as they once were.

Good progress is made up to the break for supper (2.30 am) after which we all feel in fine fettle for the second half of the programme.

The last carol has been sung and the singers tired and thankful that this engagement has been fulfilled retire to their homes where, most likely, the youngsters are already up and full of excitement with the toys that the (substitute) Santa Claus has brought them.

The canvassers have still a further duty to perform, namely, collecting the 'Dibs' upon which depends so much the jaunts we all enjoy during the summer when the memory of a distant Christmas is only very dim. Secten

The report from the following year is very descriptive:

Christmas Eve 11pm.

Our conductor begins to get all hot and bothered as to who will be there and whether they will be in a fit condition to sing, but by 11.30 pm the ever faithful are all present – assisted by the new members, and all are in excellent trim for a strenuous evening's work. Perhaps, being Sunday, the 'party' was quieter than usual but we had not been on tour very long before we were invited to drink the good health of Mr. and Mrs. Atkinson at the Jubilee Hotel. That of course put us in real good fettle right up to the interval when we adjourned for supper – Rabbit Pie!!! No Bill Johnson to do it justice. "What was the matter Bill, feeling the effects of last Christmas, or had the wife put her foot down? We missed you Bill but never mind, other members – registered or otherwise – made up for you." How many pies can be made from one rabbit, for there was only one, I'll be bound, because there was only one head this being given to Arthur C –: he liking plenty of jaw.

I wonder if anyone noticed that CHF didn't have any pie? Did he know something? He said it was indigestion, and two members promptly suggested good cures, but Mark went one better and mixed him a bottle which, you will be pleased to hear Mark, affected a cure. Next time we have pie Cecil, take a bottle with you and enjoy yourself.

Continuing our singing after supper we had the usual 'Command Performance' in Roseberry Street. The old lady who waits up for us each year accused our tenors of shouting. Now tenors you 'Cock Angels' what about that? However, to pacify her we sang her something soft and sweet – Peaceful Night. This was beautifully sung and the old lady seemed satisfied.

Shortly afterwards we had opposition from a one-man-band concertina party who quickly packed up when our party including CHF's violin and Frank's guitar struck up.

Full credit is due to members' wives for their cuteness; husbands innocently trotted out their Xmas boxes consisting of CoronaTwofors, Turkish, Woodbines, Flagedge etc. and the aromas are blown on the night air instead of in the best parlours. Any damage done however can be put right with aspro.

After doing their bit in preparing and clearing supper, the ladies kindly joined up and gave us some assistance when numbers had dwindled, and the help was most appreciated.

Jennie gingers up the dawdlers and so we finish, respectably, another Christmas Eve

engagement in the Leeman Road district and to the residents we wish many more happy Christmases. May we have the pleasure of proclaiming the 'Glad News' for many years to come?

CHF and the writer accepted a kindly lift from an old member and we travelled home to Burton Lane at speed. That's Christmas Eve – that was, and so to bed. The secretary Jan 1934

There is a different mood in the description carried in January 1936 of Christmas Eve 1935:

Despite an attempt on the part of the weather to put a 'damper' on our carol singing effort a fairly large and efficient party met at Albany Street and as midnight struck, commenced a four hour sing in the Leeman Road district. An experiment was made this year in the method of grouping the streets which proved most successful.

We cannot say that anything exciting occurred in the district and, but for a few revellers returning from parties, and an occasional burst of song from homes indulging in the true spirit of Christmas one would have thought that it was some dreary night in November rather than Xmas Eve.

By 2 am we had wended our way back to Albany Street – this reminded us of the rabbit pie that awaited us. It was a grand sight that met our gaze upon entering the mission room. Jane, Kathleen, Mrs A.Colley and Mrs Henry Brough were busy serving the pie and the tables were well filled with good fare. Almost in silence the company did justice to the excellent repast, for conditions outside were terrible, which no doubt put an edge on the appetite. So comfortable were we that to turn out again into that awful fog again needed a supreme effort......We completed the whole of the district by 4.30 am which instituted a record. PN Jan 1936.

I doubt even this request made to a canvasser that year by an old lady in Jubilee Terrace could bring a smile to their faces:

When you come on Christmas Eve please sing 'Peaceful Night' but mind you knock hard!

It is not perhaps surprising to read in December 1936:

For the first time in eleven years the Philharmonic will not go carolling. Weather conditions have been very trying during recent years and the fact that we have tacked on the eleven years to our ages, well, it makes one think. We shall miss that good old Christmas supper though.

However, Cecil was not able to enjoy a choir-free Christmas Eve.

Big Ben had chimed 12 o'clock on the radio and CHF & Co. were just retiring. Outside the street was quiet and deserted. Suddenly a series of groans broke the stillness "What on earth!" exclaimed Mr. CHF white to the lips. "It must be Mrs. Molton in a fit" "Listen!" said CHF as a series of fierce snarls accompanied by a piercing shriek came through the letter box. A few more blood curdling screams were followed by a terrific tattoo on the knocker.

HF [Harold, Cecil's son and also a choir member] *shouted to pop, that he'd seen red light on the tower of the N.R. Mental Hospital (a custom of the authorities to denote that a patient has escaped) " And he's at our door" shouted Miss JF* [Harold's younger sister Joyce] *sleepily.*

Through the night came further agonizing moans and piercing shrieks "That sounds very much like Jim" said CHF "and that's Porky" exclaimed Mrs. CHF. Then all of a sudden it dawned on the terror stricken family that it may not be an escaped patient or even a wild beast show and after much persuasion CHF went to the door.

Behold! On the step stood Porky from Scarboro – Flanaghan (without Allen) and Uncle Ed from Malton. Yes sure enough it was the original Tiger Rag Boys complete with an Austin 6 or was it 7 (I never can remember the date). "What are you boys doing out at this time of night?" demanded CHF. "We're looking for Santa Clause" replied the driver of the chariot (better known as the butter wagon) " You-shee we're full (hic) of the (hic) Christmas spirit".

After a good sing (in harmony?) accompanied by Mrs. CHF on piano, the party broke up and did a scram (that means cleared off).

A report on the 'do' should have read the singing was lovely and not lousy. This was a printer's error. Sub editor.PN Jan 1937

The style of this piece signed by a sub editor suggests it may have been written by one of the children.

The AGM held of January 1937 included this item:

During other business a reference was made to carol singing. One member voiced the feelings of certain Leeman Road residents and said that great disappointment prevailed in that district because the Philharmonic did not go carol singing on Christmas Eve 1936. It was decided to do all we could to enlist a representative party to sing carols in Leeman Road on Xmas Eve 1937. PN Feb.1937

The AGM decision was an endeavour not a promise. In November of that year support was canvassed and members were asked to sign up. However the PN of January 1938 makes no reference at all to Christmas Eve, so we do not know whether any carolling took place or indeed how Cecil and his family spent the evening.

Summary of the decade

The latest issue of PN in the archive is May 1938 so it is at this point that we can summarise the growth and success of the choir during this decade.

The Phil won fewer competitions as the years went by. This was mainly due to the choir entering the 'A' class in competitions attracting the largest and best of male voice choirs in the region. As has been noted in male voice competition, size matters and the Phil was never able to put sufficient numbers on stage to challenge the best. So to gain a third prize at Cleethorpes in June 1937, with only 33 against choirs of 50plus – beaten only by Scunthorpe and the Moorland Gleemen – was success. Small size and lack of public recognition at the highest competitive level could have contributed to the choir not achieving the ambition of broadcasting on the BBC, and being able to stand alongside Old Priory, Monkgate, and York Male Voice in this respect. This desire was also felt by some concert-goers as can be seen in this thank you letter from Acomb Adult School:

Once again we give our sincere thanks to Mr. Fletcher and the members of YPMVC for their generous help to Acomb Adult School (on January 2nd) in giving so generously both of their time and musical abilities, a big sacrifice indeed and secondly for the beautiful rendering of their music items.

The more we hear the more we are captivated. To stress this point, so attentive was the audience in some of the items that one could hear a pin drop which is sure sign that the choir has gained its objective. It is the wish of all at Acomb that the choir will go from strength to strength and give pleasure to thousands instead of tens and we are hoping in the near future to have the pleasure of hearing the choir 'on the air'. It is the wish of all at Acomb that 1938 may be one of your most successful years. C. Addinall PN Jan 1938

Any disappointments felt however must have been offset by the, probably undreamt of, success of both the Three Choirs Concerts and the Inter-Choral Competitions.

By 1938, as has been recorded, that contest had been opened to soloists, male and female, and quartets from other choirs. Plans were in place to open it further to small choirs in the district. It was now able to attract the support of conductors of the stature of Luther Greenwood to act as an adjudicator, and was on the point of becoming a worthy successor to the discontinued Yorkshire Choral Festival. This was an astonishing success brought about primarily by commitment and enthusiasm of the whole choir and by the financial support and good organisation by Cecil and the choir committee. The whole venture was fully supported by both Jack Forster and Archie Sargent, adding considerably to its later success.

The original intention of the contests, that of encouraging members to gain confidence, was well rewarded, as members used their talents in other groups. Here are two examples:

*'La Vie Parisienne' a comic opera by Offenbach was presented by the Rowntree Players in the Joseph Rowntree Hall........Two Philharmonic members (Bill Cade and Harry Birkley) are members of the Rowntree Players and appeared in this opera; they showed ability as actors as well as singers.....*PN April 1938

Having a few members of the Philharmonic Choir in the York Amateur Operatic and Dramatic Society we were interested this year in the performance of the Vagabond King........

Our chief interest; that is from a choir point of view was, – how would Jim Hardisty fare as Captain of the Scotch Archers and how would he put over that difficult Scottish Archer's Song. Well we say right now without fear of contradiction that his performance was excellent. Others of ours who did good work in the chorus are to be commended in the naturalness of their acting. PN March 1938

In a footnote we see that the Vagabond King was also a recruiting opportunity:

We welcome Mr. George McQuattie, a baritone, to the choir. George took the part of Jehan Le Coup in the performance of the Vagabond King referred to above. He has also sung in choirs conducted by Sir Hugh Roberton. We hope he will enjoy a long and happy association with the Philharmonic. PN March 1938

The Monkgate Three Choirs Festival was conceived by Archie Sargent but – as the name suggests – could not be brought to fruition without the full support of both the Philharmonic and Old Priory choirs. The Massed choir concert held in 1934 in support of the Yorkshire Choral Competitions promised a body of 400 plus, singing the 'Hallelujah Chorus' and 'The Heavens are Telling', yet the report suggest that the audience was small and the concerts and the Festival eventually failed. In contrast the Monkgate Choir Sunday – essentially a church family occasion

– became so popular as to question whether one performance was enough:

...It was the third year of an annual event which has become exceedingly popular with the public of York. This year the attendance broke the record and the church was full to overflowing. We felt that the singing was of a higher standard at this event than at the previous ones and the arrangement of the programme was all that could be desired.

*Choir Sunday at Monkgate is certainly established and judging from outside comment J.H.Forster, A.W.Sargent and C.H.Fletcher (the conductors who originated the event) will have to consider a repetition for several people have stated that they wish it could be repeated, and others that they could not get there on the date. That the public who attended on this occasion contributed £13 was an indication they enjoyed it and do appreciate good choral singing.....*PN April 1938

A full to overflowing church meant an audience of 1000.

The choir social life now included an annual dinner held in honour of wives and the womenfolk whose support was so vital in so many ways. The first was held in March 1936 as a tenth anniversary dinner and immediately became a fixture. Close friends of the choir were also invited, as can be seen in a thank you note from Janet Sargent:

We always set off for the 'phil' dinner in an unusually carefree fashion. To be free of responsibility is an unusual experience, but even the making of speeches does not constitute responsibility here.

The whole atmosphere is happy – we are workers having time off.

This was my third 'phil' dinner and I have enjoyed each more than the previous one. Many thanks to Mr.F., Committee and Choir for inviting us!

From my heart I wish the choir success. The Inter-Choral competitions were most enjoyable and the work of the choir in promoting these annual events will I am sure bear fruit in years to come.

All the very best to you all, and whatever success may come may it not spoil the happy spirit of comradeship and mutual help. Janet Sargent PN March 1938

The words of Arnold Rowntree used at the beginning of this section on the 1930s *Just as Vienna was a city of music so York was known all over for its music* in which he attributes much of this success to these three conductors and their choirs was a huge compliment, perhaps better understood now at the end of this chapter. That speech was given in spring 1938; just 13 years earlier a group of men, an embryonic choir, was meeting in a small room in Leeman Road Adult School to learn to sing together helped, or hindered, by what Jane Brough described as *'a piano that was terribly out of tune, (a number of notes absolutely refused to play at all)'*.

This is truly a story of success and in the last editorial we have written by Cecil Fletcher in May 1938 he was still looking forward:

.....The choir will continue with the usual weekly rehearsals in preparation for next season's programme. The Inter-Choir Choral Contest, which is to be held next December, will occupy much of our time during the summer months; the syllabus for the contest will shortly be available.

The past season has been an extremely busy one for all connected with the Philharmonic and some good work has been done. Rehearsals and concerts, on the whole, have been well attended, and, in thanking all members for their loyal support, we hope they will see to it that next season will be more successful than any previous. CHF May PN 1938

As we have seen the Phil worked very closely with York Old Priory led by Jack Forster, and with Monkgate Methodist led by Archie Sargent. The Priory school had one building in Nunnery Lane and another alongside the large Wesleyan Chapel [now the Rock Church] in Priory Street, opposite a large Baptist Chapel, along the street from a large Presbyterian Chapel and a short walk from the excellent facilities at Victoria Bar Methodist. Monkgate chapel, on the other side of the city, being newer, had an even better organ. The Wesleyan complex in Priory Street comprised a chapel to seat 1500, day schools, Sunday schools and a preacher's house. It was completed in 1857 at a cost of £10,936, and had been built to replicate the size and facilities of Centenary [now Central] Methodist in St. Saviourgate. That had opened in 1840 – as a cathedral to Methodism – and these days serves the Phil, and also York Musical Society, by providing rehearsal rooms. Such were the facilities available to these choirs with which the Phil had close connections.

In Leeman Road the infrastructure was modest. The choir had started in the front room of Tom Clark's house. It transferred to the adult school which proved to be neither big enough nor adequate to meet its needs. It then moved around the corner from the adult school in Stamford Street to the Albany Street Methodist Chapel. This had been built in 1900, to replace an earlier wooden structure, and was a functional building in which rooms could be opened or divided for various uses. It could hold a maximum of 250 people and had cost £678 – only 6% of the cost of the Priory Street Wesleyan complex. As this chapter has shown modest facilities could not hold back an ambitious, talented body of men.

All the large chapels described above can still be visited [Victoria Bar now residential]. However in April 1942 the Luftwaffe was unsympathetic to both the history and sensibilities of the Phil:

> Tom Clark's terraced house was hit and the family relocated within the district.
>
> The Leeman Road Adult School was badly damaged and had to be demolished. It was never rebuilt – the site remained empty until sold to the city corporation in 1967 for £100 and redeveloped for housing.
>
> The Albany Street Chapel was destroyed and was later replaced with premises in nearby Salisbury Terrace.

With hindsight it is clear that in 1938 the choir was at one of the high points in its 90 year life. But, as Cecil's editorial suggests, he did not feel that the choir had reached its peak but still had more to achieve. There was much still to do but all ambition was soon to be disrupted by war; disrupted but not destroyed.

1940-1946
Wartime stress and peacetime despair

The choir archive is empty of any wartime information. There are only two later references from the 1970s, when founder member Henry Brough was asked to record his memories for the choir newsletter. Limited to a few hundred words on each occasion, this is what he recalled. In 1977 he wrote:

During the war years, the choir had many 'ups and downs', including changes of practice rooms and loss of members, but we managed to keep going, sometimes only four members being at rehearsal.

Seven years earlier in 1970 he wrote:

Monday has always been 'choir night' and in those days we did not break for holidays. During the war years we rehearsed in various places, I remember one night in Brook Street School when there were only four of us – strangely enough – one of each part so we had a rehearsal.

Henry was an engine driver, an essential and arduous war time role, and his use of the phrase 'many ups and downs` suggests a level of understatement such as to bring a smile to the lips of a modern reader. But of all that he might have said about choir life during the war he recalled that night in Brook Street School. The symbolism and spiritual impact of that evening stayed with Henry such that more than thirty years later he was able to express it so simply and so eloquently allowing the reader to share the significance of the moment:

I remember one night in Brook Street School when there were only four of us – strangely enough – one of each part so we had a rehearsal.

In the 1942 air raids the choir was bombed out of Leeman Road and, as Henry says, had a nomadic existence for the rest of the war. Brook Street is in the Groves, in many ways similar to Leeman Road, but closer both to the city centre and to the Rowntrees Cocoa works which, at this time, was also a munitions factory. Younger singers had been called up to the armed services; those remaining added home guard, fire watch and other duties to already busy work schedules; and there was always the need to tend gardens and allotments to boost food supplies. Yet at the point of greatest pressure, when only four were able to attend, there was a first tenor, a second tenor, a baritone and a bass – a quartet – the core group required to sing a part song. It was a quartet which started the choir in 1925; it was a quartet which ensured it did not buckle under the pressures of war.

We know that Cecil Fletcher did all in his power to keep the choir meeting at this time. We must also expect that, given the nature of the choir, this would have included a determination to keep performing and serving the public. It is an obvious observation to make, but still one of relevance, that male voice singing was one aspect of war-time life which the women of the country, who did so much, could not fulfil. The assumption is that the Phil, with its reduced resources sought to maintain, as far as possible, its normal programme of concerts. It also worked with others on the additional request made to all performers e.g. Holidays at Home concerts and entertainment for service personnel. We know that Archie

Sargent continued the November performances of Messiah, and almost succeeded in maintaining the Three Choirs Festival. In 1939 the three choirs: Monkgate, Old Priory and the Phil met as usual. In 1940 there was no concert. In 1941 Monkgate and the York Male Voice Choir performed with no ladies choir. In 1942 the original three managed to get together, and in 1943 Monkgate performed alone. 1944 is a mystery and in 1945 the Phil joined with Monkgate. The stress of war can also be seen in this diary entry by Janet Sargent following this 1945 concert:

'March 18th 1945; Choir Sunday: The afternoon was very good, though the 'phil' is but a shadow of its former self.'

During the war years the mixed voice choir of Monkgate Methodist Church gained remarkable success and importance as a broadcasting choir, being heard not only at home but also, by short wave transmissions, across the world. This led them to be invited to do other work outside the church e.g. Holidays at Home, so as the war progressed it became increasingly busy. Both the choir and Archie Sargent became well known, and he became the most significant of the three conductors who had contributed so much to York's musical life in the years leading up to the war. It is reasonable to assume that the Philharmonic men would have supported this work in whatever way they could. Also, early in the war, Jack Forster withdrew from active involvement with York Old Priory, another factor which might have pushed the choirs to work more closely together. At a time when so many struggled to survive, Monkgate, which could be described as part of the 'war effort' thrived.

At the outbreak of the war the government issued emergency orders closing all cinemas and theatres until further notice. This was a 'gut reaction' no doubt made in good faith and fearful of what might be about to happen. The order was cancelled within a few days, but blackout regulations came into force which not only affected cinemas and theatres but every evening social activity. The importance of having entertainment available for all citizens both in and out of uniform was soon recognised, even to the point of allowing cinemas to open on Sundays. But blackout regulations made it necessary to make changes. For example York Musical Society, the oldest of York's musical groups, and another used to working in an autumn to spring season did very little winter work during the war. It arranged instead for a major concert each July, and in 1943 performed on a September Saturday afternoon to avoid the blackout. The Philharmonic was already a choir which rehearsed throughout the year, but nevertheless any extra pressure put on the summer months could not have been easy to arrange.

As well as his Monkgate choir, Archie Sargent also conducted the Rowntree Choral Society, which folded during the war years. This extract from his memoirs illustrates how dramatically life was changing:

And now, one of the most emotionally disturbing concerts in which I have ever taken part, comes to mind. This was after the war had commenced, and there were organisations all over the country endeavouring to bring to refugees from the continent, not only some of the necessities of life, but such consideration and compensating happiness which circumstances made possible in all the varying war conditions in which our people found themselves.

The Rowntree choir were asked to give a concert in one of the halls in the city, without any precise knowledge of the type of audience to whom they would sing, and they accepted the engagement.

That evening, however, the rain literally poured down, and as we set out for the hall, I remarked to a friend who was with me, 'I could find it in my heart to wish that we hadn't to come out tonight.'

We reached the hall and my wish vanished, for it was almost filled with refugees who had just, and only just, escaped Hitler's clutches. The only clothes they had were those in which they were dressed. They looked utterly dejected, without a hope in the world, and it was to these that we had to sing.......

Before each song was sung, an interpreter gave to the audience in the tongue of our visitors the words being sung, and they followed the programme with great intensity, receiving each item with tremendous enthusiasm. At the conclusion after thanks had been expressed, a spokesman came to the front and shook hands with me. He was a grand fellow, and as we looked at one another, the evil and the futility of war reduced us to the inarticulate.

This incident is reminiscent of 1914 when the city welcomed refugees fleeing from Belgium. Also reminiscent of World War 1 was the opening of the Mansion House to give entertainment for troops:

As *York's Military and County Hospitals received more and more wounded soldiers from the Front, the Lord Mayor and his Sheriff hit upon the idea that brought everyone a great deal of pleasure and the Mansion House a new role to play. On 5th January 1917 they invited 140 wounded men to an 'Entertainment' when, as well as tea being served, local artistes gave their services free and a VIP made a speech.* [Lords of the City Knightly / Semlyen YCC1980]

In 1941:

On Sunday 15th June 1941 the Clearing Bankers of York were the hosts of a Mansion House Tea party and Entertainment for the forces and their friends.

The group asked to supply the entertainment that afternoon was Monkgate Choir.

Other wartime special events included a Carol Service for HM Forces in the Theatre Royal on Sunday 22nd December 1940, and regular July concerts in the Tempest Anderson Hall as part of the York Holiday at Homes programme:

A large and appreciative audience which foregathered in the Tempest Anderson Hall on Sunday afternoon July 25th, warmly endorsed the sentiments expressed by the chairman in thanking the conductor Mr. A.W.Sargent, the two artists for their delightful singing, and to the choir for a memorable performance, that one of the highlights of the city's Holidays at Home programme was the concert which had been provided by the deservedly famous Monkgate Methodist choir. A big crowd of people were unable to gain admission, but their disappointment was removed to some degree, by the fortunate provision of loudspeakers.

The Three Choirs Festival still brought the choirs together. Here is a report from 1940:

It is good to find that with so many things thrown out of gear by the war, the festival can still go on. The hearty co-operation of Mr. J.H.Forster and the Old Priory Choir, and Mr. C.H.Fletcher and the York Philharmonic Male Voice Choir make it possible......The times may have got a little out of joint musically, but this effort shows that there are quarters where there is no discouragement.

In 1945 the Rev. Charles Randell wrote: *...but to find the 'Three Choirs Festival' again so excellent in choice of programme and in performance of the same, was a very great* *joy to all who were present that afternoon.....*

There is some uncertainty over the contribution made by York Old Priory later in the war. In 1942 Duncan Forster lost his battle with TB and his father semi-retired to Goathland on the North York Moors, spending less and less time in York. In 1945 a celebration, with 100 guests, was held in honour of Jack and Ada's Golden Wedding and his formal retirement from the choir. The YEP report of that occasion stated that in 1945 the Old Priory choir had not met for rehearsals for four years.

Even the annual performances of Messiah were brought into the war effort. One year there were two performances, both to full houses. Lady Churchill had launched a fund for Red Cross Aid for Russia. In support of this it was decided to repeat Messiah, but this time taking it to the even larger Centenary (now Central) Methodist Church. A full house raised a remarkable £50. The end of the war saw the November 1945 performance – the 'Celebration Messiah'– sung with a massed chorus of 220.

On Archie's first Sunday morning in charge of Monkgate choir in 1930 there were eight members of the choir. By 1945 there was a remarkable 105, made up of 50 sopranos, 16 contraltos, 14 tenors and 25 basses. These are named [VPP], with four names being recognisable as Phil members including Harry Birkley, a bass with Monkgate, baritone with the Phil and also a member of the Rowntree Players. The enhanced choir for the performance of Messiah in 1945 totalled 220, with 74 sopranos, 52 contraltos, 32 tenors, and 62 basses. The increase in male singers is considerable, suggesting that a number of Philharmonic members are likely to have taken part.

We know that the Phil played a part in launching the broadcasting career of the Monkgate choir. That was a remarkable achievement of 22 broadcasts, with the conductor and choir learning considerable skills in using microphones. Archie Sargent, who had been a naval wireless operator in the 1914-18 war, embraced the technology and was able to lead the choir in learning recording techniques. The response to these broadcasts was such that they could be considered to have been part of the war effort. Letters of praise and thanks were received from around the world. One comment received described a group of British soldiers in North Africa, who found and repaired an abandoned German radio. When they turned it on the first broadcast they received was a half hour of hymns by Monkgate Choir with Mrs Janet Sargent singing a solo.

If these broadcasts could be thought to be part of the war effort then so should be the work of the conductor. In 1942 Archie was promoted within the Inland Revenue, which necessitated a transfer to another office. He was to be sent to Darlington. An appeal was launched with a letter sent to London signed by 19 prominent citizens of York. In addition Mr Arnold Rowntree, who was not in York at the time and so unable to add his signature, wrote a personal letter to the authorities. It must be a rare event in an ancient city such as York for the citizens to petition the Crown to keep a tax collector. Although the appeal failed, arrangements were eventually made for a transfer back to York. Archie became a weekly commuter arriving back in York on a Friday evening with a heavy weekend of choir work to complete. To accommodate this change the Monkgate choir moved its rehearsal night from Thursday to Saturday.

The working relationship between the three conductors Jack, Cecil and Archie came to an end during the war. Following Duncan Forster's death in 1942, his father Jack sold the business, and, with his wife Ada – known as Ma – retired to Goathland. Duncan left a young widow Renee, who was also well known to the Phil, as she was a fine soprano and had won the 1938 Inter-Choir Choral Competition open class with a rendition of 'One Fine Day' from Madam Butterfly. Thankfully Renee did not retire completely, and post-war did perform recitals accompanied by Brian Sargent. However, Cecil and Archie remained close, as sometime in 1944/45 Cecil took over the leadership of the Haughton Road Methodist Choir in Burton Stone Lane. The Philharmonic gave a concert each year in Haughton Road, and it was this church that had apologised for the poor condition of its organ some years earlier. Haughton Road was under the oversight of the larger Monkgate Chapel, so Cecil was assisting Archie in taking on this role. The celebratory performances of Messiah in 1945 brought this wartime period to a close with the massive choir performing both at Monkgate and, with the help of a fleet of five buses, in Pocklington.

The Phil had ended 1938 on a high note and was looking eagerly forward, despite growth and ambition being cut short by war. Beaten down, but not defeated, it continued to entertain to the best of its ability. With peace the Phil could, one more, look to the future with confidence. This hope was to be very short lived, as in March 1946 Cecil unexpectedly and suddenly died. He was only 52 years old.

The minister of Monkgate Church, Rev. C. Randell, who a year earlier had been praising the Three Choirs Festival, now had the task of leading the funeral service for one of its conductors and one of his own chapel choir masters. Cecil, the apprentice grocer of 1911 now described as a civil servant, was laid to rest in York Cemetery [plot 5538c]. His widow Alice was not to join him at rest for a further 23 years. The grave has no headstone, indeed has no markings at all. When visited in July 2015 it could only be found with the help of cemetery volunteers. In 1946 he had been laid in well tended lawns alongside a path, but this part of the cemetery is now overgrown. At the foot of the grave stands a crab apple tree, the branches of which arch over to the head. Beneath this canopy lies a thorny carpet of brambles. There is then no stone memorial, but his name lives. As soon as it could be arranged, the choir held a meeting and agreed to make the choir a memorial to its founder conductor. The choir adopted the additional title of: The Cecil H. Fletcher Memorial Choir, a designation that is still part of the choir's charitable registration.

FUNERAL OF MR. C. H. FLETCHER

THE funeral took place at the Burton - lane Methodist Church, Haughton-road, York, of Mr. Cecil H. Fletcher, of 31, Ratcliffe - street, York.

Mr. Fletcher.

Mr. Fletcher, who was conductor of the York Philharmonic Male Voice Choir and had been associated with the choir for 21 years. During the last 18 months he was a member of the Methodist Church choir.

The chief mourners were Mrs. C. Fletcher, Mr. H. Fletcher, Miss J. Fletcher, Mrs. D. Fletcher, Miss A. Fletcher, Miss G. Fletcher, Mr. and Mrs. Moss, Mr. D. Moss, Mrs. T. Moss, Mr. B. Graham, Mrs. Graham, Mr. and Mrs. Acomb, Mrs. Culleton, Miss Ventress, Mr. J. Patrick and Mrs. Redfern.

OTHER MOURNERS

Other mourners included. Mr. A. P. Sargeant (Monkgate Choir), Mrs. E. Wetherell, Mr Cade, Mr. Mitchell, Mr. Smallwood, Mr. Wright, Mr Brough, Mr. J. Hardisty, Mr. G. Flanagan, Mrs. W. T. King, Mr. C. R. Evers, Mrs. M. Bell, Mr. Worfork, Mr. J. H. Forster, all of the York Philharmonic Choir and Old Priory Choir, York.

Mr. G. Bodly, Mr. J. W. Kalan, Mr. Dutton, Mr. G. W. Sherrington, Mr. J Flanagan, Mr. J. Steel, Mr. F. Kay, Mr. W. Dickson, Mr. J. Berry, Mr. E. Harris, Mr. W. Honley, Mr J. C. W. Potter, Mr. J. Milner, Mrs C. Smith, Mr. J. S. Osborne, Bell Master Dickson, Mr. Perring (Salvation Army) and Mr. F. W. Slegg

Here is the funeral notice as published in the York Evening Press and a tribute published later that year by Archie Sargent in the 'Carillon', the annual newsletter of the Monkgate Church Choir.

The sudden passing of our friend, Cecil H. Fletcher, conductor of the York Philharmonic Male Voice Choir, was a shock to all who knew him. We at Monkgate felt it keenly. For many years, Cecil and his men contributed to our Three Choirs Festival at Monkgate, and the long continued collaboration was a most happy one. Then, too, he had taken over the leadership of the choir at our Burton Stone Lane Church, and was doing splendid work for them. It is a loss to those whom he was seeking to serve, for his was a genial and attractive personality, and, apart from his musical gifts, he will be greatly missed. But we know that it will be possible now for his gifts to be fully extended in a larger and fuller sphere of service. Our deepest sympathy goes to his wife and family to whom the loss of his physical presence is so keen.

The magnitude of this loss was expressed by Archie in another Carillon entry: *With the passing of our friend Cecil Fletcher, the final link with the Three Choirs Festival was broken and this year [1946] we gave a choral programme with Doris Gambell as guest artiste – Dora Gilson accompanying her.*

Chapter 2
Sefton Fearne Jnr.

Survival and Revival

The few months following Cecil's death must have been traumatic, as the choir sought to reorganise itself. On April 26th 1946 a choir meeting was held and a clear decision was taken:

Meeting called to discuss future of the choir and the possibility in carrying on due to the death of our late and popular conductor. It was the decision of the members to continue as a choir and this be recorded as a Minute. It was decided that for the first year the membership fee would be 5/-, and that the donation at each choir practice will be 6d per member. Mr. Fearne was appointed as conductor.

Stability was restored when Sefton Fearne Jnr. stepped forward and took on the leadership. Sefton joined the choir in September 1937 and in the October 1937 issue of PN published this piece [reproduced in full] entitled *Impressions of a New Member:*

On being approached to become a member of YPMVC I confess that I received the invitation with rather mixed feelings. You will understand, of course, that anyone who loves Male Voice singing for itself alone, cannot remain inactive, and I had been for a matter of two years. I naturally felt I wanted to 'join up'.

On the other hand I am in a job (like most men I know) which prevented me from being sure of giving 100% of myself to the choir and, as I feel that a member of any organization should pull all his weight, this factor weighed with me quite a lot. But I felt that even if I was not a 100% man, and I pulled all I could, you would not judge me too harshly. So I came. I was constantly being told by my friends (already members of your choir) that you were all really one large and happy family. This was very much impressed on me when I became one of you, and I am sure that, so long as this feeling exists, success (social and musical) must follow. I have only been with you a few weeks and I have already been made to feel very much at home by everyone. I thank you all for this, for you will all know what it is to be a new member and the feeling that each is wondering who the new chap is, and incidentally making him feel rather 'awkward'. That state of affairs did not occur to me.

I wonder if I dare to be so bold as to make an appeal. Since I have been with you I have felt that your (sorry 'our') choir is not doing justice to itself on account of the under strength of the 2nd bass line, and the choral pieces must, to an audience, sound very thin: this could surely be overcome by each one of us trying to introduce men who we know could strengthen that line. Can't we try?

Please don't think me too presumptuous, but I am only saying this as an interested choir member (I may not get another chance) and I feel sure, you who have the interest of the choir at heart will forgive a new member calling you attention to something which when rectified, cannot help but increase the enjoyment of all.

Good luck to the choir, and, Good Hunting! Sefton Fearne Jnr.

Little was he to know how he would serve the choir, probably giving more than

100% at times. Sefton Junior will be referred to later in the chapter on York Male Voice Choir in which his father, Sefton, and his uncle had both been prominent members. The presumption is that Sefton junior's reference to 'being away from male voice singing for two years' suggests that he too had been a member.

In 1947 the choral community of York suffered another loss with the passing of Jack Forster. Sir Hugh Roberton (Conductor of the Glasgow Orpheus Choir) had been a friend of Jack and was in regular correspondence with Archie Sargent. In November 1947 he wrote this in a letter to Archie:

I enclose a Lute [magazine of the Glasgow Orpheus] with a notice of dear old Jack Forster. By the way, is York going to do anything in his memory? I would like to see some official recognition, and suggest a bronze plaque let in one of the city walls 'in commemoration of one who did much for the cause of music in this city'.

York did not erect a bronze plaque but the Forster family, in memory of Duncan, had already placed two park benches for the enjoyment of all in the moorland village of Goathland, and Jack, like Cecil, has a living memorial in that his music lives on in the York Priory Choir, now ladies only.

In his tribute to Jack, Archie Sargent quoted Sir Hugh Roberton:

... and as we remember his personality with love, and his work with gratitude, we should like to record a tribute from our mutual friend, Sir Hugh Roberton, who said. 'Jack Forster represents a type of social-serving and self-effacing creatures who, down the ages have, often unwittingly, done more to preserve culture and sweetness in society than the loud-mouthed demagogues who prate about it.'

This photograph is, perhaps, the most poignant in the Phil's archive:

All that is written on the reverse of this photo is: *1947 Joint Choir YPMVC Old Priory*. By the way the choirs are dressed it is not mid-summer, but we don't know at what point in that traumatic year it was taken, or why the choirs had come together. The only public building in York to match this location is the County Court at York Castle. Both choirs had lost their founder conductors; the austerity and rationing of post war Britain was tough; the winter of 1946/47 had been one of the worst on record; and in the spring of 1947 York had been badly affected by floods. We don't know exactly when or why this photo was taken, but with both choirs at a very low point they came together in mutual support. Sefton Fearne Jnr. is in the centre of the front row. The younger man two places to his right could be Harold Fletcher. The lady second in from the left on the fourth row is thought to be Elsie Senior, a highly respected contralto who also sang in the Monkgate choir and Sargent Singers, showing again how closely these choirs were linked. On the outer side of Elsie could be Douglas Holder, a tenor soloist with the Phil and also a member of Monkgate choir, as well as the smaller recording group the Sargent Singers. During the war Douglas, a special constable, used to sing a humorous duet called 'We're the extra-special Constables' with bass and police sergeant Fred Clarke, possibly front row far left. It is no surprise, however, that there is one easily recognisable face in this photo, one which stands as a statement of commitment and consistency. Henry Brough, a stalwart founder member of the Phil, who sang for a total of 65 years, stands on the back row fourth in from the left.

Sefton Fearne began the task of restoring the Phil, and was joined in this task by a 16 year old music student, Brian Lister. Brian was a schoolboy friend of Lawrie, Sefton's son, and the two families knew each other well. Lawrie joined the choir and his school friend played the piano, whilst Sefton conducted. It was not unusual for a talented teenager to take on such a role, but this appointment is highly significant. In 1946/7 the choir was at the lowest point in its history. Brian Lister was there when the recovery began, later to return in 1962 as Music Director. He would then lead the choir to its greatest ever achievements – from the depths of the valley to the top of the mountain.

In 1946/7 it was important to the choir to keep going but it took some time to recover, with the first recorded performance being in spring 1947. The YEP reported:

First Concert of York Choir

About 150 people attended the first concert given by the York Philharmonic Male Voice Choir under their new conductor Mr Sefton Fearne, in the Baptist Church Priory Street York.

As a tribute to the founder of the choir Mr. C.H.Fletcher, who died a year ago, the choir will, in future, also be known as the Fletcher Memorial Choir.

The programme consisted of many well known songs, great appreciation being shown of the choir's interpretation of 'The Holy City'. Other works included the always popular sea shanties of 'The Jolly Roger' type.

Not the most memorable of reviews but another from November 1947 showed improvement:

The York Philharmonic Male Voice Choir is getting well into its stride as winter advances, and this week two popular concerts have been well attended and enthusiastically received.

At St. Barnabas Church Hall the choir gave a well chosen programme of choral items, while Arthur Green, Harry Shipman, Jim Busby and Albert Snowden presented solo items.

At Monkgate Methodist Church the choral programme was supported by solos from Arthur Green, Fred Clarke, Harry Shipman, Jim Busby and Albert Snowden, and on both occasions the choir was conducted by Sefton Fearne with Brian Lister as accompanist.

In February 1948 the choir returned to the Baptist church; what a difference a year had made:

The Philharmonic Male Voice Choir on Wednesday visited the Baptist Church Priory Street and provided a real musical treat. Immediately the choir began to sing one was struck by the excellent tone and good balance, and these were maintained throughout the programme. A notable feature was the concentrated attention of the choir given to the conductor. The programme was well chosen especially 'Martyrs of the Arena' and Bairstow's 'Music when soft voices die' which were sung with intense fervour. 'The Old Woman' was a highlight. In addition to the choral items, solos were sung by Messrs. A.Green (tenor), F.Clarke (bass), A.Snowden (bass). The humour was provided by J.Busby. The accompanist was Mr. B.Lister. The concert was in aid of the Baptist Sports Club. [Yorkshire Gazette 20/2/1948]

On the 13th March 1948 the YEP reported:

York Philharmonic Male Voice Choir continues to enjoy great success in the city with its exceptional vocal achievements. Two recent concerts by the choir were in aid of the Leeman Road Old Age Pensioners and Haughton Road Methodist Church.

A similar programme was given at both these concerts and received excellent ovations. The individual soloists, Mr. W.Payne (tenor), Albert Snowden (bass) and Mr. R:W.Colley (recitations) proved popular. Mr. Sefton Fearne was the conductor and Mr. Brian Lister the accompanist.

The choir had regained its pre-war verve and confidence, and Sefton was fortunate in having a large number of talented and experienced soloists available.

Brian Lister played whenever he was available but this became harder. He was studying at the London School of Music, followed by National Service in the RAF. Given his absences, Mr. William Hanley was also an accompanist.

These were austere times but, in 2015, personal recollections from two elderly gentlemen, one now 86 years old, the other now 90 remember food and laughter. In 1946 Ken Horwell, best remembered now as a member of the Yorkshire County Bowls Team in the 1950s and with one appearance in the England team, was a young apprentice at Terry's Chocolate factory. At the suggestion of his boss Arthur Green (tenor soloist), he joined the choir as a top tenor and was one of its youngest members. With an interruption for National Service, he stayed with the choir till 1952. He remembers the choir rehearsing on Mondays and Thursdays in All Saints North Street and being about 36 strong. It was still the practice that subs were paid for each rehearsal attended. The choir sang five or six concerts a year, mostly in Methodist Chapels. Ken does not remember the concerts in the city centre so well as those trips to the villages around York. The choir, together with their ladies, would travel by Pullman bus to the concerts, which Ken remembers fondly due to the lavish suppers which country Methodist folk seemed able to provide even during such times of rationing. He recalls Albert Snowden and war-time recruit Fred Clarke singing duets, and a young tenor, Reg Goodhall, beginning his long service with the choir.

Ken's memories of laughter are also recalled by Brian Sargent. Brian is the son of Archie and Janet and although he was never a member of the choir attended some concerts. The laughter, which both men remember, was provided by Harry Shipman. In Ken's words, *the times were hard and we needed a comedian.* Harry was that man, according to Ken, *a true club comic.* Brian remembers a piece which Harry would perform with such style that it would almost always be requested and invariably brought the house down. This was called 'The Song of the Windmill' a setting of a poem by Longfellow. By itself that does not appear to be comic, the opening line being 'Behold a giant am I'. Harry, in a deep bass voice, sang the words with gusto, the comic effect coming from the fact that, physically, he was a very small man.

The Phil was making an excellent recovery, and even revived the Inter-Choir Competition in 1949, when the young Lawrie Sefton won the Challenge Cup. This too was short lived, as the choir faced another crisis. Sefton Fearne was unwell and during 1949 was forced, by ill-health, to resign with no replacement available. This was at a time when the young Brian Lister was unable to offer much support as he was completing his National Service. The Phil was once more at a loss and vulnerable. It is thought that during the following months a number of choristers stepped forward and tried to lead the choir. These efforts were unsuccessful but acknowledgement must be made of those contributions by: Harold Fletcher, son of Cecil; Harold Shipman, the small in stature comic; Fred Rogers and Sefton Cotton.

Chapter 3

Archie W Sargent

The Post-War Rebuild

Archie and Janet Sargent in 1950

Archie Sargent had already played a significant part in the development of the Philharmonic and had been a Vice President for some 15 years. He now took on the task of continuing the renaissance of the choir. Building a choir was Archie's particular skill. During his thirty years in York, he already had great success at Victoria Bar and Monkgate Churches, and in the forming of the Rowntrees Choral Society. He was well known to members of the Phil and his style of conducting was similar to that of Cecil Fletcher; each sought to connect with the 'essence' of the music and to achieve an emotional connection between music, choir, and audience. In his own words:

Quite recently I have heard the idea expressed that, if it is desired to achieve success, a conductor must be 'tough' with the singers and players under his direction. In other words, the method we have come to associate with a sergeant major must be adopted in order to obtain the desired results. I do not agree, and I am completely unable to understand why this should be necessary. As I see it, there should certainly be a mutual respect and confidence between performers and conductors, but, most of all, there must be that intangible 'essence' which we might describe as magnetic communication, a sensitive understanding and appreciation, or a sense of being 'en rapport' if the healing or therapeutic power of music is to be released, involving as it does expressive shades of expression and subtleties of tone colour.

Archie was a deeply religious man, who served as organist and choirmaster at four churches in the city. His work at Victoria Bar and at Monkgate has already been noted, but in 1951 he moved to the Presbyterian Church of England, St Columba's in Priory Street, and then in 1962 to Clifton Methodist. As these later moves overlapped with his time in charge of the Phil, it too took part in occasional events at these churches. In all appointments Archie succeeded in building up both the size and quality of the choir. He was committed to performing an Easter Oratorio, and was particularly fond of 'The Darkest Hour' by Harold Moore. The annual performance of the Messiah [a total of 13] was opened up to singers from across the city. He also strove, with less success, to maintain the Three Choirs festival. Another benefit to the Philharmonic of having Archie as its leader was that Janet Sargent became accompanist, the value of which was later recognised when she became the second lady to be awarded Honorary Life membership. Our knowledge of life in these years comes mostly from Archie's memoirs and extracts from the unpublished private diaries of Janet, researched and kindly provided by their son Brian.

In *Voices Pipes and Pedals* Archie devoted a chapter to his time with the Philharmonic. Here is his introduction:

On the 15th December 1952, the choir's Silver Jubilee Concert was given in the City Art Gallery, and the notes appearing on the souvenir programme indicate briefly the details concerning the choir's formation, and the general pattern of events thereafter.

Somewhere in the Leeman Road area of York four men, keen lovers of music, approached Cecil H.Fletcher, and sought his assistance in forming a Male Voice Quartette, Very readily he consented and soon other singers appeared, resulting in the formation of the Leeman Road Adult School Male Voice Choir. Eventually the name was changed to the York Philharmonic Male Voice Choir which went from strength to strength and was successful in competitions in York, Pontefract, Barnsley, Sheffield, Elsecar and Cleethorpes.

At this time Cecil Fletcher edited and published a choir journal called Philharmonic News which quickly became a most popular and entertaining monthly production. For some years the Phil was one of the three choirs in the Three Choirs Festival held at Monkgate Methodist Church. For a considerable time, too, the choir organised annually its own competitive festival, involving solo classes for tenors, baritones, basses, male voice quartettes etc.

Then came the war, and it became almost impossible to maintain the choir owing to the demands of the Forces, fire watching, Home Guard etc. Even in those days a few contrived to meet, and, 'Cecil was always there which made it worthwhile.' The end of all things seemed to have arrived when the beloved founder conductor died suddenly. At the cessation of hostilities several attempts were made to reorganise the choir but without success, until Sefton Fearne undertook the leadership. Once more the choir fellowship was restored – concerts were given – the Phil was reborn. But another calamity followed. Sefton Fearne found it quite impossible to carry on owing to illness and most regretfully resigned....

At this point, Archie Sargent, who had been a friend of the choir and a Vice President for many years, stepped in, and during the last eighteen months, the choir has increased in numbers and efficiency – the future seems bright with promise, and a hope of greater things than the past has held.

The choir was really in a desperate situation when I agreed to take over its direction in 1950, and as may be gathered from the foregoing notes, this was due to circumstances over which they had no control. I remember remarking to one of the members that never, while I was in York, would I see the Philharmonic go down. At this time we were fortunate if we managed 17 at a rehearsal, and so we went to work with enthusiasm.

Two years later at the date of the Silver Jubilee Concert in the Art Gallery the membership was 47. There was a fine spirit in the choir and indeed it was this feature which had always attracted me. Once again concert engagements were accepted and programmes were given to churches, chapels and any charitable organisation in need. An annual concert was given each year in the Art Gallery in aid of the Lord Mayor's Christmas Cheer Fund. These were greatly appreciated and the Civic Party attended.

Archie starts his account by describing this first major concert, a Silver Jubilee celebration and a significant achievement. But the work had started almost two years earlier. The Phil had planned to take part in the 1950 Three Choirs Festival, but was without a conductor. Archie agreed to be the guest conductor for this concert and on February 13th 1950 Archie and Janet attended a rehearsal which she recorded as:

Played for the Phil in the evening at All Saints' room North Street. They rose to Archie.

Archie described that Choir Sunday festival as follows:

In April 1950 we resumed our Three Choirs Festival in very happy circumstances. My wife and I had listened on the radio to a Scarborough Children's Choir conducted by Miriam Dowson. The singing of the children was excellent, and I wrote to her asking whether it would be possible for her to bring the choir to York for the Three Choirs programme at Monkgate. There were a number of reasons why this could not be done, but Miss Dowson wondered whether I would like another choir of hers to come instead – the Scalby and Newby Ladies' Choir – and so it was arranged.

The members of the York Philharmonic Male Voice Choir at that time were passing through an extremely difficult period and were without a conductor. I had been a Vice President of the choir for some years, and agreed to act as guest conductor for the Three Choirs programme.

That day the Phil sang six pieces: *Deep Harmony* arr. Luther Greenwood; *Lonely Woods* Lully; *I'm gwine to sing* Spiritual; *The Old Woman* Roberton; *Music when soft voices die* Bairstow; and *Feasting I watch* Elgar. These were all known to the pre-war choir and ones in which they would have felt comfortable. The joint item for all three choirs was also an old favourite having been sung in earlier festivals: *Non Nobis Domine* Quilter.

The Phil had not been musically challenged, but had taken part and had succeeded. A promising future looked to be on the horizon.

The 'guest conductor' stayed on during that spring and led the choir in a concert at St. Hilda's on June 13th, followed the next day by another at Monkgate, when Janet noted:

The Phil gave a concert at Monkgate. Mr. Salmon sang beautifully. It was a fine concert, but we are so worried – the Phil want Archie!

It seems that by default Archie and Janet officially took on the task. In September, Janet and Archie joined the choir on a day out to Ripon, Reeth and Richmond and that autumn saw three more concerts at York chapels. The spring of 1951 saw a change of rehearsal room to the Guild room of the Salem Congregational Church in St. Saviourgate (demolished in the 1960s). Brian Lister was home in March and played at a rehearsal. He was back again in July, when he resigned from the choir. Although unavoidably absent for so much of the time, Brian was still an official accompanist. This situation had to be resolved and, with Archie and Janet now well established, Brian concentrated on building his career as a music teacher and establishing York Youth Choir. In 1951 the Phil gave 10 concerts and held two social events – a river trip, and a day out on the North York Moors – normal service was resumed.

1952 saw a similar pattern. Numbers at rehearsal fluctuated from a low of 17 in August to 40, and often moved between 24 and 38, which must have given some rehearsal challenges. However, the commitment was there and in October, 41 turned out for a concert. In preparation for the Silver Jubilee concert, the choir gave four performances in larger city centre chapels during October and November so was 'match fit' and ready for this late running anniversary.

This photograph of the Silver Jubilee concert – December 15th 1952– shows the Lord Mayor Ald. C.W.Wright having a word with Archie Sargent. *On the far left stands top tenor William Payne 'Old Bill', one of the original four – now aged 76 years;* read the caption to this press photograph. The reference to Bill and the original four makes the distinction, maintained throughout Bill's long life, between the four who had the idea of the choir and the six (or seven) who attended the very first rehearsal with Cecil, and became founder members.

The report of the concert printed in the Evening Press gave this additional detail: *Last night's programme ranged from traditional airs to spirituals, from sea songs to the devotional music of Handel. Soloists were Mr. R.Goodhall, Mr. John Boston, Mr. Henry Brough, Mr. Albert Snowden, Mr. Cyril Luford and Mr. Fred Clarke. Janet W.Sargent was the accompanist. Mr. W.G.Birch (President) said the proceeds would go to the Lord Mayor and Sheriff's Christmas Cheer Fund.*

Janet's diary report was short: *Dec.15th 1952. 'Our Silver Jubilee Concert. It was lovely no snags. Civic party were thrilled.*

Many Civic Parties since that date have also been thrilled, as 1951 began the tradition of supporting the Christmas Cheer Fund through an autumn concert, an event still held today.

The naming of the soloists shows the link between the pre- and post-war choirs. Henry Brough and Albert Snowden were regular soloists in the 1930s; Fred Clarke (a policeman who joined during the war years) and, especially, Reg Goodhall would be soloists for the next 30 plus years, with both men singing in the Diamond Jubilee Concert in 1985.

The experience of Ken Horwell illustrates the tensions that so often accompany membership of any ambitious society. When the choir began in 1925 it met only during the winter months, from the end of September till May. This was common practice in those days so members could manage summer and winter activities without conflict. This changed in 1936 when the choir started meeting all year round, which undoubtedly added to the tensions in the choir at the end of 1936. This was, however, essential if the choir was to progress. Such tensions were still there post-war, and indeed can still be seen today. As a county class player Ken was committed to bowls seven days a week during the summer months. In 1952, during the time when Archie and Janet Sargent were working hard to build up the choir, Ken and two other singers in similar situations were asked by Archie to consider their commitment. Where did their priorities lie? All three were keen bowlers and chose to leave. It was a necessary move by Archie if the goals were to be met, but it was sad to lose singers in such a way, particularly as there did not appear to be many new members until 1954 and later. Ken keeps an interest in the choir to this day, and his fond memories include one which took place during his wedding reception. Whilst still a chorister and 'well fed and watered' Ken recalls singing 'The Jolly Roger'– a pirate song – together with his uncle who was a member of Burton Stone Lane MVC. The 'Song of the Jolly Roger' is in the 2015 repertoire and is often sung both at concerts and social functions.

The Phil, although now city centre based, was still nomadic with no settled rehearsal rooms. Between 1950 and 1962 a number of rooms were used dependent on their location and convenience but more critically, on their warmth, cost and dependability. All Saints Church hall in North Street, and St Crux The Pavement, were used the most, but time was also spent in All Saints High Ousegate, Central Methodist Hall (our current home), Salem Congregational Church St. Saviourgate (now demolished), The Unitarian Chapel St. Saviourgate, St. Columba's Priory Street and New Lendal Congregational Church Burton Stone Lane. Janet's diaries describe some of these changes of locations which must have been disruptive:

Mar 8th 1954 No phil for me. There is trouble with the Unitarians. It was a business meeting about a room.

Mar 15th 1954 the Unitarians met our committee about costs. The place was freezing.

Mar 16th 1954 Committee met at Mr.Reynolds. We are to move to All Saints

Mar 17th 1958 shocking muddle at North St. Place in darkness electricity removed just candles. Dashed off to Priory Street and practised there, but it was an upset. Now we are homeless.

Jan 11th 1960 When we got to St Crux we found the whole place a mass of decorators ladders and planks! John B. slipped round to Centenary who lent us the Guild Room. It was lovely. It was a very good practice.

Despite this disruption, the work and morale of the choir improved: *'Concerts given by the men during this period were legion'* is the simple way in which Archie described the return of the familiar rhythm of choir life. Along with the hard work, the genial fun loving attitude of the choir had also been revived. Archie wrote: *Rehearsals were such happy affairs and in those days there were some real 'characters' in the choir.* There were long serving members, apart from Bill Payne, Henry Brough and Albert Snowden still singing. Albert was described by Archie as: *The genial chairman of the committee who was greatly devoted to the choir. He achieved quite a measure of fame locally for his humorous contribution, 'Three ha'pence a foot' in various concert programmes.*

The choir had, then, regained its energy, enthusiasm and good humour. These two diary entries give a flavour of choir life:

May 17th 1954: *A grand phil practice. 4 new members in 3 weeks. We haven't dropped below 30 yet.*

Jan.19th 1955: *Archie went to Harry Shipman's funeral. Concert at Priory Street. It went splendidly and there wasn't a bad audience.*

Harry Shipman, one of the choir comedians, the little man with the big voice, died young but would, probably, have been pleased that this concert went ahead without him.

The revived Phil entered its first competition at the Pontefract Music Festival in 1955. It won the Albert Ward Memorial Trophy:

...the test pieces were: 'Heraclitus' (Robert Elkin) and 'Christus Der uns Selig Macht' (Bach). Of the first, the adjudicator, Dr. Eric Thiman said, "This had the confidence and ease that comes from a first rate technical equipment. It had some charming nuances. The phrasing and diction fully brought out the sense of the poem. A fine range of tone throughout; admirable ensemble, and much tenderness in the mood."

Regarding the Bach Chorale, Dr Thiman explained its difficulties to a Male Voice Choir, and said that the presentation by the York Choir was taken at a practicable and sensible tempo which allowed a good flow and sostenuto, with the words always admirably coloured. He liked he said, the dignified and beautifully shaded performance of this work.

This report from the local press also made the following suggestion (echoing pre-war practices):

The trophy is a beautiful piece of work which, it is hoped may be exhibited on one of the main York thoroughfares so that York citizens will have an opportunity to see it.

The choir returned to Pontefract in April 1957, with rehearsals for competition starting in October 1956. The choir was unhappy with the test piece, not an uncommon problem. Nevertheless the Phil took second place.

In November 1955 the local press reported on the annual choir concert. In a review headed:

Excellent Male Voice Fare.

The annual concert by York Philharmonic Male Voice Choir and other artists at the City Art Gallery on Wednesday deserved a much larger audience, for this was excellent fare; nevertheless, the audience, which included the civic leaders, were soon on friendly terms with those taking part. There was early evidence that the choir of some 40 voices were in fine form; their enthusiasm for the popular 'Happy Wanderer' song was infectious; in contrast, Brahms' beautiful 'Cradle Song' was effective in its simplicity. The two set pieces of this year's Pontefract Music Festival which won for the choir a silver trophy, were nobly sung – 'Heraclitus' by a contemporary Robert Elkin, and Bach's chorale, 'Christus der uns selig macht.'

Further groups of songs included Elgar's setting of 'It's oh! To be a wild wind`, sung especially for the choir's President unable to be present and 'Zion's Children' a spiritual which displayed the choir's splendid fortissimo.

Reg Goodhall, tenor, sang an interesting set of songs including the 'Mighty like a Rose', while Elsie Senior, contralto, charmed with Edward German's 'Court Favour' and 'Sigh no more ladies', including in her second group two songs of the sea in contrasting mood. In the modern idiom, baritone songs by Benjamin Britten and Vaughan Williams earned praise for John Boston.

Bertha Etty, elocutionist, provided humour and pathos with recitations and character sketches which included 'An Old Maid's Story', Jim Jacksons 'Experiment' and two poems. The reception of these delightful interludes was well merited.

One almost felt that the extra item given at the very end of the concert had not been added, so stirring was the choir's climax in the 'Holy City' (Doris Arnold's well known arrangement). Undoubtedly this choir owes much to its conductor A.W.Sargent, and not least to Mrs. Sargent who ably accompanied throughout.

The proceeds of the concert will be devoted to the Lord Mayor and Sheriff's Christmas Cheer Fund.

The first musical item mentioned in this review was 'The Happy Wanderer'. This was introduced to the world by a German youth choir at the 1953 Llangollen Eisteddfod. It became immensely popular, and was a top selling record in the UK for some 16 weeks in 1954. By 1955 it was in the repertoire of the Phil. Also included were items by living and active composers, Vaughan Williams and Benjamin Britten, and the concert ended with an arrangement by the very popular Doris Arnold. The rejuvenated choir and its soloists were keeping the repertoire up to date.

The reviewer made reference to Elgar's 'Oh to be a Wild Wind!' sung especially for the choir's President, who was unable to be present. He was Walter G. Birch [younger brother to W.H. Birch who had played an important role in the choir's life pre-war] and the significance of the Phil singing this piece was recorded by Archie Sargent in a tribute paid to Walter G. Birch following his death in January 1956:

It was not until he [WGB] became President of the York Philharmonic Male Voice that I met him personally. I discovered that the more one knew of this attractive personality, the more one was drawn to him with warm regard. Apart from business acumen, his enthusiasm for the finest music, and his deep knowledge of literature, one felt that here was a man of deep compassion – one who loved his fellow men........he would come into a Philharmonic rehearsal from time to time, and when I greeted him, he would say with a smile "I should like very much, to hear the men sing, It's Oh to a wild wind" – an Elgar miniature of sheer beauty – and we would sing it for him. Archie then described the funeral arrangements.....*All the necessary arrangements were made, and a great congregation assembled including the two choirs of which Mr. Birch has been President – York Old Priory [conductor Sydney Skinner] and the Philharmonic, children from the Deaf and Dumb Benevolent Society with Mr. R.S.Oloman, representatives from the British Musical Society in York and other societies in which he was interested and had helped in one way or another.*

The review also referred to the male soloists Reg Goodhall and John Boston. Both undertook significant roles beyond normal choir concerts. An intriguing reference was made to the performance of Messiah in 1957, York Festival year. The local press announced:

All four principals in the performance of 'Messiah' at the York Presbyterian Church on November 17th this year will be York singers, says the conductor, Mr. Archie W. Sargent, who has already announced his plans to members of the chorus..........'And now for an intriguing feature of the performance this year', adds Mr. Sargent, 'there has been considerable controversy in our ancient city on the theme that some of our choirs should have been brought into the 1957 festival. We cannot do very much about that, but we can, in this festival year, engage an all York quartet of principal singers. This we have done, and they are: Stella Kemp-Welch, Gwen Hall, Reg Goodhall and Arthur Taylor.

At Easter 1962 and 1963 in Clifton Methodist Church, Reg, John and Fred Clarke together with Janet Sargent sang the lead roles in 'The Darkest Hour' and in 1965 Reg and John were the principals in a performance of Stainer's 'Crucifixion'.

An unusual style of concerts also proved popular. These were held at 8pm on a Sunday evening in the Railway Institute Gymnasium and were called '*Sounding Brass and Voices'*. In March 1957 the local press reported:

Last evening another concert in the series Sounding Brass and Voices was given at the York Railway Institute Gymnasium. The band was the Railway Institute Band under its conductor L.Bruce. The York St. Lawrence Male Voice Choir (conductor G.J.Stacey), The York Philharmonic Male Voice Choir (conductor A.W.Sargent), and the York Railway Institute Male Voice Choir (conductor L.Smith) also took part.

Guest conductor Royden Knights, who conducted the band in two items, is the conductor of the choir at Wesley Chapel. The band played extremely well throughout the whole of the concert, and accompanied the choirs most admirably.

The choirs kept extremely good pitch and tone, and the diction was excellent, especially in their pianissimo passages. The dynamics of both band and choirs were superb and one can only say 'Bravo' for a fine musical performance.

Janet's diary entry stated: Sunday Mar.3rd *The three choirs at the Railway Institute went beautifully. 'I dare not ask a kiss' and 'Feasting I watch' were super.*

This must have been a popular show as Archie reported that:

...shortly afterwards the concert was repeated in the Salvation Army Citadel and the proceeds handed to the Melrose Club for the Blind.

The first time that Archie Sargent conducted the Philharmonic was in the revived Three Choirs Festival at Monkgate in 1950, but it was not until April 1959 that he was able to recreate this format. This must have been a significant event for older members, as the Philharmonic was reunited with the York Old Priory Ladies Choir.

The local press reported:

Last night at the Presbyterian Church a festival of Music was given by York Old Priory Ladies Choir (conductor: J.L.Huntington), York Philharmonic Male Voice Choir (conductor A.W.Sargent) and York Presbyterian Church Choir (conductor A.W. Sargent). The programme opened with three pieces by the Presbyterian Choir one of which was 'To

Music' (Schubert) arranged Bairstow, sung with full understanding of both words and music.

Next came three pieces by the York Philharmonic, which included the beautiful 'Eriskay Love Lilt' (arr. Roberton). This was sung with deep feeling.

The York Old Priory Ladies Choir also sang three pieces, one of which was 'Nymphs and Shepherds' (Purcell) arr. Keighley. They blended well but a little more zip in the rhythm of the Purcell would have added lustre to the performance.

There was a two year gap till the next Three Choirs Concert, when York Athenaeum Ladies Choir (also led by Archie Sargent) took the place of Old Priory Ladies. In May 1962 the concert moved (with Archie) to his new base at Clifton Methodist with Clifton choir now joining the Athenaeum ladies and the Philharmonic. It seems clear, however, that the pre-war popularity of the annual Three Choirs Festival at Monkgate could not be repeated.

However, the popularity of the '*The Happy Wanderer'* did not diminish and it helped the Phil achieve one ambition which had so far eluded it. Before the war it was the only significant York choir, which had not been broadcast on the BBC. Archie Sargent had been remarkably successful during his time at Monkgate and his reputation helped in later securing broadcasts of church services from both the Presbyterian Church and Clifton Methodist. The 'Happy Wanderer' had been a huge hit in 1954, and remained popular. In 1954/55 York City Football Club enjoyed a successful season ending up in fourth place in Division three North, and reached the semi finals of the FA cup. During that year they won 11 away matches and became known as *'The Happy Wanderers'*. W.H. Sessions was President of the football club following on from 14 years as chairman. He was a good friend and Vice President of the choir. Alderman Ernest Harwood was also a director at the club and was President of the choir. As 'The Happy Wanderer' had become the club song and was in the choir's repertoire it is not surprising that these two men invited the choir to record it. This did not happen, however, until 1958 when it was recorded as part of a concert given in the Art Gallery. We believe that for a number of years the recording was played over the loudspeakers before home games. It was not a BBC broadcast but, at last, the choir had been recorded and was being broadcast. The details of this recording as noted by Archie and Janet differ slightly. Archie wrote: *Accordingly the record was made, I believe during the 1958 concert in the Art gallery....* Janet, who was still recovering from a broken wrist gave more details but again is precise:

Nov.12th 1958: *Splendid concert at Art Gallery. I managed to accompany quite creditably. Quite informal and the Lord Mayor and Sheriff and Ladies were thrilled. The Harwoods were there. The men did sing well. The Hall was full.*

Nov. 24th: *We had the recording played back. It was lovely except for one tenor!*

Dec. 8th: *We did the recording at the phil. Quite an interesting time.*

Feb. 16th 1959: *Very good practice the records came.*

It would seem the recording was made at the concert as Archie 'believed' but it may not have been the recording eventually issued. Janet's notes suggest that it was re-recorded at a rehearsal – perhaps with one particular tenor sat on the 'subs' bench.

In December 1956, the Choir accepted an invitation from the Castle Museum to take part in a Nativity Play. This was it seems a successful night but was not repeated. It was, though, a foretaste of what was to come when the very successful and long running 'Carols in Kirkgate' began in 1962.

Janet wrote: Dec.17th *The Nativity Play in the Castle Museum was lovely, and the Phil men made grand carol singers.*

The following letter of thanks was received from the curator:

I wish to thank you and your Male Voice Choir on behalf of the Castle Museum Committee, for so kindly leading the carols at our Nativity Play.

We have received many expressions of appreciation from the public, and we are most grateful to you all for providing such a perfect conclusion to a memorable play. Having seen the same play performed without your choir, I am in an excellent position to judge the effect, and I can only say that there is no comparison.

We all deeply appreciate the willing and kind co-operation from all your members, and trust this happy association will long remain.

With again our very sincere thanks for the beautiful singing and wishing you all a happy Christmas and successful New Year.

The Christmas story can indeed be told without music as this letter of thanks suggested but the Rowntrees Cocoa Works Magazine of Christmas 1937 described the enhancement that a choir [often unseen] can bring to such a dramatic presentation:

The life and soul, almost, of a Nativity Play is the 'Heavenly Chorus' the choir which links the scenes together with those carols and hymns which are, perhaps, older even than the idea of the dramatic presentation of our Lord's birth. Its music catches the heart in some mysterious way and touches even those who have no feeling for the religious side of the festival. 'The First Nowell', 'The Holly and the Ivy', 'The Cradle Song of the Blessed Virgin' and the 'Coventry Carol', the culminating triumph of the 'Adeste Fideles' – 'Come all ye Faithful' – make the Christmas play of today one in purpose with the old Mysteries. The message is the same – 'Unto us a Child is Born come let us adore him'. As the Shepherds then heard the Angels sing – 'Peace on Earth to men of goodwill and come to worship him', so does mankind today yearn for the same blessing. Christmas without this sense of worship and goodwill would cease to have real meaning.

This Cocoa Works description is of interest to our story as the Rowntrees Choral Society in the '30s had Archie Sargent as its honorary conductor. Archie recalled his memories of these Nativity Plays as follows:

One of the outstanding memories, however, relates to the production of a Nativity Play at Rowntrees Theatre for several years. The producer was a charming Roman Catholic Lady, who asked me to provide a small choir of 'Angelicals' to operate in the wings. These performances were timed to begin after evening services, and so I was able to slip across to the theatre in time to join my singers in the darkness of the stage, armed only with a tuning fork and an electric torch! All those years before ecumenical movement were operating in such profusion a Roman Catholic and a Methodist were found in happy collaboration, working out the details of the Nativity Plays! It was certainly a matter of general regret when the series came to an end owing to the departure of the producer Miss Crisp, on War service.

These productions saw the first public performances by Brian, the young son of Archie and Janet, who recalls bowing to parental pressure to play the part of an angel. Brian was another talented young musician whose first job was as the afternoon organist at Salem Congregational. In the 1930s Cecil Fletcher had been joined in the Phil by his son Harold, a young Duncan Forster had been invaluable to Jack at Old Priory, and now Brian Sargent joined with his parents by playing the organ for the Messiah. Brian gave his first organ recital, in Monkgate church, at the age of 21 shortly after graduating with a music degree from Manchester University. He was assisted in this by Renee Forster, the widow of Duncan who, in Archie's words: *'has a very beautiful soprano voice, and, what is more, she loves her art, and gives to it all the artistic resources of her personality.'*

There was a poignant reminder of the pre-war years when Joyce Fletcher, daughter of Cecil, attended the November 1957 annual concert. Eleven years after the death of her father she said to Janet that *'her father would have been proud of the Phil that night'.*

Janet's diaries contain many references to good rehearsals and a happy atmosphere in the choir: *'A most hilarious practice at the Phil. The men were fey!'* May 16th 1955. However, as the decade progressed there were signs of tension. There was, at times, dissent and conflict, but the diaries offer little explanation. Choice of music is the only specific reference made: *'Annual meeting so I didn't go to the Phil. Rather a rough do-music again'* April 27th 1959. *'Archie had a committee meeting about the YMVC music.'* April 29th 1959. The diaries also note when new members joined the choir but no details are given of their ages, whilst time took its toll on the older members. Choir comedian Harry Shipman had died in January 1955, with the choir attending his funeral during the day and giving a concert in Priory Street in the evening; in March 1958 came this lament; *'Today we had the news of Mr. Boynton's illness. We feel really sad that he must give up. We shall miss him very much as man, singer and jeweller. The Phil is being hit – tenors Mr. B.Arthur Colley, Mr. Ashby, Colin Kirkby, Bill Payne. Bass – Arthur Boddy and Charlie Olson – all belonging to the phil for so many years'.*

These periods of unrest and loss were clearly hurtful. It reached the point, in March 1959, that Archie announced his intention to retire, but was persuaded to stay. The disagreements flared up over a number of years without, it seems, getting resolved. This must have been difficult for all concerned. The choir as a whole was happy. Everyone had an immense admiration and respect for Archie and Janet. Nevertheless, resolving conflict in such a 'family' situation was not easy. The underlying strength of the choir was, however, always present and the men would always rise to a challenge, as the diary noted in November 1960: *'All the ingredients for a complete flop at the Annual concert – many colds, an accident etc. were in place, but the men gave their all, and it was a really happy affair'.*

Looking back from a distance of 60 years, and having the benefit of knowing how the choir progressed in the 1960s, some suggestions can be made as to the likely cause of this unrest. Archie had stepped into a crisis in 1950 and had done what he did best – he built the choir back to be a competition-winning ensemble at Pontefract in 1955. What next? It seems that the choir lacked any long term vision. No other competitions were entered, and a return to Pontefract in 1957 only gained second place. The pattern of performances in and around York had changed little in 30 years, but the Inter-Choir competition had not been brought back, so there were few, if any, challenges. Indeed one variant to the concert schedule, the 1956 and 1957 concerts with The York St Lawrence and Railway Institute Male Voice Choirs made the Phil vulnerable. To sing with other male voice choirs in your own city is not a threat so long as yours is the best. Indeed that way you may gain new recruits; but what if your members think the others are more attractive? We don't know if Archie had a deputy to assist him in any way with extra rehearsals etc., but we do know that Colin Kirkby [who left in 1958] took one as did Reg Goodhall. But there does not seem to have been much practical support for Archie, whose workload was such that he could give only limited time to the Phil, another constraint to any ambition.

This still doesn't explain the vexed question of music, the one issue identified in the diaries. The assumption must be that at least a few senior members wanted some changes in repertoire – a situation recognisable to music directors of any generation. What was new in music in the mid 1950s? Bill Haley and the Comets –*'Rock around the Clock'* 1954; Elvis Presley – *'Heartbreak Hotel'* 1956; Lonnie Donegan – *'Rock Island Line'* 1956; all new musical sensations which, through radio, film, television, and the culture-changing seven inch 45 rpm record, were sweeping the world. It is not surprising that such changes in popular music should lead to some debate as to repertoire.

In 1957, as he reached 60yrs of age, Archie considered retiring from his full time role at the Inland Revenue, but then continued until he was 64 in 1961. In 1960 he accepted the position of music director to the York Atheneum Ladies Choir, another crisis appointment, another choir needing to be rebuilt. This was his specialism so when retirement from the Inland Revenue came and Archie and Janet needed to rethink their workload, the choir to be dropped was the Phil; their work there was complete. Archie resigned on March 21st 1962 with the expectation of carrying on until September to allow a replacement to be recruited. This was unsettling for the choir but it was not a crisis as in previous times. The recruitment moved swiftly. Ernest Robinson – choir secretary – invited Brian Lister to apply. An interview was held on 23rd May, the appointment was made and Brian took his first rehearsal on the 4th June. This aspect of the change was not handled well by the committee; Archie and Janet were not told of the appointment until they arrived to take the practice on May 28th. Janet made the following note in her normal positive manner: *'We got to St. Crux to find it was our last night. A few people were annoyed and so were we. It was a smashing practice. Anyway it's all over now.'*

The choir responded by immediately electing Archie as President for that year, and by presenting them with a chased silver tray bearing the inscription:

Presented to
Mr. and Mrs. A.W.Sargent
By The York Philharmonic Male Voice Choir
In gratitude for their unstinted services
1950-1962

This photo copied from Voices Pipes and Pedals shows the presentation being made on October 10th 1962 attended by some 25 choir members.

[In February 2016 Brian Sargent, kindly donated this tray to the choir archive]

The final piece of this story took place some seven years later in March 1969, when Archie and Janet received this letter from the secretary at that time – Jack Jones:

Dear Archie,

This is a twofold letter – one of sadness, and one of joy. We in the choir were very sorry to hear of your continued ill health Archie, and it is the sincere wish of all your old friends and new ones alike that a full and permanent recovery will soon be yours.

We missed you and Janet at our Clifton concert, but I know that you were both with us in spirit at least, and we look forward to your return to our local concerts

Now the more pleasant part of my letter. The new committee met last week, and one of our first jobs was to review the list of officials of the choir. I am delighted to tell you Janet, that for your services to the choir as accompanist, the committee were unanimous in their decision that you should be elected to Honorary Life Membership of the choir. I did not know you both in your 'heyday' but I have read enough in minutes and newspaper cuttings to know that this election is well deserved. You know I think it must be rather unique for both husband and wife to be Life Members of the same organisation, and this fact alone shows the devotion and dedication with which husband and wife faced life together – perhaps there is a moral here for our younger generation.

Finally my personal congratulations to you Janet and my good wishes for your speedy recovery Archie,

Sincerely Jack.

Janet Sargent joined Jane Brough in the distinction of being the only two women to be granted this honour in the 43 year life of the choir.

Archie served as conductor until 1962 which is too early [by only one year] for any current member to have sung under his direction. In 2015 our longest serving chorister, Tony Sawyer, celebrated 50 years of full membership, although he first sang with the choir in 1963. We do, however, have two members who have sung under Archie in other settings. Peter Evans (bass) was a member of Clifton Methodist Choir under Archie's direction before joining the Phil in 1967, and top tenor Alan Wells remembers singing in the chorus at one of the last Messiahs which Archie conducted. Peter remembers him as a man of deep religious conviction, with a determination to get the best from any choir. He also recalls his own early days in the Phil when Archie was, at times, referred to by older singers in reverential tones as though his spirit was still within the rehearsal room.

In 1962 Archie, aged 65, was able with confidence to hand the baton to 31 year old Brian Lister – to the next generation. The last entry we have from Janet's diaries is from November 1962 when they, as Choir President and wife, attended the autumn concert. Janet wrote: *'Splendid audience and a very good concert. Brian Lister was pleased at Archie's appreciation.* In 1971 Archie in his memoirs wrote: *Although this meant saying farewell to many friends and colleagues, we have not lost touch with the choir, who are giving a great account of themselves under the extremely competent direction of my successor Richard B. Lister.*

Chapter 4
York Male Voice Choir ...and its interaction with the Phil

There is little or no knowledge of York Male Voice Choir [YMVC] amongst York choral singers in 2015, even those with 50 plus years of experience. It had disbanded c.1960 and left no identifiable legacy. It was a fine choir, predating the Phil by more than 25 years. The two choirs influenced each other but not in a publicly acknowledged way. This chapter seeks to recognise the success of the older body and tries to explain some of the dynamics and connections between the two.

An entry in the York Directory [Kelly's] for 1925 gives details of the choir and its achievements to date.

- York Male Voice Choir was inaugurated on 11/05/1899
- It performed before the King and Queen on 13/05/1903
- In 1908 and 1910 YMVC joined with York Musical Society to perform *The Dream of Gerontius* in York Minster.
- In May 1912 it won first and second prizes in an international competition held in Paris
- By 1925 it had won over 80 major prizes in competitions including the Yorkshire Challenge Shield 12 times.

The entry states that the choir existed: 'principally for competitive work with one grand concert each autumn'; and it offered: 'An invitation to possessors of fine voices'.

The choir added to its royal connections by singing for HRH Princess Mary as recorded in N&V August 1926.

YMVC had the honour of singing before HRH Princess Mary at Scriven Park. After the performance – a special one – Mr J.L.Slater conductor was presented to the Princess. It is interesting to note that of all those present only 5 were with the choir when it sang before HM the King (then Prince of Wales) at Escrick Park in 1903. They were Sefton Fearne, Fred Holmes, Jack Parkin, Jack Steel and J.H.Forster.

Alderman W.H. Birch [WHB], together with his lifelong friend Jack H. Forster, was a founder member of this choir. WHB was a good baritone soloist, as well as also being a member of a chapel choir and York Old Priory Choir. He was an active supporter of the York Music Festival, and also became a Vice President of the Phil. In 1945 Alderman Birch wrote some memoirs for his family which were never published. These memoirs have been a valuable source of information for this chapter, and extracts are reproduced here with the kind permission of Mrs Kathy Pickard, granddaughter of WHB and the current President of York Priory Choir.

As a young man WHB was a member of a Methodist chapel choir, believed to be Melbourne Terrace, and as one of a group of 16 musical friends a decision was taken to enter a competition.

...a party of 16 musical friends determined to enter for the male voice section of a competition held at Hardraw Scar, a natural amphitheatre near Hawes in Wensleydale.

We did not expect any success, entering for the joy of singing and the day's outing, and I shall never forget the trudge from Hawes station to Hardraw Scar. A lovely day, delightful surroundings and an ideal place for a performance, the platform being fixed where the listeners could hear easily from the sides of the amphitheatre, but we were new to competition work. Many people like ourselves made it a holiday and that Saturday afternoon some thousands had a joyous time. I remember walking along with Matthew Rymer, a local organist, whom we had persuaded to train us. He told me that the fruit he was eating was a Canary banana; it was the first of its kind I had seen.

The 16 of us, responding to our number which had been announced, walked in fear and trembling onto the platform, (the smallest choir of the day), grouped ourselves and waited for the signal to commence singing the competition piece, 'Wanton Gales'. Returning amongst the audience we anxiously awaited the adjudicators' comments, never expecting anything but a few complimentary remarks, but to our confusion and confounding we were awarded the third prize.

Never were men more astonished or happier; one would have thought we had licked the world. Any honorary mention would have been sufficient, but a third prize was beyond the imagination of all of us; we were completely unbalanced, singing all the way home and projecting plans for the future to build up a choir big enough and good enough to compete with the best male voice choirs in Yorkshire. It was a big idea, for there were a number of first-class male voice choirs with a competition singing force of 40 odd voices so it was no mean task that we had set ourselves. We sought right and left for singers, adding another two good altos, three extra tenors, four extra bass and two first tenors thus doubling our numbers and as Mr. Rymer could not afford the time to take practices we obtained the services of Mr. Wm Child, a local musician of first class repute, and ultimately by careful selection we increased our numbers to over 50, which was sufficient to form a certain party for competition purposes, with a safe margin for illness.

Everyman took the work seriously, putting in good attendances and learning something of our conductor's knowledge.

This was the beginning of the long and successful musical career of the York Male Voice Choir, beating some of the best choirs in Yorkshire and Lancashire in competitions at Huddersfield, Blackpool, Ilkley, Middlesbrough, Leeds, Halifax, Nelson and elsewhere....

The ambitions forged on the train home from Hawes were most certainly realised. Matthew Rymer, who had trained these singers, is listed in the 1922 city directory as being the choirmaster of a large choir of 43 singers at Centenary Chapel [now Central Methodist]. This adds weight to the idea that this group came out of the chapel choirs of Melbourne Terrace, the Priory Street chapels, and perhaps Centenary which would have allowed them access to good rehearsal rooms and facilities. Alternatively it may have been, as WHB wrote, just a group of friends from a wider circle – the Fearne family for example were members of St. Lawrence Church. As the choir became established it retained its independence both in its choice of name and rehearsal facilities, having the Micklegate Bar rooms as its base.

As well as competition work, the choir also gave annual autumn concerts. In November 1905 it teamed up with the York Symphony Orchestra in a joint concert in the Exhibition Buildings. The choir sang six pieces including *I wish to tune my quivering lyre,* by S. Wesley, set in five parts. This piece was to be sung again in a grander setting when it was an 'own choice item' in the International Choral

Competition in Paris in May 1912.

That competition billed as an 'International Musical Competition & Demonstration for Choirs, Orchestras & Bands' was organised by the city of Paris, supported by the French government, and attracted a large number of entries from across Europe and America. It was held over the Whitsun week-end 26-28th May 1912, and adverts in the Musical Times suggested that board and lodging plus rail fare for a two night stay would cost about £2. The top two classes were 'Excellence' and 'Superior'. According to the listings in the Musical Times of April 1st 1912, the London Welsh and Swansea and District Choirs had both entered the 'Excellence' class and were both taking 120 singers. York entered the 'Superior' class. The April 1st listing showed 19 choirs in this class of which York, with only 40 singers, was the smallest; the largest had 172 singers. The conductor was music teacher Harry Seymour Wilkinson who also held the post from 1922-25. William S. Child, the music teacher who had built up the choir, and in whom WHB had such faith, is thought to have died in 1909. The trip to Paris was a great success despite the fact that Seymour Wilkinson had one arm in a sling following a cycling accident two weeks earlier. The Yorkshire Herald carried a full report of the choir's homecoming on the 30th May including details of the competition given by Seymour Wilkinson:

The competition started at 9 o'clock on Monday morning. There were 6 choirs competing in the section in which we were engaged. There was an audience of between 400 and 500 people, and they were most appreciative, and applauded freely. The test piece was 'Riders of the Night 'by Laurent de Rille. All the choirs had to sing it. From the outset my choir sang with freedom, and I felt that they were doing well. After we had sung 'Riders of the Night' we proceeded to another hall where we had to sing a piece at sight. It proved to be very difficult. By careful reading we were able to give a fairly accurate rendering of the piece. After lunch we returned to the first hall, and sang a piece of our own selection, 'I wish to tune my quivering lyre' by Dr. S.S.Wesley. Here again we felt we had given a fine rendering. There was no announcement of the results, and it was not until late in the evening that we knew we had been successful. As a matter of fact I went to the hall late at night, and by the aid of a lighted candle was able to see the results which had been posted on the hall door. I found that the first prize for the selection had gone to the Orpheon des Mines de Dourges, a miners' choir of nearly 100 voices. We (The York Male Voice Choir) were bracketed with Lille (Nord) as second. There were no marks issued in the awards simply the bare announcement of the placing of the choirs. In the sight reading competition we tied for the first place with the Orpheon des Mines de Dourges, which won first prize in the other part of the competition. No third prize was awarded. The total amount we won was 1700 francs which is equal to about £68. There was another English choir in the competition – the Wren choir from Camberwell London but they were not successful in getting placed at all.

The 19 choirs known to have entered in April had reduced to six on the day. York knew it was the smallest but still chose a piece set in five parts. This was a bold act but it is likely that the choir knew this piece well and enjoyed singing it. The miners' choir numbered 96 so was always going to be difficult to beat. Lille, with which York came joint second, numbered 45. It was a tribute to York to come joint first (with the miners) in the sight-reading test, given that no other choir was thought good enough to be awarded a prize.

In the Yorkshire Herald the following day this letter was published which gave an account of just what a significant event this had been and how well York had been received:

To the Editor of the Yorkshire Herald – York Male Voice Choir Visit to Paris

Sir , – In your report in today's 'Herald' of the return of the above choir to York last night, an interview with Mr. Wilkinson is given, in which it is stated "we did not take part in the procession because I could not find it." This is rather misleading for, as a matter of fact, The York Male Voice Choir was well represented, Mr. Wilkinson and about half a dozen members unfortunately being missing through inability to get through the huge crowds to the right entrance to the Gardens of the Tulleries, where the procession was marshalled. Those of us who took part in it with our typical 'John Bull' leading had an experience we shall never forget. The choirs of other nationalities were allowed to pass comparatively unnoticed, but as soon as 'York' and 'Angleterre' caught the eye of the crowd the welcome accorded us defies description. We were applauded by thousands. Men and women grabbed us by the hand, and on all sides shouts of "Vive la Angleterre" resounded, interspersed with good humoured banter, such as "John Bull" and "jambon". The same description applies when passing the covered dais erected for the President, as everything was quiet and orderly until we arrived opposite, when the whole assembly surrounding the President started cheering – ladies waved their handkerchiefs and threw kisses, and the President bowed to us very graciously – whilst we in return waved our hats and gave them three cheers in true English fashion, and as only Yorkshiremen can. There would be 50 or 60 bands all playing stirring marches, and we marched at a brisk pace for something like 2.5 miles through dense crowds of cheering people. The route was kept by soldiers, and at the Hotel de Ville a troop of French Cuirassiers on horseback also were on duty, and looked splendid in their brass helmets and long plumes. The procession finished at the Place de'l Bastille, but on getting to the back of the Hotel de Ville we espied an underground station, and dropped out just about exhausted with one of the hardest and still most pleasant experiences it has ever been my lot as a singer to go through.

Just one little amusing episode and I have finished. We were marching along and perspiring with the heat and exertion, when someone in the crowd shouted: "Come and have a drink!" and the automatic way all heads turned in the direction of the speaker was very funny. Of course it was out of the question to accept the invitation; but, as one member remarked, that was the best bit of English he had heard in Paris.

We shall all remember our visit with pleasure and a certain amount of pride at the success of our efforts. The journey was rather long, and we have had very little sleep, but were highly favoured by having smooth passages across the briny; and the memory of our visit will linger in our minds for many a day.

I am, sir, yours faithfully Edward Swann May 30th 1912.

The reception the choir received was remarkable. Was it just because they were one of the best choirs on the day or was Paris welcoming an ally as the war clouds grew? The Titanic had been lost only a few weeks earlier on the 15th April – did this affect their reception? We cannot answer these questions but can acknowledge that on the day these singers were excellent ambassadors for our city.

The following photograph, recently found at an antique fair, is marked York Male Voice Choir, with no date or location given. It is believed to have been taken during this visit. The gentleman in the light suit has been identified as Alderman Lancelot Foster, President of the choir and a former Lord Mayor, who was with the choir in Paris. The shield shown also appeared on the photograph published in the Yorkshire Herald [not of good enough quality to reproduce] showing the choir arriving back in York.

The new technology of film making also played a part in this event with one enterprising York Cinema manager seeking to make a profit. The Yorkshire Herald report of Thursday 30th May ended with this note:

Record Development of Cinematograph Pictures of the Choir

Mr. Bert Rutter, the manager of the Victoria Hall, created what is probably a record in the cinematograph world last night by taking a picture of the York Male Voice Choir at half past six, on their arrival at York station, and showing the picture at the Victoria Hall at half-past nine. In the course of that time the picture had to photographed, printed, developed and dried. The picture was a very good one and the different members of the choir were easily recognised. In addition Mr. Rutter showed a very fine film of the choir taken at the Victoria station London yesterday morning. The film was developed in London and actually travelled on the same train as the choir. The pictures were shown together, and elicited loud and prolonged applause.

The enterprising Mr Rutter also placed this advertisement in the same edition.

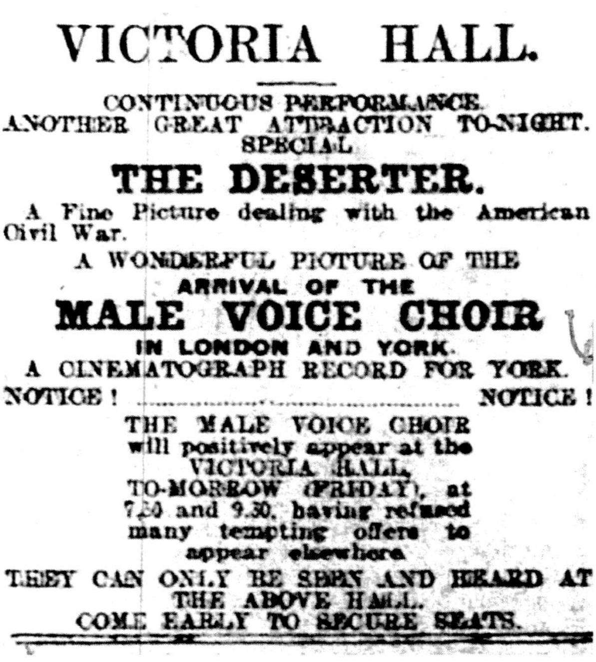

VICTORIA HALL.

CONTINUOUS PERFORMANCE.
ANOTHER GREAT ATTRACTION TO-NIGHT.
SPECIAL

THE DESERTER.

A Fine Picture dealing with the American Civil War.

A WONDERFUL PICTURE OF THE
ARRIVAL OF THE
MALE VOICE CHOIR
IN LONDON AND YORK.
A CINEMATOGRAPH RECORD FOR YORK.

NOTICE! .... NOTICE!

THE MALE VOICE CHOIR will positively appear at the VICTORIA HALL, TO-MORROW (FRIDAY), at 7.30 and 9.30, having refused many tempting offers to appear elsewhere

THEY CAN ONLY BE SEEN AND HEARD AT THE ABOVE HALL.
COME EARLY TO SECURE SEATS.

So, in 1925, as the Leeman Road Adult School Male Voice Choir was being formed, the York Male Voice Choir had an excellent reputation and performed to high standards. It was a competition choir which gave only one annual concert. Shown below is a review of the December 1926 concert as written by W.H. Birch and published in N&V. It is reproduced in full not only to describe the choir but also to give an entertaining insight into changes in musical taste which were clearly not to the liking of WHB.

I must confess to a slight bias for men's voices which may account for my unqualified delight in listening to excellent performances by Male Voice Choirs. The Annual Concert of YMVC under the leadership of its gifted conductor Mr. J.L.Slater was wholly enjoyable although some items stood out in contrast to others. Among the best results were the splendid rendition of 'Feasting I watch' and a piece of different character 'Swansea Town'. The narrative of the latter was very pleasing and sustained the interest as 'a tale that is told' should. The effect of the dramatic performance of Feasting was at times electrifying as words such as solemn, splendid, flashing, pageantry and crown should. It was in 'The Reveille' however that the choir reached a high water mark rising to the full height of the words and music and convincing the listeners of the compelling power of 'the drum' – a truly magnificent performance. 'I dare not kiss' was not sufficiently delicate – too muffled. 'Bold Turpin' was an indifferent performance, not at all convincing.

Mr. Harold Williams, an artiste whose efforts were characterised by a clarity of expression and a resonant tone, is a singer immersed in his subject and absorbing his audience with a desire to hear him again.

Some of the more delicate parts of the second half of the programme were somewhat marred by the dance music in the adjoining Assembly Rooms and we had the unique experience of listening to the sublime and the ridiculous at the same time with emotions varying from the heavens of delight to the depths of despair.

The only time I feel like murdering someone is when I hear jazz music, for of all the inventions of modern time this, like poison gas, is one we could well do without. Strange contraptions are brought into play like the tapping of wood across iron railings, curious instruments producing sounds like long eared quadrupeds in pain. Sounds like the wail of the lost in the desert mixed with various squealing force themselves intermittently on the ear of the unwilling listener with a deadly monotony, the concerted result of which defies expression. Modern dancing evidently calls for no further effort than merely walking aimlessly about with a girl, keeping time, off and on, in a desultory fashion with strange noises that take the mind back to sounds we can imagine were produced by primitive peoples who with their 'tom toms' got a glimmer of rhythm and the elements of musical sound as they articulated their emotions in their ancient mystical rites. But why we with all the possibilities of hearing the best of music set with entrancing rhythm and delightful modulations of tone and harmony enticing us to dance should stoop to wasting time with such rubbish passes my comprehension.

I think there must be something the matter with the musical and mental make up of those who spend their time shuffling along a polished floor to the accompaniment of such infernal trash.

It may be a passing phase of meaningless piffle the elimination of which would be an occasion for rejoicing, or it may be a stepping stone to higher things. I wonder, in fact I often wonder when compelled from time to time to listen to the efforts of those who evidently take their art seriously what it will lead to but to be compelled to listen to such tintinabulating nonsense at the same time as such a delightful programme as that provided by YMVC was being performed is a tragedy which should not be permitted a repetition.

By careful selection of singers and by concentrating on competition work YMVC managed to maintain a choir size of 50 plus. This was a considerable achievement, as many enthusiastic singers and potential members could not read music to the standard required. There is a life cycle in choirs which can affect the ease with which new singers can join. York Male Voice Choir had always selected the best they could find – entry was not automatic. By 1926 Old Priory members were commenting that it was harder to join OP than in earlier years and a debate was taking place over the introduction of annual tests in order to maintain membership. At the same time, enthusiastic male singers irrespective of their ability to read music were being made welcome in Leeman Road.

Recruitment was always a concern and there are frequent references in N&V to the shortage of men, particularly tenors. Old Priory never had sufficient male singers to enter Class A competitions which prompted this entry in N&V in July 1926; an entry which also illustrates both the friendship and interlinking that seemed to be part of York's Choral life at this time.

Recruiting more men!

I mentioned the idea to a member of YMVC a few days ago adding that there was no thought of opposition in my mind as far as that choir was concerned the relations between the two choirs being too friendly to allow such thoughts. Promptly came his reply 'Oh there is room in York for 3 never mind 2 choirs like the 'Male Voice'.

At that time, several members of Old Priory also sang with YMVC including Jack Steel, Bob Hodgson, and Jack Fairweather.

The comment made...*there is room in York for 3 never mind 2 choirs like the Male Voice*...displays an immense confidence, reflected, perhaps, in this 1925 photograph.

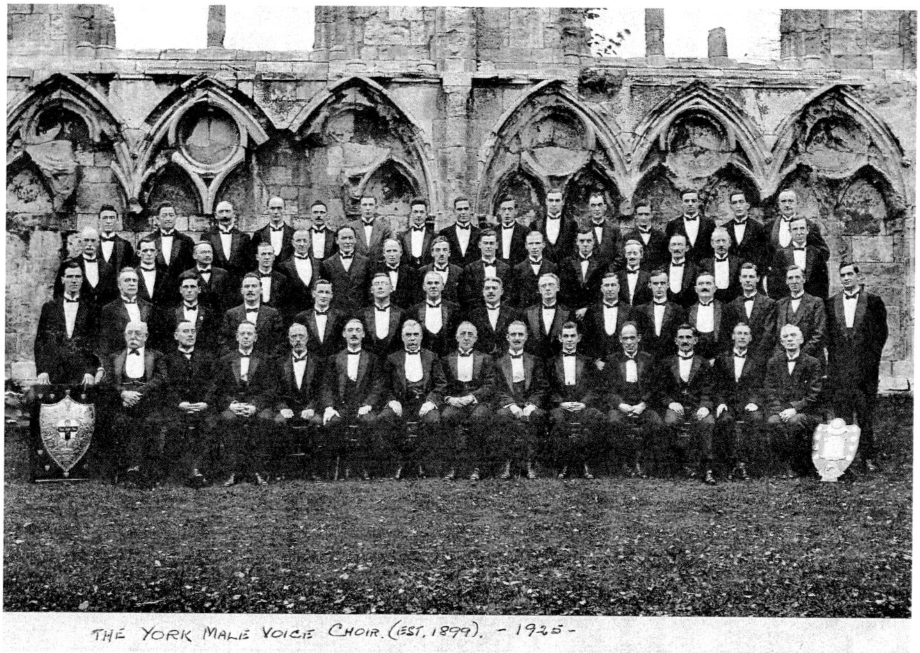

THE YORK MALE VOICE CHOIR. (EST. 1899). - 1925 -

Taken against the backcloth of St. Mary's Abbey there are 58 men present.

H Seymour Wilkinson was in his last year as conductor, and is shown sixth in from the right on the first row. Two places to the left is the well-fed Sefton Fearne, whose son Sefton junior was later to play a vital role in life of the Phil. With the exception of Jack Forster, the singers named as being at Escrick Park in 1903, and those who also sang with Old Priory are pictured. For example Bob Hodgson and Jack Steel are stood together in the centre of the second row. The younger man second in from the right on the back row is F. Clampitt – a bass of this name was a member of the Phil in 1962.

The photograph accurately portrays a large, successful, confident choir with an excellent reputation, so it is not surprising that YMVC sought to maintain this by careful selection of singers. Nevertheless, the rapid growth of the Leeman Road choir suggests that YMVC did not suit all singers, it was, perhaps, too exclusive; and maybe York did not want, or could not sustain, two or three choirs just like the YMVC. In comparison, repeated here is the first photo of the LRAS choir 1926-7.

ALL OUR YESTERDAYS: The choir in 1926-27. Mr Brough is on the back row, third from the right, with the open-neck shirt. His sisters are on the front row. Jane, left, was accompanist and Kathleen was her assistant. They are sitting on either side of the then conductor, Mr Cecil Fletcher.

Despite the visible differences in size, wealth, presentation and achievements it took only a short time – till 1929 – for the LRAS to be ambitious enough to change its name.

The importance, to the city in the 1920s of two choirs OP and YMVC can be seen in the York Choral Festival of 1928; neither choir took part, and the audiences were reported as being very poor.

By 1935 the younger male choir, the York Philharmonic, was the dominant concert choir in the city, whereas the YMVC, although struggling, could still compete and was the more prestigious of the two. The copies of *Philharmonic News* [PN] the magazine of the Phil from the 1930s offer no comparisons or comments on YMVC – indeed they make no references at all to the older choir. In the copies we have there is one indirect mention made by a new entrant to the Phil, and the older choir is only named once in a letter from Jack Forster, conductor of the OP. There are, however, several references in N&V, which is understandable given that Jack Forster had been a long term member of YMVC, and on two crisis occasions stepped in to take leadership of that choir. There is no suggestion that the younger choir set out to take over from the older, as their cultures were quite different. However, there was one time when, had events turned out differently; the YMVC might have absorbed YPMVC.

In his memoirs WHB described the choirs in which he had been a singing member, and not, as in the case of the Phil, a supporter. Therefore he gave no record of any interaction between the two. He did, however, give clues as to difficulties within YMVC, which struggled over a number of years to find suitable conductors. It seems there was a continual problem in matching choir and conductor despite the appointment of some excellent musicians. In such circumstances no choir can truly thrive.

The York Male Voice Choir suffered a grievous loss in the death of its conductor. Not many choirs have been so able led, for Mr. Child was a musician to his finger tips, his choir felt they had a leader whom it was a joy to follow, for there was a bond and confidence between us which made for success, it was always a pleasure to attend the practices, he never raised his voice above conversation pitch, he had a quiet manner of correction, plenty of patience, sure in the knowledge of what he wanted and determined to get it. His death was a loss to those who looked upon him as a teacher, also as a friend, and there were many.

This description of the founder conductor suggests a man who could nurture and build a successful choir. Despite the achievements of Seymour Wilkinson over many years it would seem, at least to WHB, that the choir never again enjoyed the long term support and leadership of one so talented.

Entries in the city indexes help us to track the number of conductors that followed. However, there are some gaps. The indexes start from 1922 but it is thought that Mr Child, a music teacher, died as early as 1909. WHB refers to Mr Tindall of St. Peter's School taking over at a point soon after the death of Mr Child, and we know of Seymour Wilkinson's contribution in 1912; but do not know whether he led the choir continuously till 1926.

1922 -1925: Seymour Wilkinson
1926 -1929: J. L. Slater [a pupil of Dr Bairstow]
Short term stand in: J. H. Forster
1930: G. Firth
1931: Owen Le P. Franklin [assistant organist at York Minster]
1932: J.H. Forster [Conductor of York Old Priory]
1933 -1938: Eric Godley
1939: Geo. Wainwright
1949 - 50: E. Pragnell [conductor of York Co-op choir in the 1930s]
1951: L.E. Wreigitt
After 1951 the index entries are reduced in size and give only contact details rather than the names of conductors.

Entries in N&V illustrate some of the problems:

YMVC has been passing through deep waters recently. J.L.Slater has left York and his successor as conductor resigned before picking up his baton. N&V October 1929

Jack H. Forster stepped into the breach and took over the baton, handing on to G. Firth and then quickly onto Owen Le P. Franklin.

Despite these difficulties the choir still took part in prestigious musical events. For example, in 1930, as a tribute to the work of Dr Bairstow at the Minster a concert was arranged entitled; 'An Evening with Dr Bairstow's Music.' The participating choirs were: York Musical Society, under the direction of Dr Bairstow himself; York

Male Voice Choir conducted by Owen Le.P. Franklin; York Old Priory conducted by J.H. Forster and the Minster choir. The local press carried the following report

The programme was well carried out, but one is less inclined to dwell on the performances than on the spirit which animated the performers. No fewer than four different choirs took part, and their hearty cooperation may safely be interpreted as a desire to do honour to Dr Bairstow, and another proof was to be seen in the large audience, which nearly filled the vast wilderness in the hall which has to serve as a makeshift concert-room till one worthy of the city is evolved.

The reference to the hall is interesting as the Festival Concert rooms in Museum Street had recently closed and this concert was held in the skating rink attached to the Rialto cinema. As the concert also included solo items, instrumental pieces for violin and piano, and for two pianos, the hall must indeed have proven to be more than adequate as a concert venue.

Notes and Views then chronicles an event which is not mentioned at all in York Phil records, and which forms no part of the oral tradition of the choir either:

Once more the conductorship of YMVC has changed hands. Mr Franklin has resigned and Cecil H.Fletcher has been invited to take his place. For some considerable time this once famous choir has been 'losing ground'. Enthusiasm has waned, interest has been lacking and members have dropped until the number of faithful is few indeed. So that Mr Fletcher has a tough job on when he sets out to rebuild the choir and help it recover some of its former glory. He is a hard worker and though young both in years and experience has achieved considerable success with the YPMVC. We, of Old Priory wish him even greater success with YMVC. N&V March 1931

Later in the same issue came this correction:

Since printing the paragraph about YMVC we have been informed that Mr Fletcher has intimated to the choir that he regrets he cannot see his way to accept the invitation to be their conductor. When the paragraph was written we had it on reliable authority that he would accept and whilst we do not wish to withdraw anything we say about his qualifications we do regret that Mr Fletcher has changed his mind.

Then in the next issue April 1931:

After declining on two previous occasions, J.H.Forster has been persuaded to accept the conductorship of YMVC. At the invitation of the President of the choir, Mr Will Birch, some 50 members past and present and friends attended a social gathering at the Feasegate Restaurant on March 16th. During the evening Mr Birch, in a comprehensive speech, reviewed the history of the choir and briefly referring to the present small membership made a stirring appeal to lapsed members to renew their association with the choir. As a result 10 or 12 promised that night that they would return and on the following Monday when 35 were present at the rehearsal J.H.Forster was unanimously elected as conductor. A week later the attendance was even better no fewer than 39 turned up and nearly everyone on time – a very good sign.

Keen enthusiasm prevailed at both rehearsals and regret being expressed at Easter Monday should break the sequence of practices it was agreed to hold the weekly rehearsal on Thursday of Easter week. It is sincerely hoped that this wave of enthusiasm will be lasting and that YMVC may again become a musical force in the city. The great need of the choir is first tenors and if this should meet the eye of any who would like to join they should communicate with the secretary Mr Reg.Clampitt.

In February 1932 N&V carried a report of a concert in Market Weighton. This was reported as the first outing [a local concert not a competition] by YMVC since being resuscitated by Jack Forster. Jack's son, Duncan, acted as accompanist. The article looked forward to ...*when YMVC makes its next appearance in the city after a long hiatus – some people thinking it defunct.* The article likened the choir ...*to a patient near to death.*

In the May 1932 York Choral competition, that wish was fulfilled when YMVC once again won the Challenge Shield (A class) under Jack's leadership. Burton Stone Lane MVC won the B class. YPMVC did not take part.

This continual quest to recruit top tenors is interesting, as a review of a York Philharmonic performance in November 1931 suggests that the Phil had a very good top tenor line.

Their singing of Bairstow's 'Music when soft voices die' was really an excellent performance. The attacks and releases were cleanly done, words were good and the mood of the piece caught. The whole interpretation gave evidence of very careful training and preparation.

The top tenors are particularly good and with all due respect to the other sections form the best part of the choir – at least this was so at the Melbourne concert – their tone always of good quality, tuneful and never forced........

Much credit must be given to C.H.Fletcher for the high standard which the choir has reached. When one recognises the handicap of having to train a body of singers many of whom had no knowledge of music whatsoever the result is little short of marvellous. N&V Nov. 1931.

The comparatively young and inexperienced Cecil Fletcher had been thought to be the man to resuscitate YMVC. As a founder conductor of a choir perhaps it was felt he had the leadership skills [as did the late Wm Child and Jack Forster] to build up a choir from 'nothing'. This might reflect the very sad state of YMVC at this time. Had Cecil accepted the invitation, the still young York Philharmonic may have died on his departure. However their cultures were so different that perhaps he, as did so many others, may have struggled to succeed in leading this competition based choir.

YMVC continued to have leadership problems. It is difficult to know why, when so many other York choirs of the day enjoyed successful long term relationships with their conductors. It could be that the narrow focus of the choir – competitions and one annual concert – met neither the aspirations of conductors nor indeed the membership. As with the short term tenure of so many football managers today, whether in the premier league or the lowest division, short term results were all that mattered!

This turnover of conductors was certainly too rapid to allow for the development of any choral group. The fact that Jack Forster, the founder conductor of the very hard working York Old Priory Choir had to take over both in 1929 and 1932 suggests a crisis situation. The memoirs of WHB assist by specifically describing the time of Eric Godley 1933-1938. Eric Godley had been a singer with the Carl Rosa Opera, and had then become a singing teacher:

Later he left the 'Carl Rosa' and took up song teaching for a living with varied success and ultimately he came to York as conductor of the York Male Voice Choir, guiding the choir through many competitions, but he never seemed quite happy with the results; one or two firsts, but mostly second or third, or outside the prize list.

At practice he tried to convey his depth of musical feeling to the choir, forgetting that soul and emotional depth varies with every individual, and although he knew what he wanted, he did not appreciate that wanting and getting it unanimously from his choir is a different proposition. His enthusiasm was often beyond his control and on occasions he vexed adjudicators with his too outspoken remarks.

He was imaginative and temperamental and sometimes difficult to understand. A steadier attitude would have taken him further on his musical pilgrimage, for without doubt he had a first class voice and great possibilities.

This temperamental leadership may have had significant consequences.

Philharmonic News always named and welcomed new members to the Phil. Where newcomers came from outside the city the entries often gave previous experience. For example, March 1933:

We welcome Mr H.Taylor [late of the famous 'Cleveland Harmonic' Male Voice Choir] to our ranks. Mr Taylor is a baritone and is familiar with most of our pieces. We hope that he will have a long and happy experience with our choir.

On other occasions new singers were merely named and welcomed. In April 1935 there was more exuberance expressed:

We are pleased to record that our membership is now 58.The way new members are joining (and good ones too) it would seem that our ambition to reach seventy will soon be achieved. To the undermentioned we give a sincere welcome and hope they will derive much pleasure from a long association with the choir.

Mr W.Dixon (tenor]
Mr J.Hodgson (tenor)
Mr Watson (bass)
Mr Colley (bass)
Mr W.Hodgson (tenor)
Mr R.Langrick (bass)
Mr Beresford (bass)

Seven good members at once, two with the same surname; and again eight months later: *We welcome Messrs. Flanagan, Powell and Gibson to our baritone line, and hope they will find their association with us a happy one.* PN December 1935

Although not stated, or even suggested, ten new members of quality strongly suggests transfers from another group [only one of these names, J Hodgson, appears on the YMVC photo of 1925 shown earlier]. There was, however, a convention not to publicise, or be seen to 'gloat' over any transfers from a York choir; but the most likely source of so many good singers would have been YMVC.

However YMVC was still impressive, and the BBC invited it to broadcast. This was scheduled for 8th February 1937. Eric Godley was ill and so the choir was led on that day by Percy Wright. N&V reported that the broadcast was of a high standard.

In 1938/39 a young man, George Wainwright became conductor of YMVC, which was still able to have an average attendance of 50, and George achieved third prize in his first competition at Huddersfield in 1938.

The two choirs, YMVC and YPMVC, may have met on competition days but would normally have been competing in different classes. However there were occasions when the choirs worked together, and with others, in support of the York Choral Competitions. In May 1932 these were so poorly supported by the public that a loss of £200 was made. To recoup this, a combined concert was held in the November which included many of the choirs which had been successful in the competitions over the years. This included YMVC, YPMVC, York Old Priory, and Burton Stone Lane MVC. From that point on, financial pressures seem to mount and the combined concerts were repeated in 1934 and 1936. However this support could not stop the eventual demise of the York Choral Festival.

In October 1937 Sefton Fearne Junior joined the Phil as a bass and wrote a letter giving his impressions as a new member. In this he wrote:

You will understand of course, that anyone who loves male voice singing for itself alone cannot remain inactive, and I had been for a matter of two years.

Two Fearne brothers were such key members of the top tenor section of YMVC that WHB mentioned them by name in his memoirs. Sefton Fearne senior held the post of treasurer in the 1920s, and was recorded in the YEP as conducting the choir during a visit to Malton in 1927. It seems in 1937 Sefton junior preferred the Phil, and his letter suggests that he could have been a member of YMVC alongside his father and uncle until 1935. As already acknowledged Sefton Junior was successful in holding the Phil together in the crisis years – 1946 to 1949 – and became a life member.

In the January 1938 PN magazine, published this letter from Jack Forster:

I have attended scores of Competitive Festivals during the last forty years a few times as a competitor in a quartette – not very successfully I regret to record – frequently as a chorister during the six years I was a member of the York Male Voice Choir when the choir was in its palmiest days – more often winning than not........

It seems that York Male Voice Choir was indeed extremely successful but was unfortunate in being unable to replace its founder conductor with a leader able to maintain and develop a specialist competition choir. In the mid 1930s this unfortunate situation was happening at a time when York had three conductors: Jack; Cecil and Archie; with a remarkable track record of leading successful and congenial choirs. Unintentionally the Phil benefitted from the problems within YMVC but in its magazines did not seek to publicise the fact.

It seems that YMVC, this fine choir, went into a slow decline. Janet Sargent, who was accompanist to the Phil during the time that her husband Archie was director, wrote this diary entry on January 6th 1958: *The 'Phil' practice was a very good one. A York Male Voice man joined us. The YMVC is fast going out.*

The YMVC must have disbanded sometime c.1960-65. There was one known attempt to resurrect the name of the choir as shown in this extract from the AGM minutes of York St. Lawrence MVC in October 1966:

Mr J Stockdale moved the following resolution. 'That the name of the choir be changed to: The York Male Voice Choir. This was seconded. After much discussion a vote was taken resulting in the motion being defeated.'

The York St Lawrence Choir was formed after the war and won a class B competition at Harrogate in 1950. Its origins are not known but it performed with the Phil in the 1950s and again in 1963. It is believed that this choir absorbed the existing Railway Institute Choir [c.1960]. It was therefore a choir with many railway employees as members. Although the resolution of 1966 proposed by Jack Stockdale – a deputy station master – was rejected, the choir was seeking to rejuvenate itself by adopting a new identity. It achieved this in January 1968 by becoming the York Railway Institute MVC. It seems that Jack's motion to adopt an unused but prestigious name was turned down so that the choir could gain the financial benefits of joining with the Railway Institute, membership which offered free rehearsal rooms at the Institute. And so it would seem that Yorkshire financial prudence and pragmatism rather than ambition led to the final loss of the name.

In the absence of a published history of York Male Voice Choir it is hoped that this chapter is, in some small way, a tribute to what must have been a fine body of singers of which the city could be justly proud.

Part 2
The Second Generation
1962-1993

Sweet is the work, my God, my King,
To praise thy name, give thanks and sing;
To show thy love by morning light,
And talk of all thy truth at night.
Deep Harmony: Parker / Watts – signature tune 1950s-70s

Chapter 5
Richard Brian Lister

1962-70: National and International Acclaim

Richard B. Lister is the name that appears on concert programmes, press reviews and record sleeves during this most successful period in the choir's life. There were two Richards in the Lister household. Richard senior was known as Dick and Richard junior, from an early age, was known by his second name Brian. The press reports, shown earlier, of the teenage Brian as accompanist of the choir in 1947, refer to him as Mr Brian Lister. It is after his return as director in 1962 that his public title became more formal.

During the 16 years 1962-78 the Phil set itself many challenges and succeeded in them all. As a creative period it compared well with the first 15 years 1925-40. Many choral directors can leave their mark, perhaps a written record of competition and concert success, or a collection of audio recordings. Only a few leave a living legacy to match that of Brian Lister. In 1962 'Carols in Kirkgate' was born; in 1969 came the twinning with the male voice choir in Münster. The way in which these innovations were conceived and nurtured by Brian brought them immediate success, and made it possible for successive conductors to carry on the work. These ventures have played such a key role in the life of the choir that both have extended chapters later in this narrative. Believing his work to be done, Brian resigned from the choir in 1980. Very sadly, in June 1990, he died – at the tender age of 59 – unable to see and appreciate the lasting success of his visionary leadership.

Brian graduated – LLCM and Teaching Diploma – from the London College of Music in 1949, and on completion of National Service in the RAF, was fortunate enough to return to York as head of music at Beckfield County Secondary. We know that he stepped down from his role as accompanist to the Phil in 1951, and then spent several years building up youth music in both the school and the city. He acted as accompanist to director Bernard Porter in the formation of the York Youth Choir in 1954, later taking over the baton. This choir evolved into the York Youth Operatic and Choral Society and in 1959 he directed, with his school colleague Eileen Robinson as producer, its first stage show 'The Gondoliers', performed at the Joseph Rowntree Theatre.

These photos (copied from: 'York Youth – The First 25 Years – An Appreciation') show Brian conducting their rehearsal in the Tempest Anderson Hall, with, below, the 1959 cast of the Gondoliers. This successful production launched the society, yet both Brian and Eileen stepped aside, with John Warburton starting his many years as director in 1962.

The Youth group was not a great source of new singers for the Phil, but its influence is still being appreciated today. Eileen Henderson, now Eileen Grey – accompanist and Honorary Life Member of the Phil – was a member. With five others from York Youth she formed 'The York Madrigal Group', which performed with the Phil from 1968; later, in 1975, she recruited former members to join the 'Kirkgate Ladies'. Dilys Fletcher and Graham Firth, who both appeared as soloists in the first year of 'Carols in Kirkgate' in 1962, were members, as was Simon Braithwaite, who accompanied the choir in the mid 1970s and plays on the audio recordings of that time.

In this short section three music directors have been named: Bernard Porter, Brian Lister, and John Warburton. All three were music teachers in local schools, with each going well beyond the 'day job' to enhance the cultural life of the city.

At school Brian worked with colleague Eileen Robinson – a keen amateur actor – on productions of Gilbert and Sullivan Operettas, Lionel Bart's 'Oliver', and two shows of his own – 'The Runaways' 1955 and 'Gipsy Birthday' 1964/5.

This cast photo of Gypsy Birthday shows the scale and success of the work – nearly 10% of pupils must have been involved.

Brian and Eileen also produced carol concerts which drew audiences from beyond the school; Archie and Janet Sargent *enjoyed it greatly* in a visit in 1957. These Christmas productions were later to find national acclaim as part of 'Carols in Kirkgate'.

In 1961 Brian married Barbara Marshall, another graduate of the York Youth, whose parents Herbert and Edith proved to be staunch supporters of the Phil. They were instrumental in setting up the support group 'Perimeter' formed in 1966; and Herbert, although not a singing member, acted as concert secretary for a number of years.

Brian had never lost his interest in the Phil, and so was a natural choice to succeed Archie Sargent in 1962. That transition was swift, reflecting both the enthusiasm of the young Brian for the new role and his established links with the choir. The appointment process was made easier as the secretary at the time was Ernest Robinson, husband to Eileen. Brian took his first rehearsal on the 4th June 1962.

We know, from Janet Sargent's diaries, that from 1957 onwards there was unease in the choir; it was coasting with little or no ambition. By comparison, look at the choir of 1967 as described in these extracts from an extended article published in the York Evening Press 31/10/1967:

Mr. Lister mentioned that during the past few years discipline has been tightened up considerably. At first it came as a shock to a few of the old hands who regarded choir practice as a social night out. But today members appreciate that discipline is the key to success. "We regard regular attendance at rehearsals as essential" he said, "We also keep a register and persistent backsliders are out."......

..The quest for perfection has paid dividends. The choir now finds that it is able to attract the more proficient vocalist who would not be interested if activity were on the level of a sing-song...

..."One of the troubles with a male voice choir is that it is rooted in the 19th century, and people have visions of a bunch of Victorians gathered around a piano," said the director. "We have tried to move away from this sort of thing. We have also turfed out a lot of the music which was too Victorian in flavour – and which was, let's face it, in some cases downright bad music"....

....the choir all but went out of existence during the 1939-45 war, and it is only during the past five years that there has been a terrific upsurge in interest. "People tend to think of members of a male voice choir as being around the 60 mark" said the secretary, "but we started bringing in the younger element. Today a third of our membership is under 30."...

..I (the reporter) asked if the Philharmonic now riding on the crest of a local popularity wave had any big plans for the future. A tour of Holland next September is in prospect – with, it is hoped, visits to Nijmegen, Eindhoven and Boxmeer – on an exchange basis (the Nijmegen choir is coming to York in April to give a combined concert with the Philharmonic in the Guildhall). "We would also like to give a concert as part of York's next festival" said the director. "And we would like to win a major competition and become one of the front-rank male voice choirs in the country"....

This 1967 choir had a clear sense of purpose and had already achieved a number of its goals.

Details of choir life, particularly for the years 1962-70, come from: Brian Lister's personal scrap book; a 'few' copies of choir magazines from 1965 onwards; and press reports. The scrapbook contains a copy of the first annual concert directed by Brian – 14th November 1962 – in the Tempest Anderson Hall, in aid of the Lord Mayor and Sheriffs' Christmas Cheer Fund. Given the long summer break, there had been little time for any changes to repertoire or style, so it is likely that this programme was very similar to any that Archie Sargent might have chosen.

— The National Anthem —

Choir Deep Harmony ... Handel Parker, arr. Luther Greenwood
Feasting I watch ... ... Elgar
Down in a Flowery Vale ... Festa, arr. H. Roberton
On the Sea ... ... Dudley Buck

Reg. Goodhall - Tenor
Silent Worship ... ... Handel
Art thou troubled? ... ... Handel

Choir Were you there? ... Negro Spiritual, arr. H. T. Burleigh
Goin' Home ... Dvorak adaptation by W. A. Fisher
I'm gwine to sing ... Negro Spiritual, arr. H. V. Milligan
(Soloist: J. Henry Brough)

Jean Ward-Skerrow - Soprano
Romanza and Scena from "Cavalleria Rusticana" Mascagni
The Jewel Song from "Faust" ... ... Gounod
Accompanist: Neville Turner

Choir Bless this House ... May H. Brahe arr. Doris Arnold
Farmer's Boy ... ... arr. R. Vaughan Williams
In the Gloaming ... ... arr. Doris Arnold
(Soloist: Lance Dutton)
Conducted by Thomas Sparrow

Choir Entrance and March of Peers from "Iolanthe" ...
Gilbert/Sullivan
Come landlord fill the flowing bowl arr. E. Markham Lee
Widdicombe Fair ... ... arr. Donald Behenna
Waltzing Matilda ... ... arr. Thomas Wood

Reg. Goodhall - Tenor
"When the stars were brightly shining" from "Tosca"
Puccini
"None shall sleep tonight" from "Turandot" ... Puccini

Choir Serenade ... ... Schubert arr. John Bateson
Soloist: Reg. Goodhall
Hymn before Action ... ... Walford Davies
Music, when soft voices die ... ... E. C. Bairstow

Jean Ward-Skerrow - Soprano
The Little Road to Bethlehem ... ... Michael Head
The Robin's Carol ... ...Michael Head
The Carol of the Little King ... ... Eric Fogg
Accompanist: Neville Turner

Choir Fantasia on English Melodies ... arr. Leslie Woodgate
The Long Day Closes ... ... Sullivan

Conductor: Richard B. Lister

Brian upheld the tradition of starting a concert with the National Anthem; he later did his own two verse choral arrangement, which in 1968 drew this comment from a music critic: *The Male Voice choir raised the National Anthem from its all too frequent mediocrity and bestowed on it the status of a worthwhile piece of music.* In 1962 *Deep Harmony* was the first choir item. This hymn acted as a signature tune for the Phil until replaced by *The Grand old Duke of York* in 1977. Its position at the start of this programme suggests that it had been a signature tune for some time. This is highly likely, as the arranger Luther Greenwood had been a friend of Archie's, and had acted as an adjudicator at Inter-Choral competitions in the 1930s. The first two lines of this Isaac Watts' hymn show how well it introduces a choir:

Sweet is the work, my God, my King, To praise thy name, give thanks and sing.

Reg Goodhall was the lead choir soloist, a role he undertook, to great acclaim, for some thirty years. The guest soloist, Jean Ward-Skerrow, came from Hull and performed all over Yorkshire. She was a member of 'Hull Savoyards' and so, like Brian Lister, was a fan of Gilbert and Sullivan.

President : Mr. A. W. SARGENT

Vice-Presidents :

The Rt. Hon. The Lord Mayor of York (Ald. R. A. Cattle, J.P.)
Coun. L. Daley — Ald. R. S. Oloman, M.B.E., J.P.
Miss. J. M. Banks — Miss J. E. Brough
Mr. G. Baggaley — Mr. E. Taylor

Director of Music : RICHARD LISTER
Deputy Conductor : THOMAS SPARROW
Accompanist : MICHAEL ALVEY

1st TENORS :
Dawes, W
Flint, R.
Gillery, O. F.
Goodhall, R.
Green, A. W.
Mackintosh, K.
Payne, W.
Pinder, J.
Rutherford, C.

2nd TENORS :
Belton, H
Buckle, W.
Cheetham, H. A.
Dawes, R.
Ketley, W. B.
Mitchell, G.
Poole, S. A.
Robinson, T.
Smith, E.
Sparrow, T. J.
Wharram, E. V.

BARITONES :
Bell, R. J.
Birkley, H.
Burton, W.
Chaplin, D.
DeBurgh, E.
Dutton, H. L.
Green, B. C.
Iley, B.
Ogram, W.
Porter, E. S.
Robinson, E.
Sharp, G.
Shoebridge, R. H.
Smallwood, L.
Taylor, E.
Taylor, H.
Wrigglesworth, P. J.

BASSES :
Appleton, W.
Bell, J.
Brough, J. H.
Budgen, E. E.
Clampitt, F.
Clarke, A. F.
Kneale, W. E.
Olsen, C.
Patterson, A. T.
Reynolds, W. H.
Snowden, A. E.

Intending members please apply :
Secretary ERNEST ROBINSON, 178 Beckfield Lane, York

The back page of this 1962 programme gives the first list of choir members in any archive.

There were 48 singers, but it was not a balanced choir, with only nine top tenors and 17 baritones. There were regular appeals for new tenors throughout the 1960s. A music team was in place. Thomas Sparrow the deputy was a member of the second tenors, and stepped forward to conduct the choir in three items. It seems that Michael Alvey, the accompanist played for only this one annual concert.

At the head of the page, Archie Sargent is shown as the President for the year; in subsequent years he reverted to being a Vice President – a role he had held since 1935. Honorary Life Member, and first accompanist, Jane Brough was also a Vice President. The mutually beneficial close links with the city council are reflected in three councillors being Vice Presidents. A number of Lord Mayors, since the 1920s, had become choir President, and from 1968 onwards the practice of the incumbent Lord Mayor acting as patron was established. Coun. L. Daley is shown here as a Vice President, later becoming President, a part he occupied from 1964-68. The value of this link was described in a press report (YEP 7/3/66) on the annual choir dinner held in March 1966. Mr L. Daley *...expressed confidence in the ability of their musical director Mr Richard B. Lister to uphold the present high standard.*

Mr. Lister replying referred to Mr. Daley as the backroom boy of music in York, responsible for much of the work behind the scenes with the Entertainments sub-committee of the York Corporation, bringing to the city the best of musical talent.

A YEP report of April 1966 illustrated the work of this sub-committee:

A major music event has been fixed by the York Corporation Entertainments sub-committee. This is a two choir concert to be given in the Guildhall on Saturday 7th May. Choirs taking part are the York Philharmonic Male Voice Choir conducted by Richard B. Lister and the Doncaster Wheatsheaf Girls' Choir under their conductor John Barker.

The Doncaster choir will be the guests of the York choir for the evening. These girls are known throughout the North for their singing on the radio and in concerts, including regular appearances at the Spa, Scarborough...They did a concert tour of Sweden last year, travelling 4000 miles, with eight performances in four cities. The choir has also made tours in France, Switzerland and Ireland.

In 1962 these links between council and choir were in place, and had probably been growing in strength since the 1951 Silver Jubilee concert directed by Archie Sargent. However, not everything went smoothly during the concert. The front page of the programme did not carry the designation 'The Fletcher Memorial Choir'; neither did it display the logo. Both of these points were corrected in 1963. Neither did the protocol at the concert meet with Janet Sargent's approval:

A & I went to the Phil's annual concert tonight. How they missed the finesse of Mr Reynolds. The President wasn't even welcomed! Splendid audience and a very good concert. Brian Lister was pleased at A's appreciation.

This concert was followed a month later by the first performance of 'Carols in Kirkgate', a show which proved so popular that by 1965 it had changed the annual life cycle of the choir, with much more time being needed to prepare a Christmas programme.

In 1963, the soloist at the Annual Concert was contralto Rhiannon Davies, from Mold in North Wales, making her first visit to York. The choir programme included more Gilbert and Sullivan but, significantly, a set of four Russian folk songs. The Yorkshire Post (19/11/63) wrote:

...the four Russian folk songs, which were performed at the Castle museum during the York Festival this year, are also to be included. This is in response to several requests. The songs were translated from Russian by Mr Terence Ashurst, a York language teacher, and arranged for the choir by the director Mr Richard Lister.

Brian was the first of the Phil's conductors to arrange music for the choir. Given that we still sing a number of his arrangements, it is not surprising that this set of folk songs, his first contribution, was so well received that a repeat performance was requested. The ticket price in 1963 was 2/6, with pensioners and children at half price; a programme cost an extra 6d.

The Spring Concert in April 1964 included another of Brian's arrangements, this time of four sea shanties. It also saw Lloyd D. Smith as accompanist, a role he held for a number of years.

On the 13/4/1964 the YEP published this lengthy, and 'flamboyant', article by staff music critic C. H. Schofield titled:

A Model example by York Choir

A Model example of how to build a popular programme while observing good taste and fine quality is given by York Philharmonic Male Voice Choir for their concert in the Guildhall next Saturday to conclude the very successful winter series sponsored by the Corporation Entertainments Sub-Committee.

Schubert, Elgar, Vaughan Williams are here, for their music comes home universally to the bosoms and hearts of the Common Man. It is this which gives classic stature. This and not the conceited corner chattering of the fashionable cliques whose 'music' so far from being 'caviare' to the general run of mankind, is little more than a crochet for controversy. The programme for the York concert makes good the claim to be so varied as to contain something for everyone...

Not a style of writing to be found in today's press, and the article continued in this vein for some time; but we must deduce from it that Brian Lister was approved of by this critic.

That same month, April 1964, saw the choir win its first competition under Brian's leadership. It was at the Pontefract Festival, where Archie Sargent led the choir to success in 1955. The Phil won the Albert Ward Memorial Trophy for large choirs, gaining 90 marks for singing *Salt Beef,* and 89 for *Polish Lullaby.* The adjudicator commented:

This choir's performance had spirituality and a fine sense of reverence within its impeccable balance and blend of tone.

This was an A class competition and, as ever in the Phil's history, it was still a small choir for such a stage.

For many years annual autumn concerts were performed on a Wednesday, and the printed programmes often named the members. On 16/11/1966 the programme included the duet *We're called Gondolieri,* sung by Tony Sawyer and Eric Taylor. The list of members showed a total of 42, six fewer than in 1962. However, there was a shift in the makeup of the choir. Two new top tenors, Mike Johnson and Tony Sawyer, were young teenagers (and are still members in 2015), with Tony already a soloist, and the second tenors included Trevor Cooper, who in 1963 was one of the boy soloists at 'Carols in Kirkgate'. Two years later, in 1968, the choir had increased in number to 58 – 16 new recruits in two years – most of them comparatively young. In these two years the bass section increased from nine members to 17, giving rise to perpetual adverts for tenors. The policy on recruitment and disciplined commitment, as described by Brian Lister in the 1967 press article quoted above, was now bearing fruit.

In the years 1962-8, the Phil also gave concerts at Filey, Scarborough, Whitby, Malton, Hull, Ripon and Richmond. One summer outing which was particularly enjoyed was a 'Dales Tour'. This took place for at least three years 1965-67, before changing location to the North York Moors. The first of these was described by the Yorkshire Post 7/7/1965:

The York Philharmonic Male Voice Choir, which is more than 40 strong, is to be heard singing in the open air in the Yorkshire Dales.

Leaving York in the early afternoon on Saturday they will travel to Grassington, where they will sing on the cobbled market square for about 20 minutes from 3pm.

The journey will continue into Wharfedale with a performance outside of Kettlewell church at about 4pm.

Further up the Dale at Buckden, they will be heard at the Buck Inn, about 5pm, and the choir then moves into Wensleydale to visit Castle Bolton at 6pm.

Lord and Lady Bolton have invited the choir to perform inside the Great Hall of the castle. After these performances the choir will sit down to high tea in the castle restaurant.

Collections organised by people of the villages will be taken during the singing, and will go to aid local charities.

At Buckden the proceeds are to be given to the Parish Church, and at Kettlewell they will go to the Invalid Chair Fund.

The choir, under its conductor Mr Richard B. Lister will sing a programme mainly of English traditional songs suitable for the occasion.

The Phil at Bolton Abbey, July 1965. Brian Lister is seated in the front row in the light coloured jacket. The young Tony Sawyer is seated far left next to Reg Goodhall. This was Tony's first concert as a full member, having served a two year apprenticeship whilst his adult voice developed. He celebrated the occasion by being one of the soloists.

The Dales tour of 1966 recruited a very keen supporter who became one of the furthest travelled members of the 'Perimeter' support group. This letter appeared in the YEP November 1966:

Sir – last July I went to Bolton Abbey to hear York Philharmonic Male Voice Choir sing in the Priory Church. Their performance was so outstanding that I followed them up the dale to Burnsall and Grassington. The fascination of this choir was twofold. Firstly the quality of the singing was very high, and secondly, it was very obvious that every member was thoroughly enjoying himself.

Later, at home, I made efforts to get in touch with someone connected with the choir, with the object of obtaining a syllabus of their future activities and chiefly owing to the assistance of the Evening Press I obtained the address of Mr Jones the secretary and Mr Lister the director. As a reward for my Yorkshire tenacity I was presented with a complimentary ticket for the choir's annual concert in the Tempest Anderson Hall on November 16th.

The distance from Ripponden to York is 45 miles making a double journey of 90 miles, and I am bound to say that the concert was well worth every yard of it.

I shall certainly be in Kirkgate at Christmas to hear the carol service

I am etc.

W Stocks

Ripponden Halifax.

The 'Perimeter' support group was formed in June 1966. Looking back, it seems to have been a natural development in the choir's life. It was, however, unusual in male voice circles, and so was often commented on in newspaper reports. For example, the extensive article in the YEP of 31/10/1967 quoted above was headed: *This York choir has its own supporters' club.* It was, perhaps, unusual in being a 'formal' body with a management committee.

Perimeter was introduced to the public on the back page of the programme of the autumn 1966 concert:

Members of the public who are interested in the activities of the choir are cordially invited to join this Society. The annual subscription is 5/- and, in addition to providing valuable financial support, members enjoy certain booking facilities for each concert.

Within a year, membership exceeded 100 (by 1972 more than 200), and in 1969 the society introduced its own quarterly magazine 'Perimeter Post'.

That magazine listed the officers of both the choir and 'Perimeter' and described the support group:

YPMVC
Patron: The Lord Mayor of York
Music Director: Richard B. Lister
President: Councillor Wilfred Oliver
Chairman: John Nattrass
Secretary: Don Crawford
PERIMETER
Chairman: Peter Wilson
Secretary: Mrs. Grace Wilson
Treasurer: Mrs. Henderson
Remainder of committee: Miss J. Sadler and Miss J. Brough
Choir Delegates: Ces Rutherford and J. Tierney.

The innovator was Ernest Robinson, a choir member of long-standing, whose efforts for the choir have been and still are tireless and numerous.

So, in June 1966 Perimeter was born, the fond parents, as it were, being Peter Wilson and Ian Woods. Perimeter's successful growth to its present day membership of 147 – 31 new members enrolled during 1969 – is largely due to the untiring efforts of these two gentlemen...

...The ways in which Perimeter aids the choir are manifold. For example, the promotion of coffee mornings, jumble sales etc. enabled perimeter to generously donate £150 to the choir with the express purpose to defray the considerable expense of this year's Continental tour.

Not described in this list of activities is the contribution made, by the ladies of Perimeter, to catering for the choir. This was to be seen at its best in the first visit by the male voice choir from Münster in May 1970. [Readers may also note that a committee member was Miss Joan Sadler, a lady who gave a lifetime's support to the musical life of York].

Over the years the name and emphasis of this support group evolved so that in 2015 we have two bodies: 'Friends', primarily an interest group; and 'The Phillies', an active group of women close to the choir, who offer regular practical assistance, and have a social calendar of their own.

In 1967 Perimeter membership numbered more than 100, all willing to spend 5/- a year to show support for the Phil. This must have encouraged the choristers as the hopes and ambitions of the choir grew. In particular, in 1967, it must have made it easier to agree to invest £450 in new uniforms. This photograph, taken on the steps of the Castle Museum in 1967, shows the uniformed choir standing tall.

Next to Brian Lister (to our right) stands Lance Dutton who joined the choir in 1929. Two places to the other side of Brian stands Trevor Cooper in his second year of membership.

The Phil of the 1960s had much in common with the pre-war choir and often looked back to it for inspiration and support. In May 1965, with the choir 40 years old, the Phil revived a magazine called 'Philharmonic News and Views'.

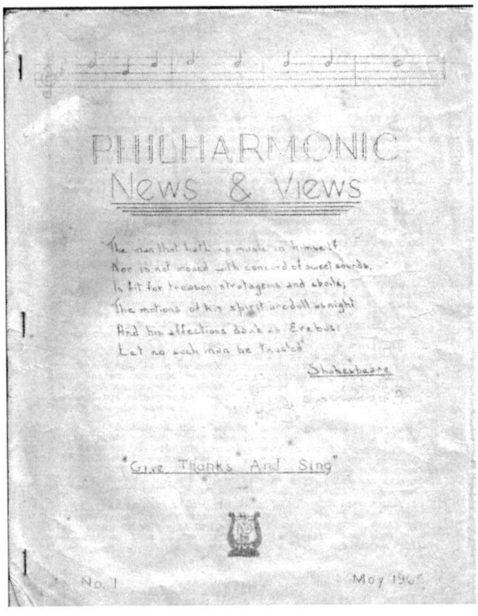

It looked back to the inspiration of Cecil Fletcher in the 1930s, and it set out its intentions on the front cover, which included a quote from Shakespeare's 'Merchant of Venice':

The man that hath no music in himself,
Nor is not moved with concord of sweet sounds,
Is fit for treason, stratagems and spoils;
The motions of his spirit are dull as night,
And his affections dank as Erebus,
Let no such man be trusted

The cover also printed the first line notation of *Deep Harmony* along the top with key words from that hymn 'Give Thanks and Sing' along the base.

When short of material, the 1960's editor used to reprint articles from 30 years earlier. Unfortunately we have only a handful of these magazines available, with nothing between the launch edition and 1969, so details about the choir during 1962-69 are somewhat patchy.

Throughout the 1960s rehearsal space was still an issue but, unlike the 1950s, was driven more by the needs of the expanding choir rather than the shortage of suitable venues. St Crux, the 1962 start point, was replaced by a room at the Railway Institute. In 1967 that proved to be too small, and the choir moved to the gym of a school in the city centre. Not only was size and suitability an issue, but also availability, as the choir now rehearsed regularly on a Wednesday as well as every Monday. Three Wednesdays per month were rehearsal days, with the fourth being committee night.

A review of 1968-1971 shows the rewards of all this activity. By 1968 A class competitions were regularly being won. In April, at Lytham St Annes, the Phil won the male voice class, and also the Kenham Cup for being the best of the 20 choirs who competed that day. In May, for the second year running, the choir won the Feversham Shield at the Ryedale Festival in Beadlam. Concerts, that year, were also given outside York in Malton, Hull, Ripon, Richmond and Scarborough. In December, the Phil joined with the York Musical Society and the York Symphony Orchestra in a concert in the Minster in support of the Minster restoration appeal. This level of cooperation had not been seen since the older York Male Voice Choir had worked with the YMS before the 1914-18 war.

There was also a recording made on behalf of Leeds United Football club. In the autumn of 1958 the Phil had recorded *The Happy Wanderer* on behalf of York City. Ten years later, the choir worked with the Rowntree Band (now the Shepherd Group Brass Band) to record 'Up United'. The YEP reported:

Leeds United fans will be adding another song to their repertoire at the home game with Sheffield Wednesday tomorrow, Words and music by Mr Jack Morgan, a retired York musical director, will be ringing out round Elland Road before the kick-off.

With the blessing of Leeds manager Don Revie, Mr Morgan has had his 'Up United' song of encouragement recorded and a tape recording is to be relayed as the players come out.

It is a stirring song put over by the 60 strong York Philharmonic male Voice Choir under its director Richard B. Lister, and the Rowntree Band conducted by Mr. Les Lambeth.

But the year was brought to a close by a significant first in the life of the Phil. Yorkshire Television recorded a 25 minute show of 'Carols in Kirkgate' which was broadcast at 11.30 pm on Christmas Eve.

Competition success carried forward into 1969. The Huddersfield daily Examiner of 17/02/1969 carried this report:

In the 'Mrs Sunderland' finals at Huddersfield Town Hall on Saturday, David Ward of Tadcaster was successful in the lieder and men's operatic solo classes, and York Philharmonic Male Voice Choir won two choral trophies, including the Centenary Trophy for the best performance of any one test piece by a choir...

In the Lieder class, David Ward was accompanied by Alan Bloomfield, who also accompanied the Phil.

In the Male Voice Class, the Phil gained 349 points, Skelmanthorpe was second, with 337 and Thurnscoe third with 334. A 12 point difference between choirs at this level of competition was unusual. This was the greatest competition honour the Phil had won in its 44 year life.

In April, the Phil travelled to Germany and Holland, starting a whole new chapter in the life of the choir (covered in detail in a later chapter).

As well as looking enthusiastically to the future, the choir also took time to reflect on the past. The choir learned that Archie Sargent was unwell. In a letter of good wishes sent in March 1969, the Phil also conferred Honorary Life Membership on Janet Sargent, seven years after her retirement as accompanist. Archie and Janet still hold the unique distinction of being the only married couple both of whom have Life Membership.

On June 16th the Phil auditioned for the BBC radio competition 'Let the People Sing!' and was accepted. The next stage was to be a recording that autumn.

The Guildhall concert in July was part of the York Festival, and was in some ways a 'family affair'. The Phil was joined by: the York Madrigal Group; with David Ward as baritone soloist; and Agnes Nattrass, wife of choir chairman John, as soprano soloist. The YEP suggested that the audience...*must have left reflecting how satisfying it was that local talent should provide such a splendid contribution to the Festival...*

The choir seemed to be invincible, and was now preparing for two major competitions. The Blackpool Musical Festival was on Saturday 25th October, which required the singers to leave York at 8.30 am to be sure of arriving on time. The following Tuesday, at 7.30pm, the Phil was to record four items for 'Let the People Sing' at the BBC studios in Leeds.

Musical Festivals can be hard to predict. Despite recent successes, the Phil failed miserably at Blackpool, coming fifth out of eight. The full report of Brian's inquest was not recorded. The treasurer added to the misery by pointing out that the trip incurred a loss of £29. 10s. 0d.

Let the People Sing!

Three days later, no doubt still smarting from this humiliation, the Phil went to Leeds to record for the BBC. Perhaps the defeat at Blackpool ensured there was no complacency as the recordings made that evening propelled the Phil to its greatest ever competition success. However, on the day of recording the treasurer, still upset at the loss incurred the previous Saturday, was at pains to point out that the trip to the BBC studios had cost a further £3.17. 6d.

The first heats were regional, and were judged in November 1969. The Phil beat six choirs, including the much respected Felling, and Thurnscoe. Representing the North of England, the Phil was then pitched against the West of England in the inter-regional heats, and on 17/03/70 beat the best of Cornwall – the Treviscoe Male Voice Choir. In the last round, the National, Royal Tunbridge Wells Orpheus Male Voice Choir was vanquished and the Phil won the right to represent the UK in the international heats. That National Final was broadcast at 11am on the 14th April, and the adjudicators were Maurice Jacobson, John Alldis and David Willcocks, all eminent choral directors and adjudicators.

The comments made by the adjudicators during the broadcast were reproduced in the Choir magazine of May 1970; the three pieces being judged were: *Bushes and Briars*, Vaughan Williams; *Music when soft voices die*, Bairstow; and *The Wanderer*, Elgar.

In the magazine report Brian Lister underlined the points he felt to be most important:

Maurice Jacobson:

Bushes and Briars: *Mellow sounding – maturity in voices and approach. They chose a goodish programme – well integrated and thoughtful work. There were one or two curious pauses in their Bushes and Briars.*

Music when soft voices die: *Would have been more successful with a minim beat instead of what appeared to be a crotchet beat.*

The Wanderer: *Seemed to be a new choir – new colours with lots of apt and very good vivid and verbal good touches. I had hoped for something extra in the way of resonance and ring in the final climaxes. Overall very attractive work.*

John Alldis:

A good choir which cares about accuracy and detail rather more than others we've heard. Dark tone but a sense of fun and drama coupled with a careful appreciation of the need of a legato line when it is required.

Bushes and Briars: *Very restrained and thoughtfully done – voices were well covered and yet they project the notes physically and to the right place.*

Music when soft voices die: *Carefully prepared. Mood and intonation were right but sense of continuity became a little bogged down through over-painting the syllables.*

The Wanderer: *Showed a wide and exciting dynamic range and the contrast between legato and pointing was well done. A very good top line.*

David Willcocks:

The feature that pleased me most about this choir was its attention to words and mood. The conductor and singers were constantly striving to make the singing fully responsive to the words. I think it was that feature which led to some of the pauses which Maurice Jacobson didn't like in the Vaughan Williams. The place they paused was 'all for to hear the small birds sing'. They felt as if they wanted to linger and hear the birds but it does destroy the flow of the melody.

Several things I like about their singing – the imaginative touches – the confidential whisper as they sang 'sometimes I think I will go to my love' and in the Elgar they were able to get vital enunciation in the words 'with a heart of furious fancies'. They were able to get suppressed excitement and mystery in 'ghosts and shadows'.

All these things showed very careful preparation and imaginative responses.

The comments which Brian thought important enough to underline both compliment the choir, and give a constant reminder to keep to the basics. Brian did not seek a discussion on the 'over-painting of syllables' but highlighted:

– A good choir which cares about accuracy and detail rather more than others we've heard

– ...yet they project the notes physically and to the right place.

– *A very good top line.*
– *All these things showed very careful preparation and imaginative responses.*
Comments which in essence say: 'Hard work pays off'.

The UK competition was in the male voice class. In the international heats, competitors were equal voice i.e. either male or female, but not mixed voice. Competing choirs came from 25 countries, so a number of rounds were required to select finalists.

In round one on 5/05/1970 the Phil beat 'Gesangverein der Basf' from West Germany.

In round two on 25/06/1970 the choir beat 'Chorale de L'École Normale D'Institutrices Delémont' from Switzerland.

In the semi-finals on the 15/7/1970, the journey came to an end when the Phil was beaten by a ladies choir from Sofia in Bulgaria.

In the final on 25/7/1970 this Bulgarian choir met with a ladies choir from Ireland – The Lindsay Singers – and shared the first prize.

There was no 'sing off' for third place, which led to linguistic challenges for copy writers. As two choirs had shared first place, some writers considered that the other semi-finalists shared second place. Therefore, dependent upon the source read, the Phil is either described as 'coming second' or as a 'semi-finalist'. Irrespective of which description is used, it was a magnificent achievement and the highest honour ever won by the Phil.

In the midst of these broadcasts the choir hosted the Münsterscher Männergesangverein on its first visit to York.

There were no 'live' competition successes in 1970. A return to Huddersfield in February ended in failure, and entry into the prestigious Teesside international Festival had to be withdrawn due to a lack of second tenors. As a consequence, it was still hoped to attend but to compete in the smaller choir class. This too had to be cancelled as this small class was held on a week-day. From a competitive point of view it was a year of reflection; like many sports teams it is one task to win a league, and yet another to retain that title.

The concert programme was much as normal but with two new interesting venues. In June, the Phil sang in the recently opened Lyons Concert Hall at York University. This was in aid of the British Legion, which had formed a branch on the campus as there were 40 ex-servicemen on the staff. Also the earlier competition success at Huddersfield led to an invitation to perform in the town hall. This was held in July and was an enjoyable affair held jointly with the Huddersfield Choral Union and a local junior brass band.

The evening press report on the November annual concert once again described a choir 'at the top of its game':

...Old favourites like the Keys of Heaven contrasted with Elgar's songs from the Greek Anthology. In boisterous (Wandering the King's Highway) or reflective (Were You There?), or whimsical (Do You Remember an Inn Miranda?) mood, under the meticulous direction of Richard Lister and ably accompanied by Sydney Herdsman the choir never failed to

evoke the right response.

One can never hear this choir without being very much aware of the tremendous concentration of all its members, and of their dedication to producing the best performance of which they are capable, and that is nearly always very good indeed.

Reg Goodhall, ever popular as the resident soloist, produced great sweetness of tone. His is a sincere rather almost didactic, rather than passionate approach to Italian opera and his most effective song was Grieg's lyrical 'I love Thee'...

1971- 80: Building a lasting Legacy

Despite critical acclaim Brian Lister was concerned for the future. In the Autumn 1970 issue of the choir magazine he wrote a thought provoking article ... *to encourage all of us to personally examine our feelings and attitudes towards the living-breathing entity which is our choir...*

The year ended with an additional performance of 'Carols in Kirkgate' – the 'private performance'. The report in Perimeter magazine highlighted one unexpected consequence of this innovation – increased membership – but no-one had an idea of just how important this additional night was to prove in years to come (see later chapter).

The response to 'Carols in Kirkgate' is always so overwhelming that this year the Choir put on a special performance just for their friends and Perimeter, thus enabling more tickets to be sold to the public, and we had our own special show. This was a great success and was, I am sure, one of the main reasons for such a rise in membership. But as both the Lord Mayor and Sheriff's Christmas Cheer Fund and our own funds benefitted, we thought it an excellent thing.

It was at this time (1971) that the Phil moved yet again to different rehearsal rooms. The choir was not to know that this would end the earlier nomadic lifestyle. The medieval St Williams College not only offered excellent facilities but also became home for the next 35 years. In 1969 Councillor Wilf Oliver had become President and John Nattrass the chairman. Wilf Oliver invited a young councillor, Keith Wood, to join the Castle Museum committee, and by doing so introduced Keith to the choir. Councillor Oliver served as President for at least ten years; Keith Wood was then elected to the post, which he still holds. This has given great stability: only two effective and supportive Presidents in 47 years. John Nattrass served for three years as chairman, covering the periods of the German and Dutch visits, and then returned for a further time in the middle of the decade. This too helped to consolidate the choir.

1971 also included a rather unusual 'first' for The Phil. The YEP 19/6/1971 published this article:

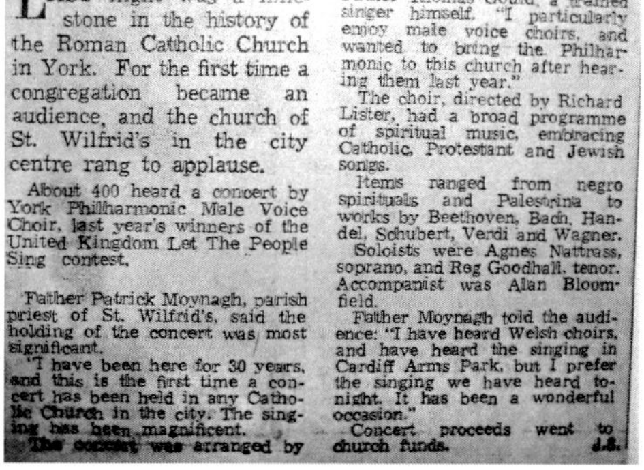

Choir makes church history

LAST night was a milestone in the history of the Roman Catholic Church in York. For the first time a congregation became an audience, and the church of St. Wilfrid's in the city centre rang to applause.

About 400 heard a concert by York Philharmonic Male Voice Choir, last year's winners of the United Kingdom Let The People Sing contest.

Father Patrick Moynagh, parish priest of St. Wilfrid's, said the holding of the concert was most significant.

"I have been here for 30 years, and this is the first time a concert has been held in any Catholic Church in the city. The singing has been magnificent.

The concert was arranged by Father Thomas Gould, a trained singer himself. "I particularly enjoy male voice choirs, and wanted to bring the Philharmonic to this church after hearing them last year."

The choir, directed by Richard Lister, had a broad programme of spiritual music, embracing Catholic, Protestant and Jewish songs.

Items ranged from negro spirituals and Palestrina to works by Beethoven, Bach, Handel, Schubert, Verdi and Wagner.

Soloists were Agnes Nattrass, soprano, and Reg Goodhall, tenor. Accompanist was Alan Bloomfield.

Father Moynagh told the audience: "I have heard Welsh choirs, and have heard the singing in Cardiff Arms Park, but I prefer the singing we have heard tonight. It has been a wonderful occasion."

Concert proceeds went to church funds.

J.S.

It was a surprise to members to be the first to perform in this church.

The rest of 1971 was largely uneventful until December, when Yorkshire Television returned to film a 60 minute show of 'Carols In Kirkgate' in colour (see later chapter).

In 1972 the Phil competed in the Teesside International Festival, which brought home the challenges faced when working at this level. In truth, choirs most likely to succeed in such competitions at this time were either youth groups, or large regional ones, supported by solid financial sponsorship. The YEP carried this report:

York Philharmonic Male Voice Choir was definitely outnumbered at the Teesside International Eisteddfod this week-end.

The choir was the smallest in the class of 11 choirs most of them from the continent.

Holidays had taken away many of the York choir's harmonious voices top strength about 60 – leaving only 47 singers at the Eisteddfod the fourth held on Teesside. And the opposition was tough. The winners a choir from Czechoslovakia had 78 members.

The York choir came fifth in the event, but were not too disappointed. Mr. Richard Lister the choir director said afterwards. "Because of our small size we don't think we did too badly".

Within ten years of taking over as conductor, Brian Lister had achieved all the goals he had publicly declared to the YEP in October 1967: the Phil was recognised as one of the best male choirs in the country; it had enjoyed success in an international competition; and had undertaken a continental tour. Not imagined in 1967, but now a reality, the Phil, via Yorkshire Television, was also part of Christmas day in homes throughout the land.

There was but one aspect of choir life yet to be achieved: the recording and marketing of a long playing record. This ambition was reached in 1974 with the launch of 'Carols in Kirkgate', recorded with the Beckfield School Choir. It is good that this was made before the school stopped taking part in the show. It was also appropriate that this recording of 12 carols included six arranged by Brian Lister.

The first copy of a record made by York Philharmonic Male Voice Choir was handed to the Lord Mayor, Coun. William Burke, at the Mansion House today. The choir has recorded 12 carols as featured in its Christmas concerts which take place annually in Kirkgate in the Castle Museum. The presentation was made by Coun. W. Oliver, left, and looking on is Mr. J. Waggott, the choir treasurer. Also featured on the record is the Beckfield School Choir, which joins forces with the Philharmonic for this annual event. It is being released for sale at the end of this week. Carols in Kirkgate will take place as usual in December and will be seen on Yorkshire Television during the Christmas period.

Launch of first LP on 11/11/1974

A second recording under the same title was made in 1976, this time with the Kirkgate Singers. This had 16 tracks, eight of which had been arranged by Brian.

By now the Phil was now confidently playing a full part in the life of the city. In April 1972 it hosted the National Association of Choirs Annual Conference. This was the first time the conference had been held in York. As the city representatives, the choir hosted the event at The Tempest Anderson Hall, and gave an evening concert together with the Hull Ladies Festival Chorus and the Kingston-upon-Hull Choral Society.

In July 1972, the choir took on a more daunting musical task. A concert was held in the Minster as part of the 500th anniversary of the completion of the current building. The choir numbered only 45 and, to an audience of more than 600, sang a programme of music spanning the same timescale as the Minster itself. The challenging programme was a profound test, particularly given the acoustic qualities of the cathedral.

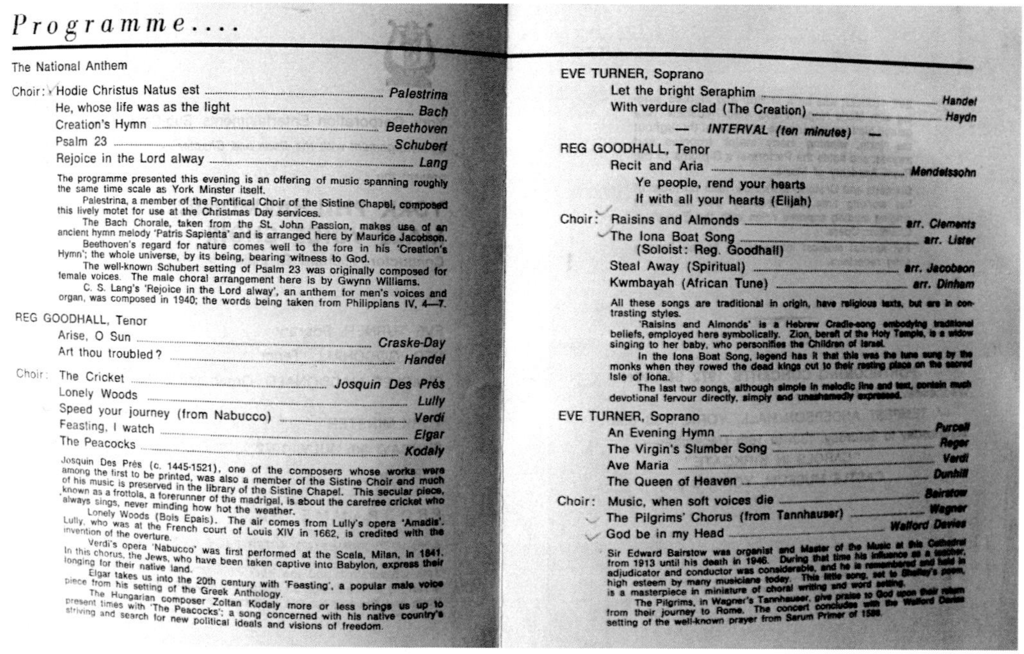

Programme....

The National Anthem

Choir: Hodie Christus Natus est .... *Palestrina*
He, whose life was as the light .... *Bach*
Creation's Hymn .... *Beethoven*
Psalm 23 .... *Schubert*
Rejoice in the Lord alway .... *Lang*

The programme presented this evening is an offering of music spanning roughly the same time scale as York Minster itself.

Palestrina, a member of the Pontifical Choir of the Sistine Chapel, composed this lively motet for use at the Christmas Day services.

The Bach Chorale, taken from the St. John Passion, makes use of an ancient hymn melody 'Patris Sapienta' and is arranged here by Maurice Jacobson.

Beethoven's regard for nature comes well to the fore in his 'Creation's Hymn'; the whole universe, by its being, bearing witness to God.

The well-known Schubert setting of Psalm 23 was originally composed for female voices. The male choral arrangement here is by Gwynn Williams.

C. S. Lang's 'Rejoice in the Lord alway', an anthem for men's voices and organ, was composed in 1940; the words being taken from Philippians IV, 4—7.

REG GOODHALL, Tenor
Arise, O Sun .... *Craske-Day*
Art thou troubled? .... *Handel*

Choir: The Cricket .... *Josquin Des Prés*
Lonely Woods .... *Lully*
Speed your journey (from Nabucco) .... *Verdi*
Feasting, I watch .... *Elgar*
The Peacocks .... *Kodaly*

Josquin Des Prés (c. 1445-1521), one of the composers whose works were among the first to be printed, was also a member of the Sistine Choir and much of his music is preserved in the library of the Sistine Chapel. This secular piece, known as a frottola, a forerunner of the madrigal, is about the carefree cricket who always sings, never minding how hot the weather.

Lonely Woods (Bois Epais). The air comes from Lully's opera 'Amadis'. Lully, who was at the French court of Louis XIV in 1662, is credited with the invention of the overture.

Verdi's opera 'Nabucco' was first performed at the Scala, Milan, in 1841. In this chorus, the Jews, who have been taken captive into Babylon, express their longing for their native land.

Elgar takes us into the 20th century with 'Feasting', a popular male voice piece from his setting of the Greek Anthology.

The Hungarian composer Zoltan Kodaly more or less brings us up to present times with 'The Peacocks'; a song concerned with his native country's striving and search for new political ideals and visions of freedom.

EVE TURNER, Soprano
Let the bright Seraphim .... *Handel*
With verdure clad (The Creation) .... *Haydn*

— *INTERVAL (ten minutes)* —

REG GOODHALL, Tenor
Recit and Aria .... *Mendelssohn*
Ye people, rend your hearts
If with all your hearts (Elijah)

Choir: Raisins and Almonds .... *arr. Clements*
The Iona Boat Song .... *arr. Lister*
(Soloist: Reg. Goodhall)
Steal Away (Spiritual) .... *arr. Jacobson*
Kwmbayah (African Tune) .... *arr. Dinham*

All these songs are traditional in origin, have religious texts, but are in contrasting styles.

'Raisins and Almonds' is a Hebrew Cradle-song embodying traditional beliefs, employed here symbolically. Zion, bereft of the Holy Temple, is a widow singing to her baby, who personifies the Children of Israel.

In the Iona Boat Song, legend has it that this was the tune sung by the monks when they rowed the dead kings out to their resting place on the sacred Isle of Iona.

The last two songs, although simple in melodic line and text, contain much devotional fervour directly, simply and unashamedly expressed.

EVE TURNER, Soprano
An Evening Hymn .... *Purcell*
The Virgin's Slumber Song .... *Reger*
Ave Maria .... *Verdi*
The Queen of Heaven .... *Dunhill*

Choir: Music, when soft voices die .... *Bairstow*
The Pilgrims' Chorus (from Tannhauser) .... *Wagner*
God be in my Head .... *Walford Davies*

Sir Edward Bairstow was organist and Master of the Music at this Cathedral from 1913 until his death in 1946. During that time his influence as a teacher, adjudicator and conductor was considerable, and he is remembered and held in high esteem by many musicians today. This little song, set to Shelley's poem, is a masterpiece in miniature of choral writing and word setting.

The Pilgrims, in Wagner's Tannhauser, give praise to God upon their return from their journey to Rome. The concert concludes with the Walford Davies setting of the well-known prayer from Sarum Primer of 1558.

This format was repeated in June 1973 with Cynthia Glover as guest soloist. The reviewer from the YEP acknowledged the challenges faced:

The York Philharmonic Male Voice Choir's programme in the Minster last night showed a nice balance, both on content and in voices. All their well known crispness in attack was needed to overcome the acoustic difficulties, but they definitely won...

There was a delightful footnote to this review in the YEP:

Way after midnight last night, a very smart group came into the club wearing collars and ties and black blazers. It turned out they were members of the York Philharmonic Male Voice Choir fresh from their concert triumph in the Minster. I gleaned my information from Cecil Rutherford who has been with them for 25 years. As I left they were giving new life to Danny Boy. Beautifully!

In April 1974 the following incident caught the attention of the Hull Daily Mail:

Hull Fire engines on their way to a trawler fire on Saturday night roared past the City Hall just as a male voice choir was singing about crickets at the Hull Musical Festival. But York Philharmonic Male Voice Choir didn't turn a hair or lose a note, showing self-control which earned the praise of the adjudicator Prof. Philip Cranmer,

"I'm astonished that the out-side out-of-tune noises did not make any difference to your singing". He told the choir. "It shows great concentration that you were not put off".

On the contrary the choir sang so well they won the class for adult male small choirs. That day the Phil also won the large choir class.

It was in 1974 that the choir first reached a membership target of 70. Average attendance at a rehearsal in February 1974 was 55. A year earlier it had been 42. The choir had 72 listed members and could now expect 60 on stage. Brian Lister had the ambition to add a further 10 to these numbers, but that was never to be. A large choir, with regular recruitment, did need to consider the cost of membership. Maintaining a 'uniform' look is never easy as trousers and blazers wear out and it is not easy to replace like with like. With the 50th year anniversary being celebrated in 1975 there was a move to introduce evening dress. This was deferred, on grounds of cost, and was not in fact resolved for another ten years. In 1974 the members understood that yet more uniform requirements would mean prospective members being faced with a bill of more than £100, a sum which would surely be a barrier to entry.

In 1975 – Jubilee Year – a dinner dance was held in the Gimcrack rooms at the Racecourse with music by the Derek Dunning Quartet. Before the guests sat down the choir sang a short concert; and was delighted to welcome one particular guest of honour, Tom Clark. As described in part one, the embryonic choir first met in Tom's front room. Bombed out in 1942, Tom and his family moved to another house in the same street where he still lived in 1975. At the dinner, Tom was given the honour of being made a Life Member.

An annual dinner was a feature of choir life, as it had been pre-war, and through the years the menu didn't seem to change much. In March 1966 at Betty's Restaurant the choir dined on:

Creamed soup; Fillet of Place; Roast Turkey; Peach Melba; Cheese and Biscuits; Coffee

At the Jubilee Dinner in April 1975 the menu was: Cream of Vegetable soup; Roast Turkey; Fruit and Cream gateau; Coffee with Mints.

This 'anniversary' photograph was taken at the entrance of St. William's College in May 1975, after the Phil had won first prize at the Wharfedale Festival.

The Jubilee concert was held in the Assembly Rooms (now an Italian Restaurant) on Friday 4th July 1975, with Brian Kay as the guest soloist. At the time, this York born singer, was particularly well known as a member of the 'King's Singers'.

The programme included items from all stages of the choir's life; the second item was *Hymn before Action*, the test piece in the first ever competition, and ended with *Moon River*, a recent 'pop' hit.

In the mid 1970s the tourist industry in York was expanding and the Phil accepted invitations to entertain visitors in hotels; for example the bookings in 1977 included four concerts in the Post House hotel. There were also occasional outings as Tudor minstrels at medieval banquets in the Merchant Adventurers' Hall. These were popular at the time, and featured chicken and chips in a basket with copious amounts of wine and ale. It was, however, thought that the choir did not look good in baggy hose. This was the time when the economy of York took a significant shift towards tourism.

There seemed to be but one goal still to be achieved, the recording of an LP of non-Christmas music. The quest to make this record as 'good as it could be' required a number of recording sessions and considerable studio time.

This article appeared in YEP 17/11/1976:

YORK CHOIR RECORDS ITS THIRD L-P

A NEW VERSION of The Grand Old Duke of York, specially arranged by Gordon Langford — who does arrangements for the King's Singers — promises to be the highlight of a new LP record being made by York Philharmonic Male Voice Choir.

The choir has completed three recording sessions at York University's Lyons Concert Hall and expects to have enough material for the record after one more session.

"After one more session we will have recorded about 18 songs and I would think about 14 or 15 will be chosen for the record," said choir secretary Donald Crawford.

When the disc is released next year, it will be the choir's third LP on the market. However, the first two are both of Christmas carols, whereas this latest one will include a variety of songs — the choir's first "straight" record, as Mr. Crawford calls it.

But recording is not the only item on the choir's busy agenda. Tonight, for example, the singers are joined by Scottish mezzo-soprano Marjory Anderson in a concert at the Tempest Anderson Hall, York, in aid of the Lord Mayor and Sheriff's Christmas Cheer Fund.

Three recording sessions had been completed with another being planned. The editing then took several months, as the copyright date on the LP is 1978. Given the inclusion of Gordon Langford's arrangement of *The Grand Old Duke of York,* the natural title for the LP was 'Dukes of York'. Fourteen tracks were included with three arranged by Brian Lister.

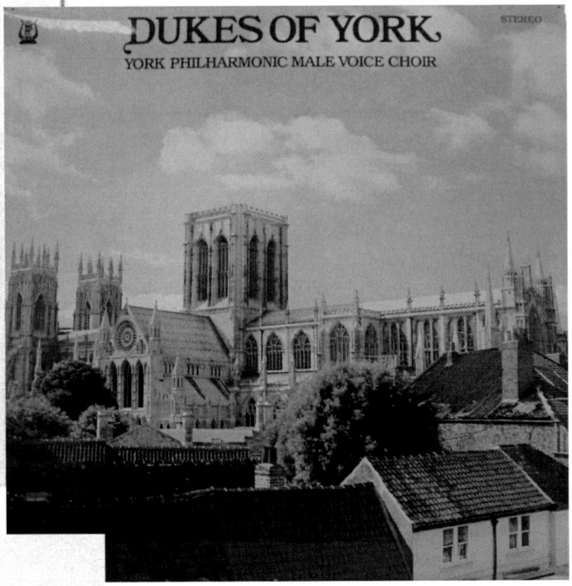

Side A

1. **The Grand Old Duke of York.** *Traditional North Country rhyme arranged Langford.*
2. **Do you remember an inn, Miranda?** *Words by Hilaire Belloc. Music by Harold Noble. Published by Ascherberg, Hopwood and Crewe.*
3. **When the saints go marching in.** *Traditional American arranged Lister.*
4. **Steal away.** *Negro spiritual arranged Jacobson.*
5. **Glory and love to the men of old.** *From Gounod's 'Faust.' Published by Banks & Son (Music) Ltd.*
6. **Speed your journey.** *From Verdi's 'Nabucco.' Arranged Northcote. Published by Ricordi & Co. Ltd.*
7. **The Pilgrims' Chorus.** *From Wagner's 'Tannhaüser.' Published by Banks & Son (Music) Ltd.*

Side B

1. **Creation's Hymn.** *Beethoven arranged Lister.*
2. **Three merry ghosts.** *Words by Thomas Love Peacock. Music by Max Saunders. Published by Alfred Lengnick & Co. Ltd.*
3. **Loudly let the trumpet bray.** *From 'Iolanthe.' Words by W. S. Gilbert. Music by Arthur Sullivan. Published by Chappell & Co. Ltd.*
4. **The Owl and the Pussy-Cat.** *Words by Edward Lear. Music by R. de Koven. Published by Banks & Son (Music) Ltd.*
5. **When the boat comes in.** *Traditional Tyneside song arranged Lister.*
6. **The Fighting Temeraire.** *Words by Sir Henry Newbolt. Music by Granville Bantock. Published by Roberton Publications.*
7. **Close thine eyes.** *Words attributed to King Charles I. Music by Ieuan Rees-Davies. Published by Curwen.*

The first 'Carols in Kirkgate' LP was recorded in July and was on sale in November, five months later. A second Carols LP, with the Kirkgate Singers, was recorded early in 1976 and was on sale that year. In 1978 a marketing company produced a double album using material from both recordings and so the show stayed available. But the 'Dukes of York' was different and took almost two years to plan and produce. The end result was (is) both a delight to the eye and to the ear. This combination of whimsical, operatic, classical, spirituals and folk pieces included one piece popular at the time. *When the Boat comes in* had been used as the signature tune in a popular TV series, and its inclusion pleased the number of Tynesiders in the choir. *The Fighting Temeraire,* a lengthy, robust song in a style associated with male voice choirs, was placed next to the prayerful lullaby *Close thine eyes.* The interesting selection showed off the range of musical styles the Phil had mastered. The LP was well received and indeed was featured a number of times on radio programmes, including David Jacobs on Radio 2, who played *The Owl and the Pussy Cat.*

The LPs recorded in the 1970s - Greetings was a double album compilation

Brian Lister strove for perfection, and was always working towards a new goal. There is, perhaps, some significance in the fact that the last entry in his personal scrapbook is the press article of 17/11/1976 giving details of the recording of the 'Dukes of York'. He continued to lead until July 1980 and yet, it seems, there was nothing more he felt he could achieve, nothing more he wished to add to his memorabilia.

There were many similarities between this choir of the 1960-70s and the pre-war Phil. As well as singing there was an active social life, with Dales tours trips, river cruises, bowls and cricket matches. During the summer recess, some still gathered on a Monday evening for a social. This led, in April 1979, to an attempt to revive one of the most successful pre-war events, The Inter-Choir Competition. This was planned, with the care and attention of 1938, to include 10 classes and was scheduled to start at St. William's College at 2pm, with no finish time stated. The winning quartet was to receive the S.P.Wilson Rose Bowl, the winner of the Finalist Class the C.H.Fletcher Challenge Cup. This was an ambitious plan, as it sought to reproduce the scale of the competition during its most successful years, but as an idea it failed. Through lack of support it was not repeated.

This photograph shows Chris Poole, Reg Goodhall, Tony Sawyer, and Don Crawford with the rose bowl and cup on the day of the competition. Jim Waggott was the last winner of the Challenge cup in 1979, which he displayed in his office for many years. Although the rules state he was to have it for one year – he holds it still.

Chris Poole, Reg Goodhall, Tony Sawyer and Don Crawford. Jim still holds the cup in 2016

Between 1962 and 1976 Brian Lister led the Phil on a journey of discovery which took it to levels of achievement way beyond the expectations of individual singers. An experimental, one night, Christmas show in 1962 led to national coverage on television, and grew to a five night concert run. A request to take part in a twinning exercise with Münster had grown into a lifelong friendship. The choir which, in the 1950s, sang mostly in local churches, could now successfully entertain large crowds in the Minster. The Phil, still only just big enough to be confident in 'A' class competition, was now a regular winner. In 1970 the 'Let the People Sing' competition placed it at the head of UK male voice choirs, and it came close to being voted the best in Europe. Success on radio and television was followed by three long playing records giving the choir an accessible and enduring legacy.

What was there left to achieve? This was an amateur group; the conductor, the accompanist and all the members had 'day jobs'. There was no commercial sponsorship and still a naivety in the choir with regard to the commercial aspect of performing. Squabbles with the record company over payment of royalties went on for some years; and, with the wonders of hindsight and knowledge of the small amount of money which changed hands, Yorkshire Television did well from the 'Carols in Kirkgate' recording. The Phil was on the 'cusp', on the limit of what it could both achieve and control.

So the choir stuck to its roots and kept doing that which it did best – entertaining the public – to the high standards that had been reached.

With no more goals to strive for, Brian Lister felt his work was done, and so in July 1980 he took his last rehearsal.

Pressman's Diary

York choir's director retires on a high note

MR. RICHARD LISTER last night took his bow as director of the York Philharmonic Male Voice Choir.

He conducted his last concert with the choir before retiring as director.

The concert, specially commissioned by the National Trust, was at Beningbrough Hall.

Forty-nine-year-old Mr. Lister's decision means an end to a happy and profitable relationship with the choir. Altogether it lasted 18 years.

"I feel that I need a change and so does the choir," said Mr. Lister, who lives at 27 Maple Grove, York. "But we are leaving on very amicable terms."

Mr. Lister, who is head of music at Beckfield Lane Secondary Modern School, became director of the choir in 1962. Since then it has doubled its size — to 60 members — and has achieved national and international fame.

In 1970 the choir won the BBC competition Let The Peoples Sing and then represented the BBC in Europe. They came second to Bulgaria.

The choir is also well-known for its Christmas carols in Kirkgate. The choir produced four records, and tracks are sometimes played on the radio.

A successor to Mr. Lister is being appointed this week.

"I only intended to stay for one year to begin with, but I enjoyed the job so much that I stayed for 18," Mr. Lister laughed.

A spokesman for the choir said that "it was with surprise and dismay that they had heard of Mr. Lister's decision to resign. But the choir wished him well in future projects."

Mr. RICHARD LISTER, retiring choir director. (See lead Diary note).

The Phil was now faced with the critical organisational challenge of recruiting a new music director. The choir had no prior experience of this: in 1946 Sefton Fearne stepped out of the choir to lead; in 1950 the choir appealed to Archie Sargent for help; and in 1962 Brian Lister had been waiting in the wings.

Since 1962 the Phil had enjoyed success after success, it had been an exhilarating time. What was to happen next? Were there new challenges still to be discovered or was the biggest task to be maintenance and survival? In choosing a new director there were, undoubtedly, some key requirements; the choir must strive to maintain the high standards reached; and must always be appealing to new members, particularly younger ones. The fear of going into decline was very real. But was there a wider ambition? Brian Lister had stepped down feeling there was nothing more he could achieve; and there was no suggestion at this time that the choir had any unfulfilled ambition. Could a new director scale new heights, to conquer America perhaps, or record the Christmas number one in Norway?

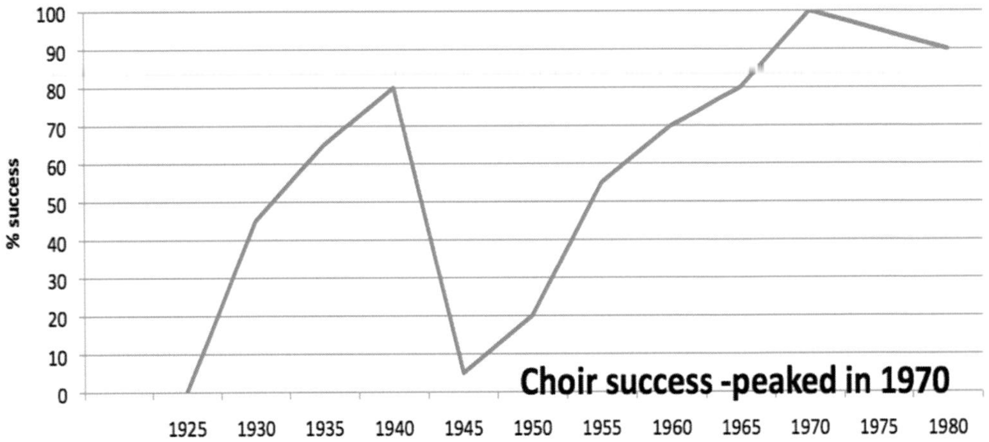

This simple illustration shows the path the choir had taken: starting with nothing; being on the point of achieving great things at the outbreak of war; then the lowest point in 1946, at the death of Cecil Fletcher; and the highest 'Let the People Sing' in 1970. Looking back from a distance of 45 years we know that the Phil has not found the 'magic ingredient' to lift overall achievements above 1970. What has been achieved is the consistent maintenance of standards. If this illustration were carried forward to the present day, the line would probably fluctuate between 70-95% of the 1970 peak. Although not known at the time, this has been the reality. No director since Brian Lister has had the heady success achieved in the 1930s and the 1970s but then no director has had to start from such a low point. Later success has come from keeping the choir 'fresh' and 'good', still able to appeal to audiences and prospective members.

What could not be foreseen in 1980 was the fact that, for a number of reasons, the Phil, which had been used to long term relationships with music directors, would need to work with seven conductors during the next 19 years.

Two of these seven had such short-term tenures that they are not named in this narrative.

Chapter 6
David Keeffe

Holding Steady – Managing the hand-over

It was a challenging task to take over a leadership role from one as successful as Brian Lister. Fortunately the choir chose well. David Keeffe, the young man appointed to the role in 1980, was ideally qualified. Born in 1956, he was 25 years younger than Brian Lister, but in this narrative is classed as being of the same generation. His credentials were excellent: a diploma in composition and conducting from Trinity School of Music, and a BA in music from York University. He was an excellent player of the French horn, being lead player with the York Guildhall Orchestra, and had directed the University of York Gilbert & Sullivan Society. In 1980 he was working on one of the emerging trends in music, the use and potential of computers.

All choirs need a constant supply of new members and it was hoped that David's youth and connections would bring some direct benefits. During his tenure the choir sought to further enhance its relationship with the University, and invited Prof. S.B.Saul to be choir patron.

In truth, his four years tenure was a fallow time. He led the Phil on a visit to Münster in 1981 and hosted a return in 1983, possibly the two most prestigious events during these years. The other change of long term significance was the appointment of Lorna Whitworth as accompanist. Jane Brough had held the post from 1925-39; thereafter it had been men. Lorna joined in 1980 and, apart from a few months in 1986, the post has been held by a woman ever since.

This lack of activity explains a shortage of photographs of David. There are, as ever with conductors, some which show the back of his head, but the one shown here was taken at the Guildhall concert in June 1981.

It is not a clear picture but is interesting because of what it shows apart from David. He is talking to the audience but just look at the Phil behind him. The choir is still using music folders – what a mess it looks! In truth these folders were not required, the choir was more than able to sing without copies, but holding a folder was a 'crutch' an 'insurance policy'. This photo was taken in 1981; in the middle of the decade the folders were thrown away, audiences applauded the move and the choir has never looked back.

The musical selections for this concert also suggest that the choir was coasting. David had planned to include *Poor Wayfaring Stranger* in an arrangement he had done himself; but it wasn't well enough known and needed to be replaced. The concert opened with *The Grand Old Duke of York*, ended with *Deep Harmony*, and included *Steal Away, Feasting I watch, The Fighting Temeraire* and *Music when soft voices die*, nothing new to excite the audience.

It was a very hard task David undertook when taking over from Brian Lister. Unfortunately, the hoped for influx of new members from the University did not materialise; but he did a good job, standards were maintained, particularly given the somewhat deflated mood of the choir; and the Phil wished him well when he left York in 1984. [In 1997 David moved to Melbourne Australia where he has gained a high reputation as a performer, composer, arranger and director].

One measure of David's four year success is seen in the fact that his immediate successor lasted only a few months. Although on paper a good candidate, the choir and this conductor were not compatible, a situation recognised and acted upon before too much damage occurred. The experience did, however, sap some of the life out of the choir.

Chapter 7
Richard Bowman

Vitality renewed

In complete contrast Richard Bowman was an excellent match and the Phil enjoyed six years under his direction. He was an excellent communicator, as befits a primary school teacher, and his vitality and musical skills brought the choir back to life.

Richard was 35 years old when he became music director. A York man, he was well known as a flautist, and was chairman of the York Recorder Society. His work with music in education was recognised when he was appointed Primary Representative on the National Advisory Committee to the Silver Burdett & Ginn Publishing Company. In 1988, whilst working with the Phil, he took his school choir, 'The Village Folk' of New Earswick Primary, on a tour of Sweden. He was known to the Phil before his appointment, as his school choir had, for some years, taken part in 'Carols in Kirkgate'.

The period 1985-91 was both busy and entertaining. It was an age of 'aspiration', of 'corporate extravagance', and a time when all sorts of events, including concerts and festivals, had to be seen to be 'bigger to be better'. The Phil first experienced this new way of living in 1986, when it was invited to sing at the opening of a head office of the Dutch Volksbank in Utrecht. Ursula Morton, whose contribution to the early success of the twinning with Münster is described in a later chapter, arranged a hotel booking for the choir to sing to Dutch tourists. The head of the Volksbank was in that group, liked what he heard and Ursula made the introductions. The Phil then enjoyed 'A day trip to Utrecht' as the bank paid for a group of 40 to take the overnight ferry to Rotterdam, then a coach to the Head Office to sing at the opening, and then back to the ferry. The town of Nijmegen is only some 40 miles from Utrecht, and is home to an excellent male voice choir (see later chapter). Perhaps taking the easy option and booking local singers, rather than overseas' ones, just did not fit the culture of the time!

There were also bookings at Castle Howard to provide 'some' of the entertainment at corporate dinners. Such events might also include a military band and fireworks. It was a new experience, and the choir always performed well, earning fees of a level which would be most welcome today – 30 years later.

It was also the first time that the Phil benefitted from commercial sponsorship. A local company, Kall Kwik Printing run by John Turnbull and family, supported the choir for a number of years, during which time two family members also sang with the Kirkgate Ladies at 'Carols in Kirkgate'. Kall Kwik evolved into Inc Dot Ltd., and is still a print company used by the choir. There were also other opportunities for one-off sponsorships, for example, Prudential Assurance backed the Summer Concert in 1990.

A review of the concert programme for 1989 shows how this feeling of affluence had spread onto the city streets. Published in May and giving commitments up to December the list included:

Two bookings to entertain tourists in hotels
Three sings in city centre stores
14 (agreed with the city centre manager) 30-minute street sings in either the Coppergate Centre or Parliament Street.

These bookings were beneficial as 1989 was to be an expensive year, as the Phil planned to visit Münster to join in the Centenary celebrations of the Münsterscher Männergesangverein. £1000 had to be found to make the trip affordable, and so these money-raising events were welcomed. Those were, nevertheless, astonishing times. Given the right time of day and fair weather, a 30 minute sing in Parliament Street could earn £100 in bucket donations. No other six year period of the choir's life has compared to 1985-91 in this respect. As an example of changing times, in the austere days of 2015, the Phil did not go to entertain tourists in their hotels; rather occasional groups of visitors came to the choir and sat in during rehearsals.

This sense that events could be big and succeed was taken up by the Huddersfield Committee of the Yorkshire Cancer Research Campaign. In 1979 the four male voice choirs of Huddersfield: Colne Valley; Gledholt; Honley; and Skelmanthorpe came together to give a concert in support of the Yorkshire Cancer Research Campaign. This may not sound remarkable, but it was the first time that these successful local choirs had worked together. Demand for tickets was so high that two concerts were given in Huddersfield Town Hall and a total of £9000 was raised. This sparked an idea, which took some years to mature and three years to plan, and led, in 1987, to 1000 Male Voices from 25 choirs joining with the Brighouse and Rastrick Band in a concert in the Royal Albert Hall, London. The intention was to raise at least £25,000 for the charity. It was a great success, which rewarded the dedication, skill and confidence of the organising body, as well as the commitment of all who took part. Not surprisingly, given its size, it had a variety of musical 'moments'. The Yorkshire Post reported:

...although there were moments when even the dedicated attentions of the conductor, Mr William Renton, could not bring strictly into line the odd under-rehearsed and wayward choir.

But also wrote:

The choir was certainly capable of grandeur in plenty – Handel's 'Sound an Alarm', for instance – but the most telling singing was in a number of quieter items which included Sullivan's 'The Long Day Closes'.

The city of York was well represented as the Railway Institute Choir also attended. The Phil was proud to be there, and many singers still have the commemorative tie and tape cassette of the concert. The Phil returned to the Albert Hall to take part in both the 1991 and 1994 events, but the consensus was that 1987 had been the best.

Royal Albert Hall 1987

THE NORTHERN MALE VOICE CHOIR CHAMPIONSHIP

The most prestigious annual competition in the British Isles for male choirs

Five prizes:
£1,000, £750, £500, £300, £200

FOURTH CHAMPIONSHIP
14th MAY, 1988

HUDDERSFIELD TOWN HALL

Principal Sponsor:
YORKSHIRE BANK

Cassettes of the Third Championship on sale now at £2.85 each including postage and packing. Profits to be shared with Yorkshire Cancer Research Campaign. More information – Harry Woodhead, Tel. 0484 712965

Huddersfield was also the centre for the Northern Male Voice Championships. This advert appeared in the souvenir programme of the Royal Albert Hall concert.

As can be seen, this was a prestigious event with substantial prize money. It is also a credit to the organisers that they planned to make a profit and support Yorkshire Cancer Research.

In the style of the times, by 1992 the Northern Male Voice Championship had grown to be the National Male Voice Championship. The Phil took part in 1991, gaining fifth place, and in 1992 coming fourth. Unfortunately, from the point of view of the Phil, the Championship developed a traditional music festival 'disease'. The specially commissioned test pieces became very complex and hard to learn. More importantly, they had little audience appeal, and so were of no value to a choir like the Phil which placed concerts above competitions. Two photographs are shown below of '91 and '92. This gives an opportunity to see together the music team of Richard Bowman and Mary Stockdale and, a year later, Margaret Martin and Frances Hughes.

THE NORTHERN
MALE VOICE CHOIR CHAMPIONSHIP
SINGING ORDER
2
PROGRAMME ORDER
13

THE NATIONAL
MALE VOICE CHOIR CHAMPIONSHIP
SINGING ORDER
1
PROGRAMME ORDER
8

These photographs show again the comparatively small size of the choir when competing at this level. Richard Bowman had 46 singers on stage; Margaret had 56 and moved up a place in the results.

There were still the traditional regional competitions to enter and in these the choir, led by Richard Bowman, had considerable success:

Blackpool 1988: 1st place

Harrogate 1990: 1st place plus Best Choir in the Festival

The greatest success was achieved in Morecambe in 1989:

- Male Voice class A large choir: 1st place
- Male Voice Choir B small choir: 1st place
- Sacred Music Class: 1st place
- Best performers of the day
- Best Music Director of the day

This was a total of five trophies, an achievement recognised by this photograph in the York Evening Press:

Richard Bowman and Chairman John Addinall hold aloft the largest of the trophies won.

There was another contributing factor to the success of the choir that day. The actual date is not recorded, but within a year of his appointment Richard convinced (commanded) the choir to put away the folders and to sing without copies. The 'prop', the 'insurance policy' was taken away to the distress of some and the delight of others. Now the full attention of the choir could be given to the director and audience. The singing took on a fresh vitality. With all eyes on him, Richard was able to vary tempi, and to ask for greater dynamic contrast. It seems such a small change to make, but in terms of the ability to interpret and communicate, it was a significant advance.

Having spent time polishing these trophies before their return in 1990 the Phil had to compete again, winning both the sacred choral class and the prize for best choir in the festival.

In addition to the normal round of concerts, Richard was also able to enjoy the 25th Anniversary of 'Carols in Kirkgate'. He also led the choir in Münster in 1989 in the Centenary concert of the Münsterscher Männergesangverein, in which Nijmegen also performed. This concert was recorded, and so Richard achieved his first audio legacy. In 1990 this was followed by a tape cassette 'Music for Pleasure' containing 21 tracks, the first recording by the Phil for twelve years. The opening number was *A Yorkshire Welcome* composed by Bruce Taylor, a member who also composed carols for the children to sing in Kirkgate.

There was a more poignant moment in 1990, when choristers gathered around the hospital bed of founder member Henry Brough. 82 year old Henry had been a singer with the Phil for 65 years. He was a regular bass soloist with the choir, and his commitment had been an inspiration to many. For example, there was a time in the 1970s when doctors ordered him to take a rest from singing. He did as he was told, but still attended rehearsals so that he would know the music when able to return.

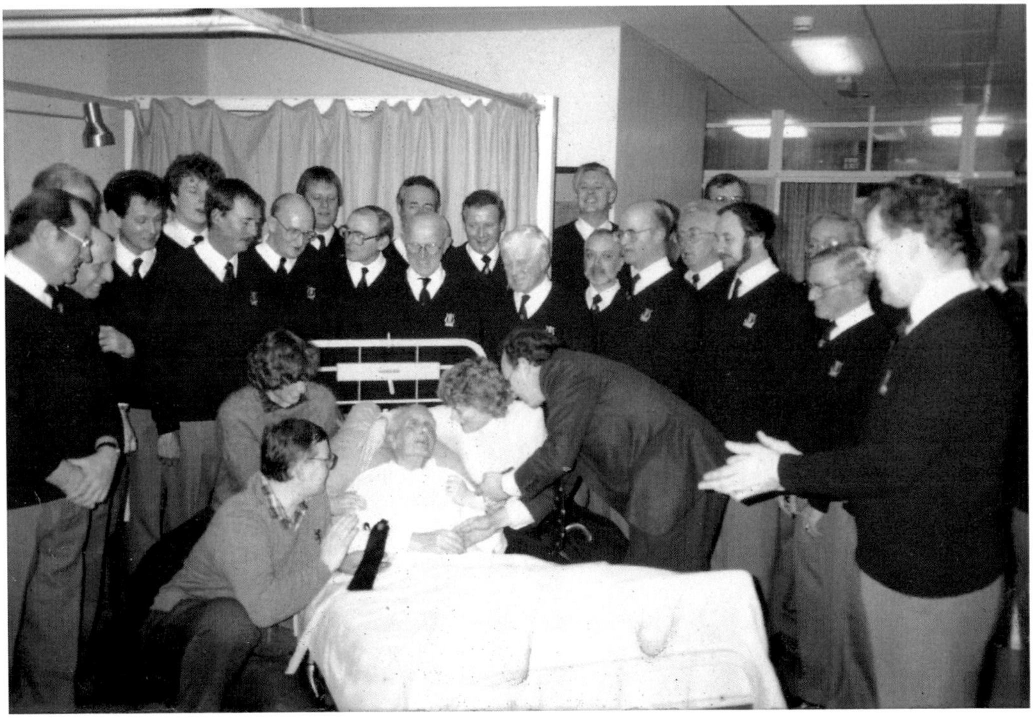

This photo shows Keith Wood presenting a silver salver to Henry marking his 65 years membership. Those gathered around the bed, from the left, are: Alan Price, son-in-law; Alison Brough, granddaughter; and Marianne Price daughter. Songs were sung and Henry joined in what was to be his last concert. As the YEP reported: *As the choir crowded round his bed, a smile broke across his face and he started to sing along.*

The first half of the decade had been rather listless; the second half was full of activity. The choir did not reach any new heights as in the Lister years, but enjoyed a number of new experiences.

The Summer Concert held in the Tempest Anderson Hall on Sunday 22nd July 1990 celebrated the 65th year of the choir. It was also the year that President, Keith Wood was Lord Mayor of York The concert also saw the start of the transition of music directors from Richard to Margaret Martin. Richard directed the choir, with Mary Stockdale as accompanist. The guest soloist was Frances Hughes, accompanied by Margaret Martin. By October of the following year those roles were reversed, when the music team had become Margaret Martin accompanied by Frances Hughes. Frances had already played for the choir a number of times when Mary Stockdale had not been available. This concert gave her an opportunity to step forward and sing. The review in the YEP written by Martin Dreyer is given here in full:

The Phil celebrated its 65th birthday last night with A Midsummer Medley of truly professional standard and scope before a packed house.

There are several remarkable features about this choir these days, which I do not recall from previous experience of it.

Not the least is that, even from a seat in the third row, it was impossible to detect a single individual voice, so smooth was the blend.

Furthermore, all music is sung by heart, so that all eyes are riveted to the conductor Richard Bowman, who thereby achieves very tight ensemble indeed.

Some 18 numbers ranged from a dramatic George Stead arrangement of 'Psalm 126', through operatic choruses by Adam and Gounod to several extracts from musicals, notably a zippy heartfelt 'There is nothing like a Dame'. And sentimentality never got a look in.

Just occasionally the transition from piano to forte is more bumpy than gradual, a result of enthusiastic anticipation over musical expediency. But balance that with impeccable tuning built upon a bass line of rich consistency: an unaccompanied account of the Haigh arrangement of 'The White Rose' was superbly controlled, the highlight of the evening.

Frances Hughes put her well rounded mezzo to excellent use in four operatic selections, while two choristers, James Waggott and Colin Hockridge weighed in with amusing interludes. Margaret Martin and Mary Stockdale alternated with more than competent piano accompaniments.

If you have not heard this choir recently, I recommend an early visit; you could be in for a delightful surprise.

There were 74 members in this 1990 choir, with 17 top tenors, 17 second tenors, 21 baritones and 19 basses, and it was in very good health. Unfortunately the choir never managed to sing with all 74 on stage. As shown above at the prestigious National championships in May 1991, there were only 46 on stage.

It was with a sadness that the choir learned of Richard's intention to stand down in the summer of 1991.

Chapter 8
Margaret Martin/Ian Colling
Safe Hands

Margaret Martin agreed to act as interim director whilst a replacement for Richard was recruited. She was an extremely accomplished performer, teacher, and producer. She had moved to York in 1985, and soon took on the role as conductor of York Opera Group. She knew how to get the best out of the Phil, and many would have liked her to stay. She holds the distinction of being the first woman to direct. She was, also, instrumental in bringing back another important woman in the Phil's life. Frances Hughes now lived in Wakefield, and some concern was expressed over possible travel difficulties she might experience during the week-long run of 'Carols in Kirkgate'. Margaret invited Eileen Grey (née Henderson) to renew her connections with the show, and to accompany the choir. Eileen came for that week and has never left.

In her short time, Margaret led the choir on two prestigious occasions. In October 1991 the Münsterscher Männergesangverein made a fourth visit. A confident Phil took the risk of booking the Barbican centre for the joint concert. This was the debut season for this 1500 seat venue, and the hire costs were considerable. The gamble paid off, as the concert attracted an audience of 1100. Margaret included *Drunken Sailor* in the programme, an arrangement by Richard Bowman. This was remarked upon by Charles Hunt the YEP reviewer:

The York choir, commendably alert to the direction of Margaret Martin bravely sang a German song in their first section. They shone brightest in their second set, with a moving rendition of Vaughan Williams 'Bushes and Briars' an exceptional unaccompanied 'The Wanderer' by Elgar and closed with a cheerful and lively 'Drunken Sailor'.

In May 1992 Margaret guided the choir to a commendable fourth place in the National Championships at Huddersfield. With the recruitment process completed and a new conductor appointed, Margaret was able to step down.

Her successor was a disaster and very short lived.

Ian Colling

Ian Colling (centre front) as director with Eileen Grey as accompanist

With the choir in an unexpected crisis, schoolteacher Ian Colling stepped out of the second tenors to 'reluctantly' take on the task. His tenure was short – about 18 months – as he then accepted a promotion and a new post in Northampton.

Ian was able to mark his stay by leading the October 1993 visit to Münster. This was a celebratory event, as it marked the 25th year of the twinning of the two choirs. He also directed two concerts in the Barbican centre. In July 1993 the choir was joined by the Grimethorpe Colliery band in a concert in aid of Arthritic Research, Martin House Children's Hospice and Killingbeck Hospital Leeds; and, with Ian conducting his last concert, in July 1994 the guest soloist was Maryetta Midgley, a regular performer on the Radio 2 show 'Friday Night is Music Night'. Given the right level of support from guest artists, the Phil was still prepared to risk booking this large venue.

Lord Mayors and Landlords

This part of our story has covered 31 years from 1962-1993. At the start an ambitious and talented young director had taken a competent, popular, local choir and turned it into an international success. Despite the frequent changes of conductor that followed, that reputation was never lost.

These years also saw the growth of an extensive support structure. The 'Perimeter' group and then the enlarged Vice President scheme played a significant part in the success of the Phil, as did the sponsorship of Kall Kwik and later Smith (Bros).

In 1986 there was a unique event in the choir's history, one which linked the choir to another of its support arms: – local pubs. The first inn mentioned in this narrative is the Jubilee in Leeman Road, where the choir took shelter in the early hours one Christmas morn. The City Arms (now no more) was also very important to the pre-war choir as the base for Inter-Choral Competitions, and the location for the 1935 tenth year dinner. In the late 60s and early 70s committee meetings were held in the Tiger Inn in Market Street, and for many years the Snickelway Inn in Goodramgate has been the post-rehearsal venue. But one hostelry was, and remains, particularly close to the choir's heart: The Blue Bell in Fossgate. There is a paradox in the fact that such a large body of men should be so attached to the smallest pub in the city, a grade 2 listed Edwardian gem. The clue lies with the redoubtable landlady from 1963-1991, Mrs Edith Pinder. As landlady and a 'York character' Mrs Pinder deserves a book of her own. Nevertheless any internet search today will find references to her, as per the one below:

Edith Pinder – the doyenne of York publicans who had lived and breathed her mini-empire since childhood and built up a huge loyalty among her clientele. Edith, though frail, was a formidable woman and never one to be crossed. Not only did she not suffer fools gladly – she didn't bother suffering them at all.

Edith Pinder was a great supporter of the choir, and was regarded with affection, indeed awe, by many choristers. At the annual dinner in 1986 she was made an Honorary Life Member. There are only four women who have ever been granted this award, three pianists and one publican, so this was, most certainly, a unique occasion.

Singers notch up 309 years of harmony

31st Oct 1986

SEVEN members of the York Philharmonic Male Voice Choir were presented with long-service awards at the choir's annual dinner at Alcuin College, York University.

They were, from left, Ces Rutherford, Andy Patterson, Reg Goodhall, Fred Clarke, Ernest Robinson and Henry Brough. Lance Dutton was unable to attend.

Outstanding

The singers have clocked up a combined 309 years of service and were praised for their outstanding dedication and commitment.

Mrs Edith Pinder, who runs the Blue Bell Inn, Fossgate, was made a life member of the choir in recognition of her contribution.

The choir's planned programme for the next three years includes singing at the Royal Albert Hall, London, in aid of cancer research in a 1,000 Yorkshire Male Voices Choir.

In recent years the Monday night post-rehearsal 'concerts' have attracted media interest as in this large picture and copy published by YEP in 2002.

Nowadays, with so many tourists in town together with the wide reach of social media, the choir finds itself being regularly filmed and photographed.

The support of sponsors and landlords/ladies has, and always will be, appreciated, but of greater long term significance has been the continual good relations with a succession of Lord Mayors.

The Lord Mayors only hold office for a year, but there have been many who have gone on to be either a President or Vice President of the choir. It is good to have this endorsement, and to feel part of the fabric of the city. In return the choir is always willing to respond to any requests for help. Support for the Lord Mayor's Christmas Cheer Fund first started in the 1930s and has been a regular feature since 1951.

No one person demonstrates this close link more than the Hon. Alderman Keith S. Wood. Keith is the President of the choir, a post he has held for some 35 years [it has been so long no one is sure of the start date]. His contributions to choir life appear in various parts of this narrative and have been (are) of immense value. He has provided practical help, in providing and operating stage lighting for 'Carols in Kirkgate'; organisational skills, particularly with regard to choir tours, and liaising with the City authorities; and is always available to offer 'wise counsel'.

The next two chapters tell the story of 'Carols in Kirkgate' and the twinning with the Münsterscher Männergesangverein, both on-going stories spanning many decades. The narrative then continues with the third and current generation.

Chapter 9

Carols in Kirkgate [1962-2012]
Christmas in Fossgate [2013-15]

Kirkgate in the Castle Museum

The relationship between the choir, the Castle Museum and Christmas began in 1956, when, in the words of the museum curator, the choir won praise for *...leading the carols at our Nativity Play.* The letter of thanks from the curator published by Archie Sargent in his memoirs gives the suggestion that the choir added to the event primarily by leading community carol singing ....'*We have received many expressions of appreciation from the public, and we are most grateful to you all for providing such a perfect conclusion to a memorable play. Having seen the same play performed without your choir, I am in an excellent position to judge the effect, and can only say that there is no comparison.*' Despite this success the Phil was not asked back.

However, the show conceived and launched in 1962 as 'Carols in Kirkgate' was different. It was not a Nativity presentation in the traditional manner, but was envisaged as a Victorian Christmas entertainment aimed at bringing life to the recreated Kirkgate Street within the museum. The curator who had the idea was Robert Patterson. He shared his thoughts with Eileen Robinson, a drama and history teacher, who worked at Beckfield Lane School with music teacher Brian Lister. Eileen and Brian were already well known in the city for their work with youth groups. For a number of years they had produced Christmas shows at Beckfield School. These attracted audiences from outside of the school; for example Janet Sargent wrote in her diary on 12/12/1957: *We went to Beckfield Nativity Play and Carols – enjoyed it immensely*. Outside the school, Brian and Eileen produced and directed the first stage production by the York Youth Light Opera Society, *The Gondoliers* at the Joseph Rowntree Theatre in 1959. Brian had become the music director of the York Philharmonic Male Voice Choir in June 1962, a choir in which Eileen's husband Ernest was a soloist member of the bass section. Hence all the links and experience were in place to respond to this request from Robert Patterson. The performers were to be the York Phil, the boys' choir from Beckfield School, and a string orchestra made up of pupils from Beckfield and Queen Anne schools [both now closed]. Readings were to be given by Peter Blanshard, and Dilys Fletcher was invited to sing a solo from the old stage coach. In addition to items from the performers there would be community carol singing, a tradition which is still part of the show. Permission to perform was required from the City Council [responsible for the Castle Museum until the creation of York Museums Trust in 2002]. Robert Patterson approached the Castle Museum Committee and the following minute of a meeting held on the 5/11/62 planted the seeds of what became part of York's social history.

Your committee are arranging for carol singing by a choir at the museum on one evening before Christmas at which a collection will be taken for the Lord Mayor's Freedom from Hunger Campaign.

It is interesting how this short minute describes the event simply as 'carol singing'; but it also suggests, by the phrase *singing by a choir,* that it was the Phil, and not the school, which had made the request.

The one night was Thursday December 20th 1962, and the performance was called 'Carols in Kirkgate'. The York Evening Press (YEP) gave a full account of the evening, reporting that more than 500 people attended. This was an astonishing number when you consider that in recent years [with everyone seated and on the advice of fire officers] audience numbers have only been 160. Here is the report from the YEP of 21/12/1962.

Old-World scene at Carols in Kirkgate

A 'Carols in Kirkgate' concert held in the famous street in York's Castle Museum last night attracted more than 500 people. A truly old-world scene was reproduced with old fashioned dress, the cobbles powdered with snow, and members of the staff wearing authentic Victorian costumes.

Taking part was a section of the York Philharmonic Male Voice Choir, and part of the boys' choir from Beckfield School. Pupils from Queen Anne's and Beckfield Schools made up a string orchestra with Bernard Roberts (viola), Michael Walker (cello), George Rowlands (oboe), and Peter Broadbent (horn).

Readings were given by Peter Blanshard and Dilys Fletcher sang a solo from the old stage coach. Other singers were Reg Goodhall (tenor), Neil Thompson, Jamie Tristram, and Graham Firth (boy sopranos).

The museum's harpsichord which has just been completely restrung and restored to perfect playing condition, was played, for the first time, by Mr Richard Lister of Beckfield School, who also directed the concert.

Admission to the museum was free but a collection was taken.

Candle fairy lights, the fore-runners of the electric type, which consist of night lights dropped into coloured glass jars specially made for the purpose, provided attractive colouring to the scene.

The concert was arranged by Mrs Eileen Robinson of Beckfield School.

The event raised £37 6s for the Lord Mayor of York's freedom from Hunger Fund.

Dilys Fletcher and Graham Firth were also members of the Youth Light Opera. Although, historically, credit is given to the Phil for this production it could, perhaps, have been billed as Beckfield School with the York Philharmonic Male Voice choir, as the men were not the most significant contributors to the evening.

A shorter review carried by the Yorkshire Post (21/12/1962) also gave credit to the younger performers:

Carols in Kirkgate

Scenes from old worlde Christmas cards came to life in York last night when the city's most famous street – Kirkgate in the Castle Museum – was used for public carol singing. Never has a first venture been so warmly supported.

Every inch of the cobbled street was occupied by lusty carols singers. Nearly 600 people crammed into Kirkgate and its environs.

It had all the atmosphere of a Dickensian setting – museum staff dressed in period costume, members of the York Philharmonic Male Voice Choir in top hats and mufflers, and school boys perched on top of a stage coach. At one point an ostler in apron and breeches served the male choristers with what must have been mulled ale in pewter tankards.

Richard Lister, who directed the singing, accompanied the soloist on the harpsichord. He was given an excellent response by the boys from the Beckfield School choir and instrumentalists from the Queen Anne Grammar and Beckfield school orchestras.

Without a doubt the experienced team of Brian Lister and Eileen Robinson had put on a 'professional' show.

It seemed assured that there would be a repeat performance in 1963. The Castle Museum committee gave permission for two performances in 1963, but with one key condition: audience numbers were limited to 300. The shows were still free to enter, with the collection going to Oxfam. This raised £41 14s 8d, not much higher than 1962, but then audience numbers were similar despite the extra performance.

A large picture and report was carried in the Daily Express – a national daily – although this, with Fleet Street 'accuracy', attributed the Dickensian scene to the 18th rather than 19th century.

The report in the York Evening Press, also accompanied by a large picture, gave a much more descriptive account:

Magnificent carol singing in York's Old Kirkgate

There are some entertainments which, in any city but York, would cost hundreds of pounds to stage and thus call for – and get – admission fees in guineas. York sets up these entertainments casually, in some of the historic surroundings, which form part of our everyday lives here, and gives them away free.

One such event was presented last night at the Castle museum at the annual Carols in Kirkgate.

The museum's famous replica street was the background for the carolling, and a capacity audience enjoyed and shared, a programme of singing led by York Philharmonic Male Voice Choir, and boys of Beckfield Lane School, led by Richard B. Lister.

The programme included a collection for Oxfam, and the producer Stanley Davey skilfully used the setting to present the Holy songs in the form of a parable, both of the Christmas story and the campaigns against world want today.

The entertainment opened to the cry of a traditional night watchman proclaiming the hour and "Alls Well". All was not well with everyone, however, for the next figure to appear was a barefoot ragged urchin, full of high spirits, but cold, hungry and timid.

This preliminary sketch ended with the urchin discovered by a Victorian family much more prosperous than himself, presented with a Christmas gift and led away, presumably, for shelter and feeding.

Then came the carollers. The boys of the school choir swarmed aboard Kirkgate's old mail coach, and perched there for the rest of the programme singing cheerfully and tunefully.

The Philharmonic choir wore Dickensian dress with mufflers and high hats, and sang magnificently.

Soloists were Dilys Fletcher (contralto), Reg Goodhall (tenor), and trebles Graham Firth, Trevor Cooper, John Saggers and Neil Thomson. With the vocalists was accompaniment from a 12 piece orchestra of violins, viola, cello, harpsichord and oboe, led by Ronald Easey.

Carols – some solo, some sung by the choir, and some sung by choir and audience together, included some very old ones such as, 'The Coventry Carol', 'The Holly and the Ivy', and 'God rest ye merry Gentlemen', and even the older pagan, 'Here we come a wassailing'.

Later favourites such as 'Silent Night', 'Good King Wenceslas', and 'Adeste Fidelis" were also sung. The orchestra played the second movement of Avison's 'concerto in E minor', and Peter Blanshard, as 'continuity man' agreeably linked the musical items with brief ceremonial and with some well-chosen spoken Christmas verse.

The performers and the staff were thanked by Coun. P.Gales (Vice-chairman of the Castle Museum Committee).

There is to be a second performance tonight. Accommodation is limited to about 300 and all admission programmes have now been taken up.

There was an enforced change to the production team in 1963. Eileen Robinson was unable to continue, and the role of producer passed to Stanley Davey. He was the deputy head at Beckfield and produced the Kirkgate shows for many years; until at least 1976.

Large press photos accompanied the articles in 1962/3, but our copies are not of a quality fit to reproduce. Here are photos from 1964. One published by YEP, and taken during the performance, looks out from the back of the choir towards the conductor Brian Lister. The soloist and reader can be seen on the balcony above Brian. The orchestra and harpsichord are in an alcove, [now reconfigured as a toy shop] to the conductor's right.

The second appeared in the Yorkshire Post and is a composed shot taken during rehearsal.

In 1964, two performances became three with another significant change – the proceeds were now to go to the Lord Mayor and Sheriff's Christmas Cheer Fund.

Your committee have agreed that carol singing should take place in the street at the museum on the 16th17th and 18th of December 1964 at 8pm. Admission will be free but a collection will be taken for the Lord Mayor and Sheriff's Christmas Cheer Fund. [Minutes 4/11/1964]

The Phil had first supported this fund back in 1932, and had been supporting it with an annual autumn concert for more than 10 years. It seemed appropriate that this potentially lucrative event should support such a popular local cause. The fund provides a Christmas meal for elderly residents of York, so it was appropriate that money should also be raised via Christmas events. Carols in Kirkgate supported the fund from 1964 to 2002 when responsibility for the museum transferred to the York Museums Trust.

The producer was Stanley Davey; the soloists, for this third year, were Gwen Rennison (contralto), Charles Croft (tenor), Reg Goodhall (tenor), Frank Morton (bass), Graham Firth, Stuart Thomson, Trevor Cooper and Terry Nicholson (boy sopranos). Trevor Cooper, now in his second year as a boy soloist, joined the ranks of the Phil as soon as his adult voice settled.

The YEP reported...*This was the third year of the effort. Last year there were two nightly performances. Such is the popularity that the entertainment will be repeated tonight and tomorrow. Next year it may be a week.*

The Civic party was present. There were also other members of the City Council, including Coun. R. Pulley, Chairman of the Castle Museum Committee.

At the end of the splendid programme the Sheriff Coun. J.E.Coleclough, proposed a vote of thanks to the Committee, the Curator, the Museum staff, the choirs, soloists, orchestra and others, including officials.

"This beautiful and wonderful Carol service", he said, "is really a memorial to Mrs. Eileen Robinson, its pioneer, who did so much for this effort".

Eileen Robinson, teacher, actress, producer, originator of this show, and wife to Ernest – bass singer with the Phil – had died during 1964.

The YEP, in 1964, was not quite accurate in the prediction made for 1965. The show did not run for a week but did add another night – making it four performances. The show was still free entry in 1965 and the museum harpsichord was still being used, now played by the accompanist to the Phil, Lloyd D. Smith. Press interest was still high as it offered good photo opportunities. The local press was already describing Carols in Kirkgate as a regular established feature of Christmas in York even though it was only in its fourth year. The Sunday Express gave it national coverage on 19/12/1965. This added detail, not reported locally, of the number of performers – 70.

In 1966 'free entry with a collection' was replaced by pre-sold tickets. Unfortunately, no council minute has been found giving the amount to be charged. This change did not add greatly to the workload of the museum staff, as there was already a ticketing system in place; demand for places always exceeded supply. In those early years when admission was free, allocation was limited to two tickets per person. There are reports of people rushing to rejoin the queue in the hope of getting a second allocation.

In the same way that the show itself was quickly accepted as being part of a York Christmas, so too did the buying of the tickets become part of the ritual. The York Press reported, from 1966 onwards how 'all tickets sold out within hours'. The date when tickets would go on sale was always published, and there were always long queues, irrespective of the weather. This press photo from 1978 is typical.

Tickets to spare as cold cuts queue

A HUNDRED people braved the freezing fog this morning to queue for tickets for the popular Carols in Kirkgate concert, given by the York Philharmonic Male Voice Choir, in the Castle Museum, York.

But the queue was "not as big as usual," said a Museum spokesman. For the first time ever there were tickets left when everyone in the queue had been served.

The four-day concert is usually sold out by 10 a.m. on the first morning that tickets are issued.

The pre-Christmas attraction will be held on December 13, 14, 15 and 16.

The YEP report of 15/12/1966 records how the performance was still evolving:

...Music Director Richard Lister produced some memorable singing from the combined choirs, whose repertoire included some lesser known old English carols, specially arranged for the occasion.

The soloists, Jean Townson and Reg Goodhall, had appropriate positions of prominence on one of the balconies overlooking the street scene – and one of the museum's veteran stagecoaches proved a useful choir-stall.

Expertly produced by Stanley Davey, the concert will go on each night to capacity audiences. All the tickets were sold weeks in advance.

The debate on the size of the audience had, for the time-being, been agreed at 400, still a large number for the space available. The Press also reflected the fact that many people were not sure how to describe the show. This 1966 YEP review is headed: *Christmas card scene at York carol service.* In the early years it was often referred to as a service – something it had never sought to be, even though it was a very good way of telling the Christmas Story. It was also described as a show, a concert and an entertainment, all equally valid.

This report is also the first public acknowledgement that old carols were being specially arranged by Brian Lister, arrangements still used today.

Jean Townson, the soprano soloist, often sang with the Phil, and was a member of the York Light Opera. She was, later, able to reach a larger audience, as she was the soloist on the 1970 Yorkshire TV recording of the show (described below).

1966 also saw the Phil accept another invitation to sing carols, this time from the landlord of The Three Cups Inn in Stamford Bridge. It was described as a chance for people who had not been able to get tickets for Kirkgate to hear the choir. It also seems to have been a good idea for a night out, as shown in this YEP photo.

Thirsty work, carol singing

Welcome refreshment after an hour's hearty carol singing for, left to right, Ray Shoebridge, Ernest Robinson and Trevor Henderson, three members of York Male Voice Choir which sang at the Three Cups Inn, Stamford Bridge, in aid of the Lord Mayor and Sheriff's Christmas Cheer Fund.

In date order, the subsequent innovations were greater than anyone might have expected. The most significant came in 1968, with a request from Yorkshire Television to broadcast the show. A 25 minute recording was transmitted at 11.30 pm on Christmas Eve 1968, followed by Midnight Mass from Largs in Ayrshire. It was shown again at the same time in 1969. This was a black and white recording which featured both choirs and had a participating audience of 200. In style it must have been similar to 'Songs of Praise' on the BBC. Unfortunately the TV Times in 1968 described the school choir as Beckwith not Beckfield. This did not, however, detract from its appeal to the viewers. We do not have a copy of this recording but it must have been well received because the producer, Graham Watts, returned in 1971 to make a 60 minute colour recording, which was first transmitted at 8.15 am on Christmas Morning 1971. This, comparatively expensive venture by Yorkshire TV paid off, as the show was broadcast annually until Christmas Day 1974. The show was also broadcast in Holland and Germany. The choir has a DVD copy provided by Yorkshire TV in 2010. It is a quality recording which, when played now, is easy to watch and does not seem dated. We need to remember that in 1971 many viewers would be watching on small screen, low definition, black and white sets. There were also households without a TV. Mrs. Barbara Lister recalls that she and Brian bought their first TV in order to watch this broadcast.

The YEP on 10/12/1971 gave this account of the planned recording, once again emphasising the fact that it was to be in colour:

York Phil nationwide – in colour

The York Philharmonic Male Voice Choir will be seen nation-wide over the Christmas period in a colour-televised version of its Carols in Kirkgate concert.

The concert, to be recorded in the Castle Museum Street's Victorian setting on Sunday week, will be sandwiched between the five nights of public concerts, to be presented by the choir from next Wednesday.

The recording will be made by Yorkshire Television but will not feature an 'audience' as in previous black and white recordings.

The new television presentation will have a distinctly Yorkshire flavour featuring several carols that were popular in the county during the 19th century. Among the more interesting interpretations will be the 'Ilkley Moor' rendering of 'While Shepherds Watched'.

Mr. Richard Lister, choir director, told the Evening Press that different locations of Kirkgate would be used for the new presentation including several of the shops. Groups of the choir will be placed in different parts of the street, ensuring that cameras will exploit the full potential of the location.

The choir is also well known in competition and on radio and recently recorded for the BBC 'Let the People sing' competition which it won last year.

The YEP also promoted the programme when, in its Christmas Eve edition, it reported:

This year's Carols in Kirkgate Concerts presented by York Philharmonic Male Voice Choir in the Castle Museum raised the record total of £342 for the Lord Mayor's Christmas Cheer Fund. The concerts have been held for ten years and during the last eight years £1320 has been raised for this charity. The accolade for the best singing audience this year goes to the Saturday night audience says choir director Mr Richard Lister.

The carols will be featured in colour tomorrow morning at 8.15am on the ITV network.

This year the TV Times did spell the name of the school correctly.

So, on the Sunday morning, after a good show the night before, the choirs, soloists and a brass quartet turned up early at the museum, ready for a long day's work.

Watching the DVD now, on modern equipment, and listening through headphones, is to realise that the choir would have to work hard these days to achieve the visual standards demanded of a modern TV programme. The musical standards of 1971 were excellent, the presentation skills less so. The flaws which 1970s TV sets would not reveal – singers not knowing the words or looking around at the wrong time – became apparent.

We have a number of singers in the choir today who took part in that recording and are able to add to the story; but a striking feature of the recording is its authenticity. At no point was the performance enhanced by the introduction of any professional actors, singers or musicians. The readers were Peter Blanshard, and an unnamed schoolboy; the soloist was Jean Townson, and the four local bandsmen were Brian Parker, Alfred Field, George Pratt and G.P. Dinsdale. Baritone Malcolm Raw played the Watchman, and Tony Sawyer, Ian Woods, Reg Goodhall, Don Crawford and Jim Waggott all took solo lines. The young and comparatively inexperienced Jim, playing the second king in *We Three Kings,* looked anxious, as the camera zoomed in on him. Tenor Ossie Gillery and bass Fred Clarke sang in a quartet, and one of the boys played the butler. The Beckfield choir was now mixed giving greater authenticity to family scenes, and the girls' dresses added to the colour spectacle. The setting was authentic, including use of the Victorian parlour in the museum, whilst none of the music had been composed later than 1860. It was a good, realistic, amateur production professionally recorded, and as such merited its inclusion in the national Christmas schedules for a number of years. Any amateur choir would be proud of such an achievement and the Phil is no exception to that rule.

Late in the show one of the Beckfield boys, perched on the stagecoach, gave a reading. Only when listening through headphones can you hear at the end of this speech a relieved male cry of "Well read lad!" Frank Caine, a young baritone at the time, recalls that the filming had to be done in one day, and the sound team were adamant they were finishing at 8pm. The boy doing this final reading kept making errors and the clock was ticking, explaining the relief when the reading was correct. It may also explain why, on the DVD, the boy sat next to this young reader looks to be struggling to stay awake. Frank also remembers that a high wind had developed during the day. The museum roof, at that time, tended to rattle somewhat in such conditions which must have given the sound team extra problems. Frank recalls that at one point a piece of glass in the roof shattered and fell in front of the choir. Thankfully no one was injured, and with a nod to health and safety, the mess was swept up and filming continued. Jim Waggott remembers that, in the already established tradition of Kirkgate, Yorkshire TV provided a sustaining barrel of beer, which led, late on in the day, to an exasperated director calling for make up to do something about 'that man's red nose'. It was a 12 hour day and described by one chorister as being *tiresome, fatiguing and at times, exasperating.* All of which was instantly forgotten in the pleasure of watching the transmission that Christmas morn.

In 1970, sandwiched between these two recordings, came yet another significant change. An extra performance was added on the Monday of the following week. This was the time when *Monday night is choir night* was introduced, a private performance for choir families. Adding another night, not open to the public, was the only way in which Brian and the committee could ensure that choir families could get a ticket. The active group of choir supporters 'Perimeter' noted this change in its review of 1970 published in *Perimeter Post:*

The response to 'Carols in Kirkgate' is always so overwhelming that this year the choir put on a special performance just for their friends and Perimeter, thus enabling more tickets to be sold to the public, and we had our own special show. This was a great success and was,

I am sure, one of our main reasons for such a rise in membership ('Perimeter' membership rose from 147 to 195 members during the year). But as both the Lord Mayor and Sheriff's Christmas Cheer Fund and our own funds benefitted, we thought it an excellent thing.

The private evening also gave the opportunity for an end of the run party, and so Monday night became known as party night, and instantly became part of these annual celebrations.

1973 saw another variation, successful for that year, but one not repeated. Two Minster Choristers, Jonathan Boatfield and Andrew Walsh, were invited as soloists in place of the customary female singers. The two boys sang on alternate nights.

In the early years, the last major changes to the show came in 1975. Beckfield School no longer took part and the Kirkgate Ladies choir was introduced. The museum also withdrew its stock of costumes, and the fragile stagecoaches were no longer to be loaded up with schoolboys. A pattern was then established which stayed in place until the last performance in 2012, some 37 years later.

The Beckfield School choir left a legacy in the form of the Yorkshire TV programme and, in 1974, the first LP 'Carols in Kirkgate'. The debt owed to the staff and pupils of Beckfield School [which subsequently closed] is considerable. Eileen Robinson and Brian Lister, the originators of the show, were both teachers there. Stan Davey who took over the production was deputy head, and the school choir took part for 12 years. But the Beckfield legacy continues as Julie Watson, a singer with the Kirkgate Ladies, and wife of tenor Steve, first took part as a member of the Beckfield School choir.

The rest of this story does not follow a strict timeline but considers aspects of the show.

Concert style

The style of the concerts was set early on and has remained consistent. The readings used in early years are interesting because it seems they were often 'ghost stories'. Eileen Robinson invited Peter Blanshard, not a choir member, to take part in the very first performance. He was an actor with the Settlement Players (as was Eileen), and also worked with a few friends in providing Victorian themed evening entertainments. He was ideally suited to the role of reader, and is remembered for giving a powerful rendition of a ghost story. It is easy to imagine the impact of his reading in the dimly lit atmosphere of Kirkgate, a tale of hangings on the Knavesmire. This was certainly not a Christmas theme, showing once again how the show, from the outset, was a Victorian themed entertainment rather than a carol service. Peter stayed as reader for many years so his contributions must have been well liked by the audiences.

For several years the boys choir used to sit in and on the stagecoach for the whole performance, giving the suggestion that they were travelling home from school for the Christmas holiday. In those early years there were no stage props, and Ossie Gillery [a retired chorister who sang in the very first performance] recalls that a real turkey was used. This was to be passed by one boy at floor level to another on the top of the coach. One time, however, rather than pushing from below the boy on top pulled the turkey up by its neck – which stretched but did not break. As a consequence of this another young chorister, on a lower level, spent the whole show with the head and extended neck of the bird resting on his collar.

Concerts always began at 8 pm with the Street clock striking eight, the night watchman ringing his bell, and declaring 'All's Well'. More recently the night watchman has had to also cry out the fire evacuation procedures, as well as a plea for mobile phones to be turned off. Since 2011 the start time has been brought forward to 7.30 pm to fit more with modern schedules, a decision made easier by the sad demise of the street clock.

Music

The mix of music – male voice, mixed voice, solo, quartets, duets, community singing – has remained constant although the repertoire has been updated. Brian Lister's original decision that nothing post-Victorian was sung was gradually set aside; for example the introduction in 1986/7 of *Mary's Boy Child,* a hit in 1957 and popular ever since, was very well received. Further additions have included, as a secular piece, *Silver Bells,* and the excellent carols of John Rutter.

In 1964 the programme included: *Coventry Carol; Polish Lullaby; Here we come a Wassailing; Hark the Herald angels Sing; Good king Wenceslas; O come all ye faithful; Silent Night;* and *God rest ye merry Gentlemen.* With the exception of *God rest ye merry Gentlemen* and the *Polish Lullaby,* all the others have been sung in recent years. The choir has also been fortunate in having been led by some talented musicians. Brian Lister was an excellent arranger of music for male voice and his 1969 arrangement of *Silent Night* has been almost a constant part of the show. Berry Lewis' arrangement of *O Holy Night* is now held in the same light. She has also arranged *In the Bleak Mid Winter* and *Once in Royal David's City* in most innovative ways.

Given that there are so many favourites there is a challenge every year in varying the programme. Berenice (Berry) Lewis [Music Director since 2000] introduces at least one new or one rearranged carol each year, which means that some favourites occasionally get a year off. In 2011 to celebrate the 50th year the choir commissioned *The Kirkgate Carol* from Yorkshire composer and arranger Alan Simmons. This piece draws its inspiration from the magnificence of York Minster and the pioneering and enduring social work of Joseph and Seebohm Rowntree.

Since leaving the Castle museum in 2013, the Victorian link has been broken, making it even easier to introduce modern music. In 2015 the Phil was pleased to be able to give one of the first public performances of *Somewhere in the Darkness* by Tom Wells. It was well received and will, no doubt, be heard again. The old and familiar carols can work well with new and previously unheard pieces.

In the 1960s most of the programme was sung unaccompanied, with the men dressed mostly in black. Eileen Grey, who as a student first saw the show in 1963, remembers that this could make the performances seem dull. Until 1976, following on from the first school orchestra, a string section would often accompany the community carols. The last such group was the Waits Strings – leader Hazel Harrison. In some ways a small string section was easy to stage, but a piano was more practical. However, this did present some challenges.

In the pre-electric age, providing a piano was not easy. An upright was squeezed into the corner of the street by the water trough. The cobbles gave some challenges to positioning and it was never considered, by those who played it, to be the most comfortable place they had ever sat. Transporting and tuning pianos is a specialist business and in this regard the choir has been fortunate over many years to have enjoyed the support of Mr. John Oxberry. John supplied and tuned the piano up to 2007 when, with the change to hired staging, we switched to using our own easily transportable, electric stage piano.

Back in 1975 when the Beckfield choir gave way to the Kirkgate singers and primary school choirs and a piano were introduced, Brian Lister was able to give the show a lift, including the introduction of a Ladies' choir. The story of the Kirkgate Ladies is well known as our accompanist and Honorary Life Member, Eileen Grey, as Eileen Henderson, was instrumental in setting up the group.

Female soloists had always played a part in the show. A pattern was established whereby she sang two carols plus a solo verse in *In the Bleak Mid Winter*. Eileen who had done this in 1974 and 1975 also sang in other concerts. She was a member of 'The York Madrigal Group', which had first sung with the Phil in 1968. They were much admired by Brian Lister, and he invited Eileen to recruit a small choir of ladies, not only to take over the role of the school children, but also to give a lift and different perspective to the performances. Eileen's recruits were singers with either the Madrigal Group or City Opera, and so was established the practice of these singers coming together once a year just to take part in Carols in Kirkgate. During this transitional time, children still played a part, being mostly the sons and daughters of members. In 1991 Eileen became accompanist and her contribution to carols in this capacity continues to this day.

The Kirkgate Ladies have been a vital feature to the show for forty years and yet, as an 'occasional' group, have no records of members or any history outside of the show – with one exception. They joined the Phil in a concert at The Tom Stoppard Centre in Pocklington in September 2002. Through the years the group has been made up of old and new friends, of mothers and daughters, of former members of Beckfield school choir, and wives of choir members. Acknowledged and respected collectively, the individual members have always been 'hidden'. The Phil is extremely grateful to all those past and present that have done so much to enhance the show.

Chairman Brian Allinson and the Kirkgate singers 1985

This article from the YEP in 2007 shows Julie Watson who started singing in the show, as a schoolgirl in 1972. She is now a core member of the sopranos, where she sings alongside Katrina Knowles with both of them keeping an eye on their husbands, respectively Steve a top tenor, and Terry a bass. [Quiz: Spot the errors in this YEP copy]

The Press www.yorkpress.co.uk

RIGHT NOTE: Jules Watson, centre, tunes up for Christmas with Ian Burks and Lorna Siddons

Below: The 1974 Carols In Kirkgate LP

Picture: Frank Dwyer

Christmas presence for Jules

A VOICE of Christmas past is gearing up for one of York's best-loved yuletide traditions this week.

Jules Watson, 48, of Acomb, was only 13 when she started singing at the annual carol concert at York Castle Museum, and two years later was recorded on the first Carols In Kirkgate LP in 1974.

Jules, who will be belting out seasonal songs with the other Kirkgate Singers and the York Philharmonic Male Voice Choir in December, was also filmed for the Tyne Tees television event in the early 1970s.

She said: "We have a good blend of carols. Some of the arrangements for the Kirkgate Singers are far more technical than they have been in the past but, in contrast to that, some of the more straightforward arrangements can be the most effective. The sound is magic and really sets the mood for Christmas."

"We also used to wear original garments from the museum's collections, but because these are so rare and valuable these days, we now have to wear replicas."

Lee Clark, of the museum, said: "Carols In Kirkgate marks the beginning of the Christmas period because it really gets people in a festive spirit. People come from all over the country to enjoy it and find they can listen to some carols and get some Christmas shopping while they are in York."

The Carols In Kirkgate event first took place 35 years ago and runs this year from December 4 to December 8, and on Tuesday, December 11.

Tickets, including the souvenier programme, cost £12 for adults and £10 for children and are available, from Monday, at the museum's admissions desk, or from Tuesday by phoning 01904 650333.

Primary School Choirs: 1975 – c.2005

Although the senior school choir had been replaced by the Kirkgate Ladies, the Phil strove to maintain the contribution of a children's choir by working with a number of primary schools. There is, however, some doubt as to the order in which they contributed and for how many years, particularly with regard to 1975-1985.

Three made a significant contribution to the concerts; New Earswick Primary, St Barnabas Primary, and Hempland. Copmanthorpe Primary also sent a good choir in 1995, but was unable to continue the support.

From 1985-1990 Richard Bowman was Music Director of the choir. He was also a teacher at New Earswick Primary. Their choir sang successfully for some years in the early 1980s.

St Barnabas sang for several years from 1987 [or earlier] to 1995. Their choir was coached by teacher Mary Cox, who has sung with the Kirkgate Ladies since 1985, and acts as the coordinator between the Ladies group and the Phil, supports

Eileen as a page turner, and is married to tenor Steve. During the time that St Barnabas took part, both of Mary and Steve's children participated. In the choir music library is the *Starlight Carol*, composed by Bruce Taylor and his wife Megan for the children of St Barnabas. Bruce, a second tenor who sadly died young, wrote the music, with the words by Megan. She was deputy head at St Barnabas, and with Bruce made the contribution by the school possible. She used to drive the minibus to transport the children and looked after them backstage whilst Bruce accompanied on the piano.

Museum gets spirit of Christmas present

HERE'S a Christmas scene which looks as if it has stepped straight out of a Dickens' novel.

The Kirkgate Carol Evenings, at York's Castle Museum, have been as much part of the festive season as turkey and mince pies for more than 25 years. Tickets ran out before the first performance this week.

The assembled choir, who ran through a series of the best-loved carols, was made up of the York Philharmonic Male Voice Choir, the women of the Kirkgate Singers and children from St Barnabas' School, Leeman Road, York.

All proceeds from the concerts, which continue tonight, tomorrow and finish next Tuesday, go to the Lord Mayor's Christmas Cheer Fund.

St Barnabas School 1990

In 1996 the baton passed to Hempland School and introduced teacher Allan Wilkinson to the choir. Allan, a second tenor and former chairman, coached and accompanied Hempland. Allan remembers the support he received from colleagues and from parents, in ensuring that the choir was up to standard, and that the children were safely looked after and transported. He recalls accepting all children who genuinely wanted to take part which did, on occasion, stretch his abilities as coach. Allan continued to coach this choir for 2/3 years after his retirement, but it became too difficult to maintain standards, and the tradition of involving primary school choirs came to a close. In 2011 whilst recalling these times Allan wrote:

Actually taking part was a fantastic opportunity and experience for the children, one which so many of them used to write about in their 'favourite' memories before they left school. They loved the dressing up, performing and the whole atmosphere of Kirkgate. I used to have groups of 25 organised for each night but I invariably had children waiting at the gate for me each morning as I arrived at school asking if they could do extra nights – they really were so keen and enthusiastic.

Readings and Drama

In the early years, Peter Blanshard read a ghostly tale of hangings on the Knavesmire, and the scene was set by the urchin in the street being rescued. The stories changed, and extracts from Charles Dickens were introduced. By 1976 Graham Hudson, one of our basses, now a life member, but then newly joined, was reading extracts from *A Christmas Carol*. Over the years a number of different themes were introduced, including one in which Queen Victoria processed through the crowds and then looked down on her subjects from a throne on the balcony. The late Jim Rayne, another member of the bass section and a former chairman, was the last to read from the balcony. Getting access was always difficult and it fell foul of heightened Health and Safety guidelines.

In the late 1990s, in order to vary the format, Neil Wood, drama teacher and baritone, wrote and produced a Christmas Story used for two or three years incorporating all the choirs and involving the children from Hempland Junior School.

Over the years the mood of the readings has become more light-hearted and has included sketches, short pantomimes e.g. a 'two minute Cinderella', and the introduction of Tom Lehrer's satirical *'Christmas Song'* so reflecting changing tastes and expectations. This more relaxed style has encouraged members to write material for the show, especially Joe Rutherford. We have been fortunate, through the years, in having a number of members who have taken on the role of director. In recent years this has been shared by two tenors, David Pike and Ian Reavill.

Appearance

The decision to stop using the costume collection for theatrical purposes was, perhaps, overdue. The risk of damage to the stock was considerable, particularly given that most of the choir were physically bigger than our Victorian forebears. So 1975 saw the gradual move towards the hiring of costume and the end of what Peter Evans remembers as *"the general lack of colour in the 1960s – most of us were dressed in black even in the 1970 colour tv recording"*. The move to hired costume was gradual; for example, this writer first sang in 1975, and for a number of years wore his own double breasted, long, brown, herringboned patterned overcoat, the height of fashion in 1970. This was finished off with a colourful cravat home-made from left over curtain material. It then became the norm to hire costumes in a mix of styles, with gentleman, military, police, artisan and urchin all bringing colour to the show. The ladies were always dressed well and the overall effect was enhanced by the introduction of stage lighting.

The Museum committee meeting minutes for 1975 are of particular interest.

19/07/1975

The Curator of the Castle Museum reported that there would be performances of Carols in Kirkgate at the Castle Museum from the 17th to the 20th December and on the 22nd December 1975.

Resolved: That in view of the committee's previous decision that the use of the costume collection for theatrical purposes be prohibited, the Curator of the Castle Museum should consult with the promoters on the question of costumes for these performances.

Another minute from later that year tells us that admission charges were still low.

05/10/1975

The Curator of the Castle Museum reported that the promoters of 'Carols in Kirkgate' had asked whether consideration could be given to increasing the admission charge for this event in order to meet their increased expenses.

The Curator reminded the Committee that the charge is 30p and the proceeds are donated to the Lord Mayor's Christmas Cheer Fund.

Resolved: That the admission charge be increased to 50p and the choir's expenses be met from the income on ticket sales, the balance to be donated to the LMCCF.

Audio Recordings

During the years that the TV programme was being shown a decision was taken to make an LP under the title 'Carols in Kirkgate'. In 1974 a collection of 12 carols was recorded with the Beckfield choir [now a mix of girls and boys]. Beckfield School choir had been a constant part of 'Carols' yet this was to be their last contribution, so it was fitting that it should be in the form of a recording. The work was done in the church at Bishop Wilton, and Ossie Gillery recalls that one of the frustrations of the day came from RAF jets passing overhead at all the wrong times.

The continuity and commitment that has always been part of 'Carols' is illustrated on the cover of this LP. The photograph shows a young male chorister standing alongside tenor soloist Reg Goodall. The young man is Trevor Cooper, who ten years earlier had been named in the Press report of December 1964 as one of the boy soloists. In 1976 another recording was made, this time in the chapel at York St. John, but by now the school choir had been replaced by the Kirkgate Singers. In 1978, a double album remix called 'Greetings' was also issued. There were no more complete albums of carols produced until the CD in 2011 to celebrate the 50th year.

In addition to these choir-sponsored recordings, the Castle museum wanted cassettes rather than LPs to sell, and so commissioned a version of the 1976 long playing record in the new format. The following minutes give the details:

07/01/1976

The Committee considered a suggestion by the Curator that a cassette be produced by Messrs. Hearne and Jobson of a recording of Carols in Kirkgate by YPMVC.

Resolved:

[a] That agreement in principle be given to this suggestion.

[b] That 50 copies of the cassette be purchased at a cost of £83.50 including all production costs and be sold at the museum for £2.60 each.

[c] That a percentage in the form of a royalty be negotiated with the choir.

After hearing a report by the Curator on the success of the 1975 performances of Carols in Kirkgate it was resolved that a letter be sent on behalf of the committee to YPMVC congratulating them on their performance.

07/04/1976

The Curator of the Castle Museum reported that Messrs. Hearne and Jobson, the publishers of the Carols in Kirkgate sound cassettes had suggested that they pay to the Castle Museum a Royalty of 10% of their sales income [excluding sales to the Castle Museum] half of this sum to be passed onto YPMVC and further that 10% of the Castle Museum's income from sale of the cassette [excluding vat] should also be paid to the choir.

Resolved:

[a] That the suggestion that the choir and the council each receive 5% of the sales outside the museum in the form of royalty be accepted.

[b] That the choir should receive from the Castle Museum 10% of the museum's income [excluding vat] from the sale of the cassette.

[c] That the cassette be sold at £2.75 each including vat.

In the digital world of 2015 it is remarkably easy to record and to publish audio material. The minutes for 1975 suggest how unusual such events were, and how carefully arrangements needed to be made. It is also worth noting that, following this deliberation, the sales price of the cassette went up by 15p.

Audiences

Carols in Kirkgate audiences have proved very loyal over the years, and have always had to be a hardy group. You needed to queue to get tickets, seats were always unreserved, so on performance nights you needed to arrive an hour before the show time to be sure of a seat near the front, and the show could run for up to 1hr.45mins without an interval. Still, there are many York citizens who will happily acknowledge to have been coming for at least twenty years. As was noted earlier the first performance in 1962 had an audience of 500-600. This would have been a realistic street scene as everyone would have been stood and crowded together. In 1964 the York Press reported an audience of 300 and it then settled to 400. Before the roof was redone it could be noisy and was not always warm. But nothing deterred the crowds. Benches were introduced so that the audience could sit. However a bench with minimum leg room on a cobbled surface was not very comfortable. In recent years chairs replaced the benches and the cobbled surface was made smoother but it has never been an easy venue in which to offer comfort even with numbers reduced to 160. Ticketing and comfort issues were never to be easily overcome but the choir did strive to improve the evening for the audience by providing staging and lighting.

Staging/ lighting

Carols in Kirkgate is the only regular event in the street which requires a theatrical layout both in staging /lighting and audience. Therefore over the years it has been the choir which has devised and provided the means by which the show can be staged.

In the 1960s, Brian Lister wanted a set of transportable, storable, raised staging for choir use at both Kirkgate and other concerts. The late Malcolm Raw [baritone] together with life member Tony Sawyer rose to the challenge. Malcolm, a design engineer with Portasilo, designed sets of raised staging best described as being like Russian dolls. The lower levels of staging sat inside the larger so that the complete set provided a curved stage able to accommodate at least 50 singers. Together with Tony, Malcolm made these sets using off cuts kindly donated by Portakabin. The material used was the plywood sections cut from Portakabin walls in order to provide the window openings. This excellent set of staging was used for some 40 years. There were, however, two challenges to its use, one general and one specific to Kirkgate. The sets were heavy and were best transported and set up by young men. Over time these young men aged! Secondly, the uneven cobbles of Kirkgate, improved in recent years but never fully levelled, were an annual challenge to Tony's ability to set them up evenly and without movement. In 2006 this set was used at Carols for the last time, and since then staging has been hired. Nevertheless the quality and robustness of these units is such that they are still at work, in various guises, within one of the workshops of tenor Graham Edwards, who for many years stored and transported these sets on behalf of the choir.

Our current choir President, The Hon. Alderman Keith Wood, was instrumental in providing stage lighting. Keith was elected to the City Council in 1970 and was invited on to the Castle Museum committee, hence his introduction to both 'Carols in Kirkgate' and the choir. The chairman of that committee at the time was Councillor C.W. (Wilf) Oliver who was also President of YPMVC.

In the mid eighties the council bought a set of portable stage lights for use by amateur groups and, given his connection with Kirkgate and his experience as a lighting volunteer on two productions of the York Mystery Plays, Keith suggested their use to enhance performances. Over the years, with the support of the museum, and with tenor Bob Sykes acting as the electrician approved by the museum, regular improvements were made. Following a school stage refit, Bootham School kindly donated lamps to the choir, and a benefactor provided a multi-channel lighting console. Graham Edwards, a locally based trailer manufacturer, made some lighting bars, and provided storage and transport for all the equipment; and so the set-up used until 2012 was established.

Since making his kind offer to help, back in the mid-eighties, Keith has been allowed one night off. During the many years that the Lord Mayor's Christmas Cheer Fund benefitted from the concerts the Civic party were always welcomed to a performance. In 1990, as Lord Mayor and Lady Mayoress, Keith and his wife June entered into the spirit of the occasion, and together with the Sheriff and Sheriff's lady, attended in full Victorian costume.

Party Night

Throughout the life of the choir, members have always been willing to enjoy a pint of beer or two. Yorkshire TV recognised this as did the museum committee. Many current singing members can recall the barrel of beer which was laid on by the museum to sustain the choir during the show's run. Sadly this part of the tradition was phased out sometime in the 1980s.

The private performance on Monday night, introduced by Brian Lister soon became an 'end of run' party night. These were held in the Half Moon Court in another part of the museum. Members provided food, and choir ladies set up the party. The Court would be packed, ale would be drunk, sandwiches eaten, votes of thanks offered, and the choir would sing a 'pub' concert. This writer's strongest memories of these nights are: the atmosphere felt in walking down through the dark passages of the old prison past the cells; coming out into the bustle and light of Half Moon Court; the patience needed and the skills required in negotiating the crowded routes from food to beer without spillage; and the good acoustic for a 'pub' sing. After Half Moon Court was revamped as a 1960s exhibition space, the party moved to Kirkgate Street itself, still retaining the old features but with much less crowding.

Bob Sykes our electrician, and his wife Hazel, ran this bar for 25 years until 2012. This was a challenge to Bob, who helped Keith strip down and load the stage lights, and then would get to the bar at the same time as most of the singers.

Additional performances in the Grand Opera House York

In 1966 the show went, for one night only, to the Three Cups in Stamford Bridge. It didn't move outside the museum again until 1998. There was such demand for tickets that the choir felt confident enough to adjust the planned show to fit a bigger venue and did a Sunday night performance in the Grand Opera House (a 950 capacity theatre). In 1998 the show was produced by Peter Walls and was an evening of carols, readings and community carols in a Victorian setting. On Sunday 6th December 1998 800 people came to the show, an unexpectedly high number.

On Sunday 3rd December 2000 the choir returned in a show produced by Neil Wood, a drama teacher, and member at that time of our baritone section. This was a Christmas concert on a Dickensian theme of Oliver Twist. About 600 attended, another high number.

Both performances included the Kirkgate Ladies and children from Hempland Junior School, and each performance made a substantial profit.

It was in the years following this that additional performances were added to the Museum run. At first the Tuesday of week two was introduced and then the Tuesday of week one so that in 2011 the commitment of the choir was: week one: Monday night dress rehearsal; Tuesday – Saturday performances; week two; Monday concert, now primarily the choir family but with some tickets on public sale, followed by choir party; and the Tuesday final performance.

In 2011 we were proud to be able to celebrate the 50th year of performing. A new work *The Kirkgate Carol* was commissioned which spoke of the constant needs within society for love and compassion and recognised the significant contribution made by those prominent York citizens, Joseph and Seebohm Rowntree. Ossie Gillery, who had sung at the first performance in 1962, was able to attend, as did some founder members of the Kirkgate Ladies, as well as widows of some members who were active in establishing 'Carols', and a number of former Lord Mayors. The choir celebrated by recording a CD, *Carols in Kirkgate.*

CD Sleeve

Here is a selection of recent images:

Dr. John Sentamu- Archbishop of York, pictured with Berry and the late Jim Rayne, enjoyed the show in 2006

Another trip away this time at Castle Howard in 2007

Leading a community carol in 2010

Graham Kay resplendent in blue – 2010

Milestone for city singing spectacle

MEMBERS of York Philharmonic Male Voice Choir, from left, Tony Suckling, Terry Yates, Richard Kay and Colin Hockridge, celebrate the 50th anniversary of Carols In Kirkgate at York's Castle Museum.
• **Full story: Page 5**

2011 advertising

In 1962 'Carols in Kirkgate' was an immediate hit, a show for its time. In 2012 it was just as popular, and every bit as relevant, still a show for our times. Christmas is a time for remembrance, a time for renewal, a time for celebration. We all like, and need, the reassurance, and the sense of belonging that comes from reliving the rituals that stretch back to our childhood. How many reading this will put up the same Christmas decorations each year that they have had since childhood, or at least since the birth of their first child? As a year comes to a close we feel that sense of hope and expectation which encourages us to look to the coming year, and to the end of winter. Choristers feel the same and there was always a buzz, a feeling, very pleasant yet hard to describe, on walking into the museum on dress rehearsal night of yet another 'Carols'. So maybe we should not be surprised that so many of the audience come regularly, maybe we should not be surprised at its enduring success; and we should, most certainly, not be surprised at getting complaints in the years we leave out *Silent Night*.

Despite being popular and so reassuring, the show, as presented, was becoming difficult to sustain. Production costs were considerable, particularly costume hire, and the hire of staging and seating. The Museums Trust had but one objective – to get the maximum financial return. There was then pressure to increase both ticket price and the number of performance nights to a level which could no longer be managed. This may have signalled the end of an era, but it did not signal the end of the show.

Christmas in Fossgate

In 2013, after 51 years of performances in the museum, *Carols in Kirkgate* became *Christmas in Fossgate; the Kirkgate Ladies* became the *Fossgate Singers* and the show transferred to the medieval splendour of the Merchant Adventurers' Hall. To retain a Victorian theme in a medieval hall did not make sense so the choir wore evening dress; and with no need to hire either costumes or staging, production costs reduced and we reduced the ticket price accordingly. The run length was reduced to three performances, and an interval with refreshments of mulled wine and mince pies was introduced. These changes, together with the much more comfortable seating were welcomed by regular and new concert goers alike. The transfer was a great success and played to full houses from 2013 - 2015.

Ready to go – 2013

Hilarious 'radio' version of Cinderella in 2013, Mary Cox as Cinders; Ivan Chaplin as the Prince and Katrina Knowles (seated right) as Fairy Godmother.

In 2015, for the first time ever, the complete show moved outside York and a performance was given at the Galtres Centre in Easingwold under the heading 'Christmas at the Galtres'. This played to an audience of 180 and was a most enjoyable evening.

The Merchant Adventurers' Hall offered better comfort to the audience than the museum. However, there were still issues with ticketing and queuing that could not be easily resolved. The Hall is not a theatre and the Christmas show always plays to capacity audiences. In January 2016 the Hall decided to withdraw from the venture, and so the 2016 show will be in the refurbished De Grey Rooms, now managed by the Theatre Royal. In a short space of time the show will have moved from a Victorian setting to medieval and back to a 19th century ballroom. That has required three changes of name, but the show has retained its appeal, and indeed, the changes have given opportunities to refresh the performance.

Chapter 10
The twinning with Münster from 1969 and other European friendships

The idea that the pain of a Europe fractured by war might be healed, in part, by individual cities and communities entering friendship pacts across borders had first been suggested in 1946. By 1957 the idea was being actively promoted by governments. And so the cities of Münster in Westphalia and York were encouraged to come together and agree a twinning arrangement. Both cities have a long and significant history and have many similarities. Furthermore, at the time, some 12,000 British soldiers were stationed in Westphalia. It seemed to be a good match – a confidence which has been rewarded – but it was also the first time that either city had agreed to such friendship so no one was sure what to expect. The earliest significant events were both of major civic importance. In October 1958 representatives from York attended the reopening of the ancient Rathaus [Town Hall] in Münster which had been destroyed in an air raid in October 1944. In June 1960 representatives from Münster attended the reopening of the ancient Guildhall in York, likewise destroyed in April 1942.

The two male voice choirs did not come together until 1968. We understand from our German friends that the city authorities in Münster encouraged their choir to *get a move on and take some action* and from that moment plans were quickly made and implemented. We tend to think of the start date as being April 1969 when the first joint concert took place, but in Münster, November 1968 is regarded as 'zero hour', the time when the personal contacts and the agreement were made. In that month Mr. André van Hooydonk, President of the Royal Nijmegen Male Voice Choir from Holland, and the Secretary of the Phil, Jack Jones, travelled to Münster. They were welcomed, on behalf of the city council, by Joseph Niehaus, the chairman of the Münsterscher Männergesangverein [MM]. There was an understandable caution in the discussions but all agreed to reciprocal visits and concerts in order to build bridges between our communities. Josef welcomed the readiness of both choirs to accept the hand of friendship from the German singers, whilst accepting that in 1968 this might be difficult for some members of both the Dutch and the English choirs. He did emphasise the genuine desire of the men of the MM to contribute all they could to reconciliation. The significance of this act of friendship, to those who had lived through and been part of the war, is shown in the written history of the MM 1889-1989 and in their 2008 publication celebrating the 40 years of our twinning. Both acknowledge this reality and express gratitude that all choirs worked hard to build a new future.

To better understand the response of the Phil to this invitation, we need to look back to the York choir of 1967. Brian Lister, still only 36 years old, had been the director for five years. The choir was now targeting a younger generation and was adjusting to a television age. In the spring of 1967, a new uniform was introduced – including the black blazer with gold badge still worn today.

This picture was the first to appear in the York Evening Press showing the

VETERAN: William Payne, 90, centre, the only surviving founder member of York Philharmonic Male Voice Choir in 1967, with director Richard Lister, left, and back, from left, John Jones, secretary, Frank Morton, Ian Woods, Trevor Cooper and Ernest Robinson

new uniform which had cost the choir £450, a considerable sum of money, but as Brian Lister subsequently remarked *"This pride in appearance has stimulated a pride in presentation."*

The choir, now 54 strong, was singing to a high standard having won two trophies already that season and was attracting new younger members – indeed one third of the membership was younger than 30. A portable staging system had been designed and built and a concert manager appointed. Repertoire was also being updated. *"We have turfed out a lot of music which was too Victorian in flavour and which was; let's face it, in some cases downright bad music."* said Brian Lister in a news article. *"The aim now is to cater for all types of musical taste from Bach to Romberg and currently the choir is rehearsing an arrangement of 'When the Saints go marching in'."* This arrangement was one of several by Brian, most of which are still audience favourites in 2015.

The choir was fortunate in having an active supporters group [known as 'Perimeter'] of more than 100, which raised considerable funds to support the choir. The Phil had two short term ambitions. The first was to become one of the front ranked male voice choirs in the UK and to enter an international competition. The second was to undertake a European tour and to establish links with other choirs. The Phil was planning to visit Holland in September 1968 with hoped-for visits to Nijmegen, Eindhoven and Boxmeer. These plans had advanced to the point that a savings scheme called 'Tulip Time' was being run by new member Peter Evans.

It is, then, not surprising that the Phil responded quickly and enthusiastically to the request from Münster. Following the November 1968 meeting, the trip to Nijmegen was rearranged, with the Phil agreeing to visit both Münster and Nijmegen in April 1969. So the second of the short term ambitions was to be achieved, but what of the first? By the time of the tour in April 1969 the Phil had been undefeated in four years in regional competitions. It had also been accepted to take part in the 1970 International Music Festival run by the BBC 'Let the People Sing! ', so the first of the ambitions was close to fulfilment.

The Royal Nijmegen Mannenkoor was important to both the York and Münster choirs. This large and prestigious choir had formed in 1859 and was one of the oldest in the Netherlands, receiving Royal appointment in 1909. As well as the talks with the Phil and the MM, it already had a link with a choir in Grimsby, and had visited Münster as part of an earlier German tour. The MM, formed in 1889 was also older and larger than the Phil, so when the tour was planned the Phil was the youngest and smallest of the three.

A tour of this size, requiring the men to be away for a full week, must have taken some organising as well as a considerable amount of inter-family negotiation. Tony Sawyer, who celebrated 50 years of membership in 2015, remembers his wife Hazel agreeing to him going even though they had a new baby daughter, and a full week of holiday would be needed. The choir was to be accommodated and entertained free of charge by their hosts but travel costs still needed to be met. Two modes of transport were planned: by air leaving York at 10am on Saturday 12th; flying by charter flight Yeadon to Düsseldorf, returning Amsterdam to Yeadon on the following Friday: cost £16.10s; or by sea leaving York at 3.30pm on Friday 11th for the Harwich night boat to the Hook of Holland, train to Münster, returning from Amsterdam / Rotterdam the following Friday evening arriving back in York on Saturday, cost £19.10s (Railway employees with travel passes £4).

PROUD: York Philharmonic Male Voice Choir with trophies won in the 1968/9 season, pictured a fortnight before setting off on a tour of Germany and Hollanc

This picture was published in the York Evening Press two weeks before the tour. It shows a confident choir, unbeaten in regional competitions for four years, displaying new uniforms. Brian Lister is sitting on the left of the front row, with tenor soloist Reg Goodhall standing behind. Holding the trophies from left to right are: Bert Cheetham, Derek Chaplin, Jack Jones (secretary), Frank Morton (treasurer) and Alan Bloomfield (accompanist). John Nattrass, the chairman is stood to the right dressed in choir uniform.

1969(April) – Coming Together

Das Rathaus zu Münster

A print of the Rathaus given to Brian Lister during that first visit

Reproduced below is the account of the visit as published in the choir magazine – *Male Voice Monthly* May 1969 edition, but the sense of the very first meeting of the choirs is better described in the memories of one young tenor, Mike Johnson. This was recorded many years later in conversation with choir archivist James Elliot. Mike joined the choir in 1966 and remembers both the excellent camaraderie and the very high musical standards. The choir travelled to Münster in two groups one by rail and ferry, the other flying from Leeds airport. Mike was on the flight and remembers looking down at the rough sea and being thankful he wasn't on the ship. This feeling was enhanced when, enjoying the novel experience of air travel, Frank Morton walked up and down the aisle proclaiming; *"It's so smooth you wouldn't know you're moving!"*

The two dishevelled, travel weary groups came together in the evening in the Clubhouse – Gastatte Freitag. After a meal they moved into the clubhouse proper to meet their hosts. Mike described the scene. *"We went into this kind of basement laid out with banqueting tables where there were about 40-50 Münster men gathered. They applauded our entrance, so Brian Lister gathered us on the stairs and we sang a song we had been rehearsing 'Rejoice with Wine'* [*The Bandits' Chorus* from Ernani by Verdi]. *There were a few seconds of silence then the place erupted with these big Germans cheering, stamping their feet and banging their tankards on the table. It was fantastic, a wonderful experience."* It would seem that any anxieties felt by members of both choirs were dispelled at this one moment. The bridge that the choir and city officials were seeking to build was completed by the shared love and power of music. This was the time when the visitors met with the German host families and dispersed to their homes. Mike and three other young members were not with families but were billeted in a flat with a 'Hausfrau' who came in to cook breakfast.

The Bandits' Chorus was also sung by the Phil in the Rathaus the following day when the choir met the city Bürgermeister. This was an inspired musical choice by Brian Lister. There is, perhaps, no better musical 'icebreaker' for a meeting of two male voice choirs. It is an opera chorus in which a group of bandits sing in praise of wine. Full of energy and life, the choir used an a-capella arrangement ideal for an impromptu sing. On reflection it is, perhaps, the most important piece of music ever sung by the Phil in the long life of twinning with Münster. There is some irony, though, in the fact that it has never been included in the musical programme of any of the 16 major concerts the choirs have performed together. It had been intended to include the chorus in the 1989 concert in Münster, the only occasion when the Nijmegen, Münster and York choirs ever shared a platform. However, late in the day we learned that Nijmegen had prepared an extended accompanied arrangement of the same chorus, and so we agreed to change our programme.

This picture of the choir singing 'The Bandits' Chorus on the steps of the Rathaus appeared in a Münster newspaper.

The language barrier needed to be overcome and Peter Evans, stage manager in 1969, remembers this as being achieved by a lot of good natured spontaneity and humour. Ursula Morton [The German-born wife of Frank] helped prepare the choir for the trip with cultural tips and language tuition, and all the choir knew at least one sentence in German – the opening line of a song *Der Mond is aufgegangen* [The moon has risen]. One tenor is known to have approached strangers in the street proudly practicing this new language skill – no doubt to many bemused citizens.

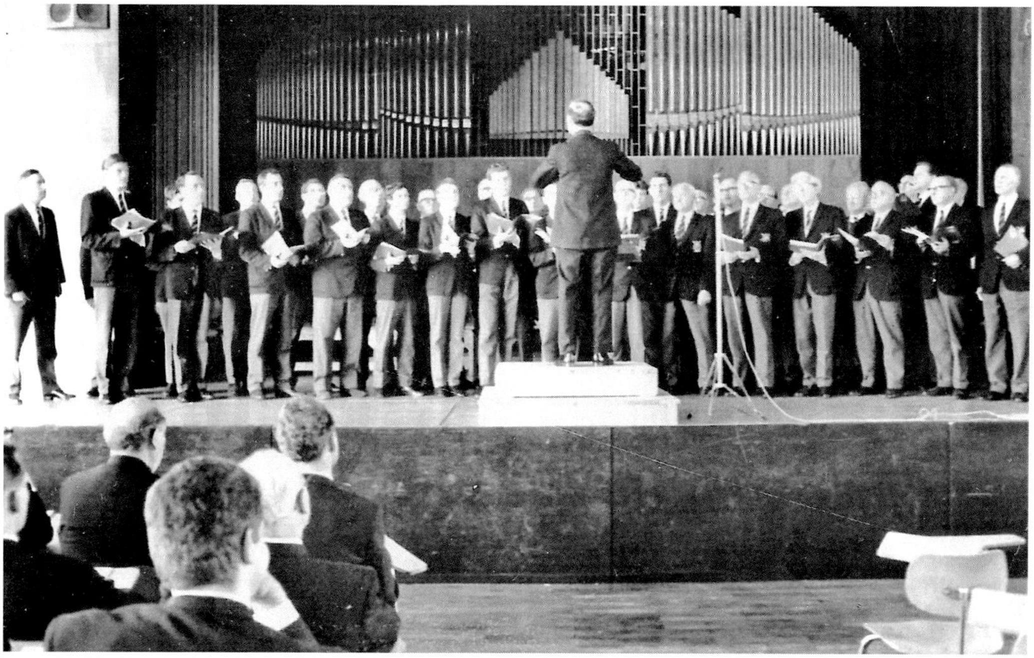

This picture shows the choir rehearsing before the concert. The tall man second from the left is the young Mike Johnson and on the extreme right is founder member Henry Brough. Members of the MM are seated in the auditorium.

The two choirs were joined in concert by the band of the 13/18 Royal Hussars and the event, promoted under the banner of the twinning of the two cities, was performed in the hall of the College of Education.

Brian Lister selected a light-hearted programme of seven items of folk songs and spirituals.

The Skye Boat Song
The Lincolnshire Poacher
My Bonnie lies over the Ocean
Steal Away
When the Saints go marching in
Widdecombe Fair
Dr. Foster

This is a selection of unaccompanied songs and the Phil only had 35 singers on the tour. It is a tribute to the quality of the choir that it achieved high critical acclaim particularly when sharing a platform with a choir twice as big as well as a military band.

The concert ended with the band and the two choirs joining together in a rousing rendition of a popular German song *Lob des Rheines* by Th. Fischer.

The concert was reviewed by two local papers

The Münsterische Stadtanzeiger wrote:

The choir which recently won the Huddersfield Centenary Cup and the trophy for the Male Voice 'A' Class at Huddersfield left a very strong impression, not the least factor of which was the great variety in their presentation. As well as the polished performance, it was the emotional atmosphere which created an incredibly lively picture of the English and

Scottish folksongs.

The jewels of this folk music were presented perfect in tone, rhythmically exact, richly shaded and colourful in sound, and the audience quite rightly showed great appreciation. At times one imagined one was listening to a professional choir, and in particular, the humorous song at the end of the first half of the programme was sung with unsurpassable precision.

The Spirituals which the choir sang, under the inspired leadership of Richard B. Lister, convinced the audience of the absolute accuracy and wide range of expression which these singers command. Their pianissimo remained expressive even in the softest moments, and the parlando (as if speaking) *brought the Spirituals close to the English madrigals. 14/04/1969*

The Münster Tag fur Tag wrote:

One thing was quite clear to anyone in the main hall of the Münster College of Education who knew anything about choral singing – It will be a very long time before they have a second chance of hearing such a fine choir as the YPMVC from Münster's British twin city of York.

Gentle, sensitive, calm and polished with a delicate sense for arrangement and a uniform blending of the voices, the choir, which consisted of the very best in voice material, sang under the leadership of Richard B. Lister, a conductor with an individual style.

Folk art in England really is art in the highest meaning of the word. Whether they are singing Spirituals or humorous folksongs, the choir from York presented everything polished to the last detail with a musical flexibility and vocal suppleness which defies comparison.

With this musical nobleness, the singers proved themselves to be true Britons, but true Britons they would not have been if they did not have a sense of humour in them, and that they most certainly did have. Merrily they altered their voices, humorous motifs being elegantly passed from voice to voice. With such light-hearted singing, a whole section of the programme had to be devoted to humour.

The Spirituals which this choir from York then sang belonged to the most beautiful part of the York- Münster joint concert. The devoutly religious mood of these songs was always exactly right because the dynamic accents were so loosely placed and the rhythm so lightly stressed that the singing created an atmosphere of immediacy and naturalness. This concert was the musical expression of the friendship between the cities of Münster and York. 15/04/1969

These are reviews any choir would be proud to receive, yet only seven short pieces had been sung, taking no longer than 20 minutes. One of the skills which raise an excellent choir director above the merely good is the ability to select a musical programme which suits the venue, the audience and the resources available at the time. Brian Lister displayed this skill to great effect on this historic occasion.

On the Monday evening the two choirs sang again at a concert in the British army Buller Barracks, joined once more by the band. Apart from the comments in the choir report given below, the only other reference is a copy of the printed programme as used by Brian Lister. This is extremely interesting as it shows how the Phil responded to the situation and changed its planned programme. There were five changes made in a planned programme of only seven items. In addition the joint item as performed the previous evening was dropped in favour of the Phil singing *The Bandit's Chorus* –'Rejoice with Wine'. This is a change that must have been suggested by the men of Münster – a very generous gesture. These changes do show the Phil as being a confident choir enjoying its work.

This mood continued with three changes being made to the planned programme in Nijmegen – not including *The Bandit's Chorus* which Nijmegen sang.

On the return of a jubilant choir the Evening Press wrote:

YORK CHOIR WINS 'RAVE' NOTICES IN GERMANY

MEMBERS of York Philharmonic Male Voice Choir today described as "fantastic and overwhelming" a week's concert tour of Germany and Holland from which they returned at the weekend.

The choir travelled to Munster, York's twin city in Germany, where it gave two concerts with the Munster Male Voice Choir and the 13/18th Hussars band which is stationed near the city.

The first concert was recorded for German radio and Mr. John Nattrass, chairman of the York choir, was interviewed with his opposite number in the Munster choir for a programme which will be heard by five million people.

Later in the week the choir of 47, with musical director, Mr. Richard B. Lister, and several members' wives, travelled to Nijmegen in Holland where they performed with the Royal Nijmegen Male Voice Choir which has visited Hull and Grimsby.

Hospitality

Mr. Nattrass told the *Evening Press* today: "The hospitality was fantastic and overwhelming. It was so spontaneous that you felt you had to rise to the occasion so as not to disappoint."

He said they had been asked to sing everywhere in Munster, including a supermarket, churches and the guildhall.

The trip was a musical triumph for the York choir which won first prize against the best choirs in the North of England at Huddersfield in February.

Mr. Lister, conductor of the choir, said: "I found the musical public in Holland, and especially in Germany, more interested in choral singing than York people.

From a musical point-of-view, the choir was very well appreciated because we use a different singing technique to theirs. The York choir is trained to sing in the Italian Bel Canto style, from the head, while Continentals sing from the throat.

Encores

"This means that our control of the very soft passages is much greater than theirs and people commented on this time and time again."

The choir was asked to sing two or three encores at every concert at which they performed and received standing ovations from their German audiences.

German music critics gave "rave" notices. One wrote: "Whether they were singing spirituals or humorous, folk-songs the choir from York presented everything polished to the last detail, and with a musical flexibility and vocal suppleness which defies comparison."

As a result of the choir's trip to Germany, where members distributed brochures about York and this year's Festival, the Munster Male Voice Choir will be making a reciprocal visit to York in May next year.

The oral tradition of the choir says that no wives travelled until 1989. However this article shows there were ladies and other supporters on this first trip, including Herbert and Edith Marshall, as the size of the travel party is given as 47 and we believe there were only some 35 singers. Herbert, a non-singer with the choir, was, however, concert manager and so needed to be there.

Here is the report as given in the May 1969 choir magazine.

<u>The recent successful continental tour</u>

This venture is deserving of written comment not only to convey to non-partaking members what happened, but to revive memories and reminiscences for those of us who experienced this memorable venture.

Our story begins at 1pm on Saturday 12th April when our Secretary, in discussions with the Münster committee hears the announcement over German Radio that "the advance party of Britain's Finest Choir – the YPMVC – has arrived in Münster to commence a week's tour of Germany and Holland". What advance publicity! Around 7.30 pm the choir are all together and both sea and air travellers are seated in the Clubhouse, Gastatte Freitag, enjoying a welcome meal and swopping tales about their respective journeys. The meal over, we move into the Clubhouse proper, where our hosts are waiting for us and greet us with a round of applause. Before meeting our individual hosts we are called upon to give a song which was well applauded. Following the distribution of accommodation, we all went our separate ways with our new hosts, to experience our first taste of German hospitality. How grateful we were to Mrs. Morton for the few pointers she gave us before we went.

<u>Sunday Morning April 13th.</u>

At the Münster Rathaus – the equivalent of our Guildhall – we were warmly received by the Bürgermeister and Oberstadt Direktor in the Peace Chamber, an ornately panelled room steeped in the history of Westphalia. Moving into a larger room, with exceptionally good acoustics, we were treated to wine and cigars, and in keeping with the mood, we sang 'rejoice with wine'. The remaining part of the morning was spent seeing the sights of Münster with our guide.

<u>Afternoon:</u> *After lunch we rehearsed at the clubhouse and then went on to the main hall of the Münster College of Education where the concert which included the Münster choir and the Band of the 13/18 Royal Hussars took place at 5pm. (I wonder how York would take a concert at 5pm on a Sunday evening). The concert was an outstanding success resulting in praise and acclaim by two Münster newspapers. Translations of these articles are attached* [see above]. *Sections of the concert were recorded for German Radio.*

<u>Evening:</u> *Following dinner at the Clubhouse, we attended a social evening, and the enjoyment we were receiving was evidenced by the way in which we all let our hair down. The entertainment was first rate, and what pleasure our own Reg Goodhall gave us and the Münster people with his solo spot.* [Not recorded in this report but remembered by Mike Johnson was the fact that Reg had broken the sole on his performance shoes earlier in the day so sang with one shoe held together with sellotape]. *During the festivities a plaque was presented to our choir depicting the City of Münster, which was received on our behalf by our Chairman, and our worthy colleagues Brian and Jack, received gifts in recognition of their efforts in making the venture a success. One of the highlights of a rather hectic day was the able manner in which our chairman* [John Nattrass] *replied to all the official speeches.*

<u>Monday:</u> *Leaving Münster in the morning by coach, we visited a number of moated castles in the neighbourhood of Münster, stopping for lunch at the Luftkurhaus Weisenburg,a delightful hotel in the country. The first stop of the afternoon was at a church where we sang for the benefit of our guide, then onto another castle and finally to the Ratio Supermarket. Here again we were called upon to sing, and the remark was overheard that this was only a rehearsal for a forthcoming series of Saturday afternoon concerts in Woolworths York. Left to do our shopping we were rather disappointed at the quality of the goods for sale. We then sat down to a meal and listened to a discourse about the Ratio organisation. After the meal we walked to Buller barracks where we gave a repeat concert to a small but most appreciative audience.*

<u>Tuesday:</u> *At 10.30 am after protracted farewells to our hosts who had treated us so* *royally we boarded the coach for farewell speeches by the chairmen of both choirs and paid just tribute to Ann Dodd, a charming young lady who had very ably acted as our interpreter and liaised with Jack during the whole of our stay in Münster.*

This first visit introduced a pattern of behaviour which immediately became the norm. Visits to either Münster or York include: a reception with the Lord Mayor/ Bürgermeister; a joint concert and social events; impromptu sings whenever possible; and, in keeping with the spirit of that first song given by the Phil, much – 'rejoicing with wine, good wine'.

On the Tuesday morning the Phil travelled to Nijmegen. The Royal Nijmegen Male Voice Choir had sent an itinerary to Jack Jones together with some information on the city.

It has 145,000 inhabitants and is situated on the bank of the river Waal [a branch of the well-known Rhine] and it is the oldest town in the Netherlands. It was built on seven hills [just as Rome] and was founded during the Roman Empire. In the town you will find many old places, as the ruins of the Castle of Charlemagne, the Town Hall, the Saint Stephens Church, the Weigh house and the old fortress-walls in Kronenburger park.

The town was heavily bombed in 1944 and the centre was nearly totally destroyed. Now Nijmegen has been reconstructed and has got a very modern image. Nijmegen is situated within 3 miles of the German border. It has a university and is the cultural centre of the surrounding area.

These short notes suggest an ancient city which would appeal to men of York. It also illustrates another consequence of war. As a potential river crossing point it was strategically important to the advancing allied troops. Sadly that act of liberation saw much of the city destroyed.

The magazine report continued:

Tuesday: *We arrived at the Kolpinghuis Nijmegen at 1pm., where we had an enjoyable meal and spent the remainder of the afternoon strolling around the city in the rain [steep rise in umbrella sales]. At 5pm we were introduced to our hosts and taken by them to their homes for a welcome wash and brush up. We returned to the Kolpinghuis for another hectic and enjoyable evening where our young guitar trio were well received.*

Wednesday: *At 10.30 am we met at the Town Hall for a most interesting tour of the civic rooms which lasted an hour and a half, then by coach to a hotel on the outskirts of Nijmegen for a meal after which we sang 'Rejoice with Wine' [I wonder why Mike Johnson was so interested in the prices of property?]. The remainder of the afternoon was spent seeing the countryside, the famous Seven Hills and the British War cemetery being among the sights.*

The highlight of the evening was the concert given with the Royal Nijmegen Mannenkoor, when both choirs gave of their best to a most enthusiastic audience.

Thursday: *At a luncheon in the Kolpinghuis, we bade our Dutch friends adieu and started our journey to Amsterdam*[Peter Evans recalls that this break was arranged and paid for by the Nijmegen choir – a generous gesture made easier by the small size of the York party]. *Now the official part of our tour was over and we were once more on our own, but why are we still talking to our fellow choir members in gestures, broken English and sign language??? Arriving in Amsterdam, we could now relax and most of us went out to see the sights. What a pleasant evening it was at the Postghorne with about 28 members under Reg's baton.*

Friday: *Awakened by the street barrel organ, the morning was spent sightseeing and shopping and at 2pm the Air party left for Schipol airport where last minute purchases of duty free goods were made. Taking off for home at 5pm we arrived at Yeadon at 6.30pm.*

Socially, musically, and in every other aspect, this tour was an outstanding success beyond all expectations. This success is attributable to each and every one of us but mostly to our Secretary, Music Director, and Chairman. To reciprocate the hospitality we received on this tour when our German and Dutch friends visit us in 1970, a lot of forward planning and serious financial budgeting will be necessary. If the spirit which has prevailed during the tour continues, then the hard task ahead of us will be made much easier.

In May 1969, Jack Jones, who had seen his hard work come to fruition, resigned as choir secretary. Donald Crawford took on the role described in the choir magazine as being one *'which will often be onerous and exacting, at times, exhausting'.* Without doubt the organising of reciprocal visits with the MM added greatly to the work load of both the choir secretary and treasurer. The financial planning for this first trip had expected a deficit, but one which was manageable, with each choir member being invited to make a £1 donation to *'replenish the much-depleted coffers.'* It was a pleasant surprise when a final review of the tour accounts showed a surplus of £88. 5s 4d; which, by popular vote, was transferred to the Reciprocation Fund.

In 1969 the expectation was that both the Münster and Nijmegen choirs would visit York in 1970. In the end Münster came in May 1970 and Nijmegen in April 1971.

1970(May) – The MM visit York

The choir magazines of March 1970 and May 1970 give both the itinerary and the report as written up by Don Crawford. Reproduced in full, these reports do show the significant amount of work that was involved to make the week-end the success that it was. The choir President at the time was Councillor Wilf Oliver. His company Whitby Oliver included an international house removal business whose vehicles carried the slogan 'Across the Street, Across the World' a phrase used in

Don's report.

Itinerary

Friday 1st May 1970

Two buses will meet and bring the party from Yeadon to the De Grey Rooms, arriving at approximately 5.30 pm and will partake of light refreshments. It is intended that choir members will arrive at approximately 6pm to welcome their respective guests and take them to their homes or Hotels, which ever applies. The rest of the evening will be free.

Saturday 2nd May

Free time up to 10.30 am when a Civic Reception will take place. Sherry will be served etc. the reception will last about 40 minutes and our guests will be met by the Lord Mayor and other Civic Dignitaries on this occasion at the Mansion House.

The rest of the stay will be free until our joint concert in the Guildhall at 7.30pm except that the Guildhall will be available for our guests for a rehearsal in the afternoon if required.

It is anticipated that the concert will be over at about 9.30pm and hosts and guests may plan their own activities thereafter.

Sunday 3rd May

A tour of the city has been arranged at 10.30 am (to be undertaken in four parties

accompanied by four guides and interpreters). We are to meet in Library Square at 10.15am. It is expected that this tour will be over about noon.

Guests will then lunch with their respective hosts and re-assemble at the Cenotaph at 2pm prompt for a tour by coach into North Yorkshire with a High Tea at the Feathers Hotel Helmsley returning to be met by their hosts at the Cenotaph at approximately 7pm.

Guests will be taken to their respective homes or hotels to wash and brush up for our party in the Merchant Taylors' Hall in the evening at 8pm. This function will finish at about 11.30pm.

Monday 4th May. Hosts will bring their guests to the Cenotaph in time for the coaches to leave promptly at 9.30 for Yeadon. March 1970

Not all the guests could be accommodated in private homes. Following the success of the York visit the previous year, there were 70 people in the Münster party, including three women. Anne Dodd had given essential translation help in 1969. Ulrike Wiede was a 21 year old reporter sent over by a local Münster paper, whilst 18 year old Birgit Sack was the daughter of tenor Willi Sack. Both spoke excellent English and, not surprisingly, caught the attention of the York Press. The cost to each MM singer was 200 DM and the choir was fortunate in that the size of the party and the significance of the trip had been recognised by the Münster City authorities who gave them a grant of 1000 DM. The MM tour leaders Rudi Grieswald and Norbert Zöllner drafted a reminder which has also been used before each subsequent visit, that each visit is not an end in itself, but part of the continuing process to build bridges between the two choirs and cities. As the report below suggests this MM objective was not only met but exceeded.

Sunday 3rd May 1970 – a sunny morning as our guests gathered for a walking tour of York.

In the May magazine Don Crawford published his review of the week-end.

The M.M visit to York 1970

A most memorable week-end, beginning on Friday afternoon when the Chairman [John Nattrass] and I met the group at Yeadon.

Seeing them waiting on the tarmac, we realised that this was the moment, the beginning of the much awaited return week-end that we had all worked and raided our 'Piggy Banks' to make possible. After telephone calls to our 'Perimeter Ladies' to commence our 'Operation refreshments' and a call to the police that we were on our way, hoping to park on the dual lines outside the DeGrey Rooms, we greeted everyone and ushered them aboard the two buses and set off for York. Frau Dodd and I checking lists, altering my already much altered accommodation list even further, each bump of the bus creating some strange spelling.

After a fifteen minute wait in Bootham, we eventually arrived and with many waiting hands soon unloaded the luggage and ushered our guests inside for some welcome refreshments.

Operation accommodation now in swing we very soon had everyone with their respective hosts and all chatting merrily made their way to their homes.

Don's report can be interrupted at this point in order to acknowledge the support given by the ladies of 'Perimeter'. Don refers to a telephone call to launch 'Operation Refreshments'. In their own magazine 'Perimeter Post', their secretary Mrs. G Wilson published this description of what was entailed.

The next big item was the visit of the Münster choir to York and we shall remember it for a long time. Tribute must be paid to about eight ladies who turned up by request to prepare refreshments for our guests on their arrival in York. They had exactly half an hour to prepare sandwiches, butter scones, arrange tables and make tea starting from scratch – even the crockery was to unpack and wash before use. As there were about 100 to cater for, this was a wonderful effort. And their efforts did not stop there, for there was all the washing up to do, the crockery to pack, and then to meet their own individual guests and take them home and start all over again. These ladies worked extremely hard, and I hope they know how much their efforts were appreciated. I could not have tackled a job like that without such dependable workers – thank you.

These few words stand as a tribute and acknowledgement of the magnificent support given by the ladies of the choir throughout its 90 years.

In the same issue Mrs. Wilson also wrote: *At the last AGM the fact that the Music Director of the choir, Mr. Lister, did not have an adequate music stand was reported, and the whole meeting passed a resolution that the committee try to find out what could be done. This was done with the help of Mr. Marshall and Mr. Lister, and a music stand was bought and a suitable engraved plaque was fitted. This is now in use and very much appreciated.*

PRESENTED TO THE
YORK PHILHARMONIC MALE VOICE CHOIR
BY
THEIR LOYAL FOLLOWERS PERIMETER
MAY 1ST 1970

Here is a photograph of that plaque showing the significant date of its presentation. The photo below published in the YEP on 11th May shows the stand being put to immediate use. 45 years later it is still used for every rehearsal.

The choir that has won international honours rehearses in the school gym at York.

Don's 1970 report continues:

Saturday morning's Civic reception in the Mansion House was truly a most hospitable occasion, our Patron [The Lord Mayor] always shows a great interest in our movement and this day was no exception, our friends were very impressed by the friendliness of our Civic Heads and soon felt at home.

After much clicking of cameras and flashing lights, our Lord Mayor was presented with an engraved tray by the MM chairman Josef Niehues, the Lord Mayor responded very warmly and both he and the Lady Mayoress were further delighted when presented with MM choir badges to mark the visit to York.

The sunny afternoon gave our guests a chance to see the shops before their rehearsal in the afternoon.

The evening concert was indeed an occasion to remember, for me, in more ways than one. The tale began with a telephone call from Brian Lister who informed me that we were oversubscribed, seating wise, by well over a 100, and though he had been able to arrange some extra seats, he had a transport problem. I said "I'll ring back shortly." The first lifesaver who came to mind was our President Councillor Oliver, I thought 'Across the Street, Across the World', he readily set his election campaign aside to help us and we were off again.

The concert was a magnificent success, both choirs under inspired conductors, our sparkling soloist's performance and our hard worked accompanist, presented a feast of music that delighted the audience and indeed brought them to their feet at the finale with a standing ovation, what a marvellous feeling it left with us.

After the concert some members from each choir accepted an invitation to the Mansion House to partake of some refreshment and have an informal chat with the Lord Mayor and Lady Mayoress.

The sun certainly did us proud again on the Sunday morning and gave a perfect setting for our conducted tour of the city, our guests were all very impressed by the sights that they beheld and were equally impressed by the interesting commentary of our Guides, members of the York Voluntary Guides Association, who deserve our sincere appreciation. The afternoon outing, again blessed with abundant sunshine, was very much enjoyed, many of our guests remarking on the beautiful North Riding scenery around Pickering and its picturesque surrounding places of interest.

We arrived at the Feathers in Helmsley ahead of schedule and this gave our guests the chance to do a little souvenir hunting before we sat down to a meal of fresh salmon and salad followed by home-made typically English cakes and pastries, which all enjoyed.

After tea, we boarded our buses and proceeded on our return journey to York through Oswaldkirk, Brandsby and Sutton, a very pleasant run, giving another bonus of our countryside scenery.

The evening social was attended by both choirs, wives and Perimeter members all of whom created a wonderful party atmosphere and did more than do justice to the English style banquet of most excellent fayre prepared with infinite care by our culinary artist, John Addinall, who well deserved the praise given by the recipients.

There was a programme of entertainment arranged but due to time, as it usually does, beating us, we had to limit this to items from both of the choirs, which was well received by the revellers.

After sincere exchanges of gifts and words by both chairmen, made understandable by the ever skilful interpretation of Mrs. Anne Dodd the MM chairman Josef Niehues delivered two very pleasant surprises. He presented some members of our choir with a gift of alcoholic beverage and honoured the President and Secretary with Honorary membership of the MM presenting them with a badge to mark the occasion, our chairman was made an Honorary Member during last year's tour by Herr Kirchhoff, who after organising this year's visit was unable to be with us owing to the illness of his wife. I sent him our best wishes and said that we would meet again in the future.

Invariably when one is having a good time the midnight hour creeps upon us and we have to call a halt to our festivities, but I am sure that this occasion will be happily remembered for some time to come.

Monday morning brought (apart from heavy eye-lids) more sunshine and (much to the surprise of by-passers) a rendering of a 'Song of Praise to the morning' by the MM on the steps of the Cenotaph, before boarding the coaches for their homeward trip.

After many warm handshakes and amid shouts of 'Auf Wiedersehen' the chairman and secretary set off with the party to Yeadon.

At the airport, as in York, there were many handshakes and 'See you all in Münster', expressions coupled with sincere appreciation for a marvellous time in York.

Before going through the barrier, someone discovered that the music copies had been left under the table in the Merchant Taylors'Hall (the librarian must have had a good party). Could we arrange their dispatch?

As the plane left the ground and out of sight, I felt a strange empty feeling, not I might add indigestion.

On arrival home after picking up the music, in three heavy cases, I rang the Cook's Travel Agency for shipping details. They suggested I contact a Removal firm,(no prizes for guessing who I contacted). Coun. Oliver arranged the packing and dispatch of the music and knowing that he reads this publication, I take this opportunity to express our thanks to him for his interest and practical help over this week-end, not forgetting the personal attention he gave to our guest Herr. Hartmann, who was, unfortunately, ill during his stay here.

It would be an impossible task to remember and report on all the week-end's events, but I trust I have covered most and apologise for any that have escaped my pen.

There were so many people who helped to make this week-end the success that it was, that I am not prepared to risk leaving a name off what would certainly be a long list, so propose, on behalf of the choir to sincerely thank everyone concerned, they must surely feel that their efforts were well worthwhile.

Having even further cemented friendly ties between our two choirs, I feel confident that we can look forward to many more happy exchange visits in the future. Don Crawford May 1970

It was standing room only at the Guildhall for the joint concert. Don's report describes the last minute rush to get 100 more chairs. The music review in the York Evening Press does not comment on the size of the audience, although a report published later by the MM refers to a figure of 600. Add two choirs to this number and some 730 people must have been in the Hall. The Phil still gives two concerts a year in the Guildhall; in 2015 the prospect of 730 people there would bring down the wrath of Health and Safety Executives.

With a full choir and an accompanist available, Brian Lister was able to expand the repertoire beyond that performed in 1969. The programme included folk songs and spirituals but added opera choruses and sacred chorales. York-based soprano Margaret Bedford was the guest soloist.

The Phil sang:

The Lincolnshire Poacher; The Isle of Mull; A Rockin'all night; O Mary, don't you Weep; When the Saints go marching in and

Ave Verum Corpus:	da Viadana
O Scared Head sore Wounded:	J.S.Bach
Speed your Journey (Nabucco)	Verdi
The Pilgrims Chorus (Tannhäuser)	Wagner
Loudly Let the Trumpet Bray (Iolanthe)	Sullivan

There was no joint choir item.

The YEP review acknowledged the contribution made by Alan Bloomfield, the pianist for the Phil who played also for the MM. As in 1969, the visiting choir travelled without an accompanist.

It is a reflection of the confidence of Brian Lister, the quality of the Phil, and the prevailing spirit of co-operation, that Brian's selections for this concert did not include the three items which the Phil sang extremely well and which had been recorded for the BBC 'Let the People Sing!' Competition. These pieces: *Bushes and Briars* (Vaughan Williams); *Music when soft Voices die* (Bairstow); and *The Wanderer* (Elgar) would all have been excellent choices for such an international concert as this; but might well, at the time, have suggested that our two choirs were meeting in a spirit of competition rather than one of celebration.

SO GOOD A THING AT GUILDHALL

IT is nearly 400 years since William Byrd, the greatest of our Elizabethan composers, wrote a couplet in the preface to his songs: Since singing is so good a thing, I wish all men would learn to sing.

Although Byrd was not represented by his music at the concert at the Guildhall, York, on Saturday evening, the spirit of these oft-quoted words certainly was.

The Munsterscher Mannergesangverein have been the guests of York Philharmonic Male Voice Choir, a return hospitality for last year's visit to Munster, and the joint concert which they presented was a main feature of the occasion.

In a speech of welcome, the international language of music was referred to, and the warm applause for this showed that audience and performers alike were sensitive to its uniting influence.

The attractive programme gave folk songs and operatic choruses of mainly English and German origin, and the two choirs were in fine voice.

York Philharmonic Male Voice Choir is, of course, one of the finest choirs of its type in the country, and its trophy list must by now be quite considerable. Richard Lister's direction of them brings out a wealth of expression and control.

In his introduction of the Munster choir's music, conductor Torsten Brand spoke in thanks of Alan Bloomfield's accompaniment, and rightly so; he ably supported a large part of the evening's music.

Jewel-like

Two female voices were heard in this male voice preserve—those of Frau Anne Dodd, who charmingly translated the speeches, and Margaret Bedford, whose delightful rendering of four operatic arias sparkled even more jewel-like in the rich setting of male voice tones.

An indication of the enthusiastic support for this concert was the fact that, long before the concert began, programmes were sold out and were achieving an interesting rarity value.

William Byrd was right—singing is so good a thing.

K. R. P.

The YEP also covered the Mansion House reception and neither the Press nor the Yorkshire Post could resist the appeal of the two young lady guests.

SIGHT SEEING. Ulrike Wiede, left, and Bigit Sack, two girl members of the Munster Male Voice Choir, look around York on Saturday during the German choir's visit to its twin city. (A Yorkshire Post picture.)

The Lord Mayor of York, Ald.R. Scobey and the Lady Mayoress thank Herr Josef Nieheus for the gift of an engraved tray from the Münster Male Voice Choir. Also pictured are Coun. C.W. Oliver and Frau Anne Dodd.

Two frauleins visit York—with 70 men

A 70-STRONG group of members of the Munster Male Voice Choir — and two girls — were officially welcomed to York today.

The Lord Mayor of York, Ald. Ronald Scobey, chatted with Fraulein Ulrike Weide and Fraulein Bigit Sack at a reception in York Mansion House.

It was the girl's first visit to England. Fraulein Wiede, who has worked for a newspaper in Munster for only three weeks, will write a series of articles for the newspaper when the party return to Germany on Monday.

"It is very nice in England . . . much warmer than in Germany," said Fraulein Wiede, aged 21, who has been studying English for about eight years.

Fraulein Sack, aged 18, is acting as an interpreter for the choir, in which her father is a tenor.

Herr Josef Niehues, president of the Munster Choir, presented Ald. Scobey with an engraved tray for his hospitality in receiving the choir at the Mansion House.

Herr Niehues said that, although the visit to York was the choir's first, he hoped they would be able to come again.

"We have brought most of our members but we had to leave a few behind, as they are aged between 70 and 80 years," Herr Niehues told the Evening Press. The choir visited Orleans, Munster's twin city in France, some months ago.

The chairman of the York Philharmonic Male Voice Choir, Mr. John Nattrass, said he hoped the visits would become a regular exchange.

Tonight, the Munster Choir, guests for the weekend of the York choir, will give a joint concert, with their hosts, in York Guildhall.

Tomorrow, the German visitors will be shown some of York's historic buildings by members of York Voluntary Guides Association, and after lunch, they will be taken on a coach tour of the North York Moors.

● Picture shows: Herr Niehues introducing Fraulein Wiede to the Lord Mayor.

The YEP (Sat 2nd May 1970) also carried an entertaining piece written by sub-editor John Stevens, a second tenor in the Phil who had hosted Jop Häming. The article described the linguistic challenges of the week-end particularly trying to find a shared understanding of the salmon which was served both at lunch in Helmsley and at the evening party. John's attempts at a German description included; *"This fish can about a metre long be; it is fat, but not too fat. It swims many kilometres and is very tired when it to the river comes. It can jump from the water and is very expensive. You can this fish either in a tin or fresh buy. Many sports fishermen seek it, particularly in Scotland". "Ah yoo!" came the cry from one of the Germans...... "Tuna".*

Within days Josef Nieheus sent a letter of thanks to the Phil which was published in June.

Dear Friends of the choir,

From the 1st to the 4th of May the members of the Münster choir were permitted to be guests of your families and the City of York.

We thank you from the bottom of our hearts, the hospitality you offered and the words of your Rt. Hon. Lord Mayor Scobey at the Civic reception convinced us of the reality of the mutual goodwill. The combined concert proved that music still has international value and loses nothing by distances and strengthens friendships. We are eternally grateful.

The organisation which had been prepared with the utmost exactness and kind attention to detail was admirable, our impressions of you, of York and of Yorkshire and our Civic Reception are very marked and of lasting value.

We leave your city so full of history and where there is so much new life and growth and forward looking initiative.

We hope to have contributed in some small way to the building of the Symbolic Bridge, which overcomes past differences and connects future friendship.

We have had an outstanding experience and send our sincere thanks to you all

Auf Wiedersehen! Josef Niehues (Chairman)

In only 18 months from November 1968 to May 1970, two highly successful tours had been planned and enjoyed. In itself this was a considerable achievement, but it is clear that the hopes and dreams of both choirs was that this friendship should continue. In September 2015 – 45 years later – the choirs met again in Münster and the planning for a 2017 meeting is underway – hopes and dreams which have been fully realised.

However, in May 1970 the Phil could not relax, as planning for the visit of the Nijmegen choir in April 1971 was underway. The unflagging support of the 'Perimeter' group continued with coffee mornings and jumble sales.

The workload, which tours add to both a choir secretary and treasurer, has already been noted. In March 1970, Frank Morton stepped down as treasurer of the Phil. David Broadbent stepped into the role, but in the autumn of 1970 was transferred to Hull and had to resign. One of the choir's newest members – baritone James Waggott – stepped into the role. Jim was a new member in May 1970 and did not sing in the concert, although he did meet with members of the MM including Jop Häming. Jim was on the next visit by the Phil to Münster in 1976, where he not only sang a solo line but, more importantly, met Jop's brother Rudolf thus starting a life-long friendship.

Jim's dedicated service to the choir and, in particular, to the development and success of the twinning with the MM will become apparent as this story continues.

1971(April) – Visit to York by the Royal Nijmegen Mannenkoor

As soon as the MM returned to Münster, attention turned to the visit by Nijmegen 11 months later. This was to be a shorter tour, as the Nijmegen choir wished to meet up with their friends in Grimsby. The experience of hosting the MM was a valuable help in planning this visit. The Phil booked the popular bass singer, Owen Brannigan, as a soloist, and received this history of the choir from the Nijmegen secretary.

The choir was founded on the 15th September 1859 and is now 110 years old. It was first called the "Zangvereeniging Nijmegs Mannenkoor" and was conducted by Albert Roothan, a famous Nijmegen musician. The choir had many ups and downs during the last years of the 19th century and especially during the First World War it had bad times. After 1918 under the President Janus van Duren and conductor Theo Wanders it made glorious times and was invited to sing all over the country and several times in Belgium and Germany.

During the Second World War the choir was forbidden any action by the Germans, (music was subject to censorship so the choir chose not to sing in public during that period). On May 5th 1945. Liberation day, the choir sang on the corner of the streets in the totally destroyed city of Nijmegen with 150 members. In the meantime the choir got the predicate 'Koninklijk'(Royal) and Queen Wilhelmina visited the choir in 1945.

In 1962 two Nijmegen choirs joined forces, the Nijmegs Mannenkoor and the De Vereenigde Zangers conducted by our present conductor Jack van de Sand. The choir again had a glorious time visiting Remscheid, Aix-le-Bains, Dortmund, Duisburg, Münster, Antwerp, Hull and Grimsby.

The choir now has 62 members and is one of the oldest in Holland.

The tour began on Friday 16th April but unlike the May of 1970 the weather was cold and wet. Once again Don Crawford published an account of the week-end.

The rather miserable Friday morning of the 16th April, cold and looking very much like rain, was the beginning of a very memorable week-end for Phil members and for six of us at the start of a very long day. At 7 am we set off from the Black Swan Inn (closed at that hour) with two buses to meet and welcome our visitors at Hull. Our friends [57 singers] *were awaiting our arrival and demonstrated their pleasure to be in England with some very warm greetings and many handshakes; I think that we really received the reception meant for our guests.*

From Hull we travelled through the Wolds country, Troutsdale and onto Thornton Dale where we stopped for a little liquid (some had coffee) refreshment before proceeding through Hutton-le-Hole to Helmsley where we dined at the Feathers Hotel on York ham with trimmings, apple tart etc. and for those who still had a corner to fill there was coffee and cheese and biscuits.

After lunch the men had a wander around the market and shops before boarding the buses for York. The weather would not allow the North Riding scenery to look its best but we had all just eaten a hearty meal plus a little northern cheer to ease it down, so thus fortified we made light of the rain and proceeded to our next port of call, the Castle Museum.

We were received here by our President Councillor Oliver who gave a few words of welcome to our guests and then led the party around the museum. Time does fly when you are enjoying yourself (or getting past 21) and it seemed no time at all before we were seated at the banquet in the De Grey Rooms enjoying the wonderful meal prepared for us by our answer to TV's Galloping Gourmet, John Addinall and served with great attention to detail. At 6.30pm our members began to arrive to meet their guests and to escort them to their places of lodging, the fun started from that moment on, Dutch and English names were called, men stepped forward, some strangers others not, but a good sincere handshake bridged the language difference anyway and away they all went.

A very swift wash and brush up was all I had time for before the journey back into the city for our social evening in the De Grey Room's very impressive stateroom; a wonderful party was had by all with singing from both choirs and some solo numbers from members of both groups, souvenir gifts were exchanged by the guests and our choir and the whole evening enhanced by the presence of our 'Perimeter' friends was I think a great success.

The Civic reception on Saturday morning was a very friendly hour of informal exchanges and was a fine opportunity for our guests to see one of our city's finest examples of historic architecture, from the inside so to speak.

Our next official occasion was our evening concert in the Guildhall where a capacity audience was thrilled by some first class male voice offerings from both choirs and a very entertaining solo programme from our guest artist Owen Brannigan assisted by his pianist Keith Swallow, another memorable evening.

The departure day of our friends was soon upon us and after a very interesting tour of the city, conducted by members of the Voluntary Guides Association, lunch with our guests etc. we found ourselves assembled on the Cenotaph steps with our wives and families bidding farewell and safe journey to our guests from afar many of whom were now family friends. After all the pre-tour preparation work and the happy week-end events, I felt that strange empty feeling as I waved to the gradually disappearing buses, I don't suppose for one moment that I enjoyed the copyright to that particular feeling.

The YEP covered the week-end with two interesting articles:

Members of the Royal Nijmegan Choir at York Mansion House with the Sheriff of York (Coun. S. Stephenson) and the Lady Mayoress (Mrs. A. J. Hardcastle).

Dutch choir sing specially for Lord Mayor

THE Lord Mayor of York, Ald. A. J. Hardcastle, did the next best thing when he found he would not be able to attend a concert by the Dutch Nijmegen Choir tonight.

He asked the choir to give him a personal recital at the Mansion House instead.

So 57 members of the choir added a musical touch to their civic reception today with several choruses of their best-known songs.

They are staying with members of York Philharmonic Male Voice Choir during their two-day visit to the city, and they spent an hour at the Mansion House.

Welcoming them, the Lord Mayor recalled a visit he made to Nijmegen a few years ago. He enjoyed it very much and was greatly impressed with Holland, he said.

He hoped the choir would be just as impressed with York and that treir visit would "wet their appetites" and tempt them to return for a longer stay.

Heer Andre Von Hoydonk, the group's leader, said they had already enjoyed what they had seen of York, and the countryside.

"York is very like Nijmegen because we are both Roman towns—but, unfortunately, we have pulled down all our old buildings, so we are a bit jealous," he said.

"We are hoping to see the Minster and the Walls, of course, but we would like to come back and see the Minster when it has been restored."

The choir, who were spending the rest of the day sightseeing, are giving a special concert with the Male Voice Choir at the Guildhall tonight.

Give us a song in Dutch, say Nijmegen choir

MARCH · 1971.

Members of York Male Voice Choir sing for the Lord Mayor of York and Lady Mayoress (Ald. and Mrs. A. J. Hardcastle) while being entertained at the Mansion House last night. Joining in at the Lord Mayor's side is Coun. C. W. Oliver, president of the choir. The reception was in recognition of concerts which the choir has given in aid of city charities.

WHEN the Nazis marched into the Netherlands the artistic freedom of the Dutch became extremely limited. Music, for example, was subject to censorship.

This censorship was so rigid that the Nijmegen Male Voice Choir chose not to sing in public.

But when Liberation Day arrived, the choir, with 150 members, sang at street corners . . . where streets could still be recognised. For the city had virtually been destroyed by warfare.

On April 17 the Royal Nijmegen Male Voice Choir (Queen Wilhelmina visited them in 1945), will sing in York. The choir now has 62 members, and is one of the oldest in Holland.

Hosts will be the York Philharmonic Male Voice Choir, holders of the BBC Let The People Sing title for equal voice choirs in Great Britain.

The concert, in the Guildhall, will feature that renowned bass singer Owen Brannigan, who, apart from solo items, will be singing excerpts from Gilbert and Sullivan with the York choir.

The York choir, directed by Brian Lister, has something of a tongue-twister to contend with. I gather that the visitors have invited them to sing IN DUTCH, and have sent to York a copy of a rousing, salty song called De Zilvervloot. The York choir is coping admirably, and has included the song in its repertoire.

The final paragraph of this article mentions the Phil singing a patriotic Dutch song, 'De Zilvervloot'. This brought a tremendous response from our Dutch guests to the extent that their music Director ran down the Guildhall and, in front of the packed crowd, embraced a somewhat embarrassed Brian Lister.

The visit was a great success and now the Phil was able to relax after 3 years of fundraising and planning. It was also able to take great satisfaction from a job well done – indeed three jobs well done. The choir had proved to be good ambassadors for the city, at home and abroad, had formed a friendship with the MM which thrives today, and had established a format for exchange visits which has proven its value ever since.

The visits of 1969, 1970, and 1971 were extraordinary and today we benefit from the comprehensive reports written at that time. However the extraordinary instantly became the ordinary and no such written reports are available for any of the subsequent exchanges, the next of which took place in 1976.

1976 – Münster

Early in 1974 the Phil received an invitation to visit Münster during autumn 1975. The invitation was readily accepted, but the date was put back a year and a party of 45 set sail on Thursday 14th October. It was a night many remember. It was a rough crossing with the ferry taking part in rescuing three sailors from a sunken East German tanker. A news letter editorial gave this report: *'We could have done with a smoother passage. Arriving tired after a sleepless night being tossed about on the High Seas, was not the ideal way to start a rather exhausting, but nevertheless very pleasant four days.'*

About half of the party were hosted in homes, the remainder were well looked after at the Kolpinghaus, which also provided the rehearsal rooms for the MM.

The concert was held in the Rathausfestsaal – a different venue to 1969 – and Gerhard (Gerd) Wild was now the music director of the MM. In 1969/70 Torsten Brand had led the choir. As a schoolmaster, Gerhard was able to bring to the concert a High School Orchestra – Der Mozartorchester der Volkschule. He also invited two soloists, Carmen Gagnon (Soprano), and Donald Rutherford (Baritone) from the Münster City Theatre Company.

The Phil sang 11 pieces, again unaccompanied, a mix of folk and opera. In 1969 *Der Mond is Aufgegangen,* a German song practiced by the Phil, was not part of the public concert. However this time the choir sang in German, performing Schubert's *Die Nacht* as its penultimate item.

The visit repeated the format of 1969 with a civic reception, concert, and social evening. Some York singers still needed help in finding their way around Münster and two baritones needed directions to the Rathaus. Approaching a young lady they slowly and loudly asked. *"Do you speak English?" "Very well" came the reply. She continued "I recognise that uniform you're from York aren't you?" "How do you know that" came the puzzled enquiry. "I saw you in concert at St. Chad's two weeks ago, my dad's the vicar. The Rathaus is down the end of this road on the right."*

On the way home the Phil made an overnight stop at Nijmegen. No concert was planned but a social evening was held with the Nijmegen choir. Steve Cox recalls that night. The hotel the choir used was it seemed in two halves with separate staircases. Steve settled down for a late night card session with other Phil members and found that the route to his bedroom in the other half of the Hotel had been locked. Stranded, he negotiated for the use of half of Sid Teasdale's bed. Back home, things did not go to plan for their ladies either. Taking an opportunity for a family visit to Oxford while the men were away, Joan, wife of Sid Teasdale and her baby son Paul travelled to Oxford with Mary Cox. The car broke down and Mary (eight months pregnant at the time) was stranded in the car in pouring rain with baby Paul and Joan's dog while Joan went to get help.

Despite the success of the 1969 and 1971 concerts and this brief visit, the friendship with Nijmegen did not develop – they preferred to put their energies into their existing friendship with Grimsby Male Voice Choir. We did, however, meet again on stage in Münster in1989.

1978 – York

Two years later in October 1978 the MM returned to York. Their preference for air travel was, perhaps, enhanced by the rough sea crossing experienced by the Phil in 1976 and so the party of 73 flew into East Midlands Airport. This time both choirs had accompanists, Herr Yserman travelled with the MM and Lorna Whitworth played for the Phil.

The joint concert was once more at the Guildhall, and the guest performers were a Ladies Youth choir from Münster which was visiting York at that time.

Münsterscher Männer-gesangverein und der Jugendchor Münster-Gremmendorf

The ladies were led by a music teacher, Frau Liesel Steinwachs. There were 21 members, most of whom had been singing together for ten years. When they grew too old to remain part of a children's choir, their desire to keep singing was such that in 1977 they formed the youth choir. After performing before a visiting group of Yorkshire Young Farmers in Münster, they started a pen pal correspondence with some and accepted an invitation to visit York. This photo of them singing a joint item with the MM at the Guildhall concert does now beg the question as to whether any of these young ladies are now tending Yorkshire farms.

The youth choir sang seven items plus a joint piece with the MM and greatly enhanced the concert, which once again played to a good audience.

1981 – Münster

In October 1981 the Phil was once more in Münster travelling by coach and ferry from Hull to Rotterdam. There were two significant changes to the party. Brian Lister had resigned as Music Director in 1980 and the choir was now led by a young man, David Keeffe. Lorna Whitworth travelled as accompanist, being both the first accompanist to travel and the first woman to join any of these tours as a performer. There were 44 singers in the party.

Yorkshire Evening Press, Friday, October 30, 1981 13

MEMBERS of the York Philharmonic Male Voice Choir, with their accompanist, Mrs Lorna Whitworth, who arrived in Munster, West Germany, today.

York choir speak language of music

LANGUAGE will not be a barrier for a York choir arriving in Germany today — for it intends to communicate in music.

Few of the York Philharmonic Male Voice Choir know German and not many of their hosts in York's twin town of Munster speak English, according to the choir's secretary, Mr Donald Crawford.

"But it does not matter, as music will be our best language," he said.

Three-quarters of the 60-strong choir are now on their third trip to Munster, as guests of the town's own male voice choir.

"The twinning of the choirs happened in 1969, and we have been visiting each other ever since," said Mr Crawford.

On its arrival today, the choir was going straight into rehearsals for its concert with the Germans on Saturday

"But it is not all music-making. We have a lot of fun too. There will be a civic reception and a party held for us," said Mr Crawford.

There is a traditional exchange of gifts between the groups and, this year, the York choir is presenting the Germans with a hand-painted plate bearing the York rose.

Some members of the choir are staying with friends they have made on previous visits and others are staying at the Kolpinghaus — which Mr Crawford described as a "sort of YMCA".

On the choir's repertoire is its theme song, The Grand Old Duke of York, written for them by the King Singers arranger.

"We also do grand opera, spirituals and comic songs. Although the Germans might not understand the language, they do appreciate our animation that goes with it," said Mr Crawford.

The only woman on the trip is the choir's pianist, Mrs Lorna Whitworth.

The joint concert was held at the Landesmuseum, the third venue in three trips and played to a full house. As guest soloist the MM invited a good friend of theirs – Ude Krekow, a baritone with the Hamburg Opera – who was accompanied on the piano by his wife Diana. This gave the opportunity for a joint item with which to finish. Both choirs and Ude sang 'The Holy City', the first joint item since the very first concert in 1969 and one well liked by the large audience.

The concert was reviewed by the Münsterschen Zeitung, a review which sparked some controversy. Some adverse comments were made, for example, about the tenors of the Phil over-singing and becoming raucous in the opening set. However the reviewer was complimentary towards later items, in particular, 'Die Nacht'. He was also critical of the MM pieces which included soloists. This piece led to some concert-goers writing to the paper to complain about unjustified criticism. These protesters included members of the Nijmegen choir who had travelled across for the evening. The photo (below) from that review shows the Phil ready to sing and being introduced to the audience. David Keeffe is stood on the extreme left behind Laura at the piano. The reviewer was unhappy with our tenors but made no reference to presentation; the choir sang wearing bow ties with a blazer – a decision which led to some 'discussion'.

Münstersche Zeitung STADT MÜNSTER

Zu einem Gemeinschaftskonzert trafen sich die Yorker Sänger mit dem münsterschen Männergesangverein im Landesmuseum.
Bild: Hänscheid

1983 – York

In September 1983, 62 members of the MM set out for York, travelling by air from Amsterdam to Manchester. However, they had some problems at the airport. The flight was overbooked and six singers were left behind. They followed on by private jet to Leeds where they were met by members of the Phil.

The joint concert was once more in the Guildhall with the York Railway Institute Band, led by G.E. Pratt, as guests. David Keeffe directed the Phil with Les Bresnen on piano. This concert was well reviewed by the YEP with no controversy.

The social evening was held in the Assembly rooms and on this occasion our guests from the MM provided much of the entertainment. Ludger Voss, a bass singer and an imposing figure, on his first visit to York, acted the role of the Kiepenkerl – a pedlar and traditional symbol of the city – and introduced some Münster traditions to the Phil. Alderman Keith Wood, the President of the Phil still remembers his introduction to drinking Schnapps from a wooden spoon. The evening also included a musical sketch 'Die fidele Gerichtssitzung'. This was a musical trio accompanied by Martin Wiese in which the three singers, Theo Mucksch, Berthold Auerbach and Ludger Voss, set new standards by performing in costume.

1987 – Carols in Kirkgate

The next visit was not scheduled until 1989, planned to celebrate the centenary of the MM. To shorten this six year gap the Phil invited the committee of the MM to join in the 25th year celebrations of 'Carols in Kirkgate'. This invitation was accepted and eight guests joined the event. The visit was enhanced by a reception at the Mansion House with the Lord Mayor, but is best remembered for the coming together for the singing of *Silent Night*. The MM singers were invited forward to join the Phil in singing the excellent arrangement by Brian Lister. It was a moment to be remembered with its echoes of the trenches of 1914.

This photo shows MM chairman Wolfgang thanking the Phil for the invitation. The setting is the 'Half Moon Court' in the Castle Museum where the choir held an end of run party; the tables laden with food can be seen in the background.

1989 – Centenary Celebrations with the MM

In October 1989 the MM reached a magnificent milestone for any choir – 100 years. Clearly any concert planned to mark this event would need to be special – and so it was. Both Nijmegen and York choirs were invited together with their wives and partners. Immediately the organisational work load increased, particularly for the MM who now had to organise a three day visit by a party of 103 from York, and an overnight stay for 154 from Nijmegen. This would be the first time that York ladies had joined the tour – so no more late night card games for Steve Cox. The sartorial ambiguity of 1981 had been resolved as now the Phil had two uniforms: blazer and tie, and evening dress – enhanced on special occasions with a white rose.

For this concert Richard Bowman directed the Phil, with Mary Stockdale on the piano. In the 20 years from Brian Lister to the appointment of our current director, Berenice Lewis in 2000, the Phil had six directors; five of whom took part in joint concerts with the MM. This rapid turnover was primarily down to our selection of talented younger candidates who moved away from York as a result of work and marital commitments.

The Jubilee concert held in the large Kongressaal der Halle Münster was presented by: the three male voice choirs; guest soloists, Daniela Stampa-Middendorf; Christiane Lülf; Heinz Kruse; and, once more, Ude Krekow; and the student orchestra of the Westphalia Music School. The concert was also recorded and a cassette of a selection of the programme was issued. Not surprisingly the ticket price at 15DM was the highest yet charged – the price in 1969 had been 3DM – but this did not deter a large crowd.

When three male voice choirs share a concert platform there is a danger that there will be little contrasting style and repertoire for the audience to enjoy. This was not the case on this occasion. Nijmegen sang opera choruses; the MM did a number of items led by their guest soloists, a performance style they do like and use often; and the Phil sang to its strengths with the following pieces: *Gwahoddiad,*

Wandering the Kings Highway, Softly as I leave you, Sound an Alarm, The White Rose, Psalm 126, finishing with the German folk song *Der Mond*. This selection was well received by the audience and the music critics. The reviews complimented the Phil on its sensitivity, its flexibility in sound shapes, and its ability to reflect the tender melancholy of the folk tunes. Critics from both Münster newspapers appreciated the singing of *Der Mond*, described as a special gesture to both the host choir and the audience and being a *'smoothly-coloured finale to the presentation'.* All three choirs came together for a joint item at the end of the first half, *Landerkennung* by Grieg with Ude Krekow as soloist. The concert ended with the three choirs and orchestra joining together in *Va Pensiero* (Nabucco – Verdi) and *The Holy City,* with Ude Krekow as soloist. It was a gala night.

Celebrations continued the following evening with a Jubilee dinner and party. Appropriate to the occasion, the MM made a lifetime award to Josef Niehues, who had worked so hard to set up these choir links, and presented some long service awards. There was one certificate of particular interest to the Phil, as it recognised the immense contribution made to the success of the York-MM twinning by Anne Kirchhoff. Anne's unflagging ability to interpret had been relied upon by both choirs and the civic authorities

The Phil made a surprise presentation when Chairman John Addinall presented Wolfgang Wächter with a birthday cake. Members of the Phil lit small candles, and stood to sing Happy Birthday to the MM. This has been recorded in the history of the MM and the photos published there are shown below.

Mit „Happy Birthday, dear MM“ gratulierten die Sängerfreunde aus York, die dazu Kerzen zum Geburtstag leuchten ließen Fotos: ohw

1990 – Inauguration of Alderman Keith Wood as Lord Mayor

In May 1990, Wolfgang Wächter, accompanied by Anne Kirchhoff, attended the Annual Meeting of York City Council to witness the inauguration of Alderman Keith Wood as Lord Mayor for the year.

1991 – York

In October 1991 the MM made their fourth visit to York, bringing a party of 94 which included wives and partners. The concert was part of the debut season at the Barbican centre, a new 1500 seat hall. The plan had been to have choirs plus Ude Krekow and the Salonorchester. Unfortunately the Salonorchester was unable to come. All previous concerts had been at the Guildhall. It was very expensive to hire the Barbican centre but a large audience justified that decision. Rather like Münster in 1989 the ticket price did have to reflect the new realities. Entry to the first concert in 1970 had cost 6/-; tickets for the Barbican were now £4- £6. The joint items to close the concert were *Va Pensiero* and *The Holy City* (as per 1989) with the two choirs enjoying the boisterous spiritual *Ride the Chariot*.

The YEP called the evening an 'exceptional concert;' which pleased the Phil as, once again, there was a new team in charge. Margaret Martin, the first lady ever to direct the choir, was assisted by Frances Hughes on piano.

1993(October) – Wenn Männer s(w)ingen!

The Phil was back in Münster in what was another anniversary year, the 1200th anniversary of the city and the 25th anniversary of the three choirs of Münster, York, and Nijmegen coming together. However on this occasion Nijmegen was unable to take part, although their committee members did attend. The Jubilee nature of the week-end was acknowledged with a letter of greeting and congratulations to the two choirs from the Lord Mayor, Councillor, Ann Reid.

The MM marked the occasion by granting honorary membership to Jim Waggott and Has van der Lee of the Nijmegen choir.

Josef Niehues, Jim Waggott, Has van der Lee

The joint concert was once again enjoyed by a large and appreciative audience – inflation had pushed the ticket price to 18DM – and the Phil was directed by Ian Colling with Eileen Grey at the piano. The Salonorchester joined the two choirs and in the joint items were two pieces of modern songs arranged by Gerhard Wild: *Raindrops* by Burt Bacharach, and *Sailing* by G. Sutherland.

1997(March) – A twin city Friendship week-end

This time the anniversary was the 40th year of the two cities twinning. The MM was joined on this trip by 22 members of the Constantia male voice choir which was also directed by Gerd Wild. This led to the largest group yet to be accommodated in York, 64 singers and 63 partners, a total of 127. In a sign of the times, one of the two buses leaving Münster was 'Non Smoking'. The joint concert was held in the Jack Lyons Concert Hall at York University. The Phil was directed by Jill Wild accompanied by Eileen Grey.

Here the combined choirs, directed by Gerd Wild, join together for the joint item 'Va Pensiero'.

Party Night was held at York racecourse, once more with a variety of entertainment.

Here we see a group of dubious looking German Nuns re-enacting a scene from the film 'Sister Act'. In 2000 the Phil added an 'interpretation' of the 'Sound of Music' to these entertainments.

The York branch of the Von Trapp family

2000 – The European Millenium Tour

As the Millennium approached, the Phil wished to mark it with a more extensive tour including another visit to Münster. A specialist music tour company was engaged to help with this planning.

The finalised itinerary led to this being the longest tour the choir has ever undertaken, starting from York on Friday 26th May returning on Sunday 4th June. To mark this extended tour, a dark blue sweater was commissioned bearing the choir logo, the year 2000 and European Tour. This was a popular choice of clothing which can still be seen at rehearsals 15 years later.

From Rotterdam, two coaches with a total of 98 passengers headed south to Dieblich, a small town in the picturesque wine-producing Mosel valley south of Koblenz. Accommodation was at the Hotel Pistono, an excellent choice. The following day – Sunday – included a tour of a hilltop chapel Matthias Kapelle and a joint concert with the Kobern-Gondorf Male Voice Choir together with a local school orchestra.

In the archive there are very few photographs taken on this tour, but there is a good selection showing the Kapelle and the area from the later tour in 2006 (see below). After the concert the Phil was presented with a share of the takings from the concert, an unexpected donation. The Matthias Kapelle stands at the top of a cliff with a steep path marking the Way of the Cross. The Phil discovered that the Kobern-Gondorf Choir voluntarily maintain the path and the Stations of the Cross, so gave this donation back with the request that a bench be placed along the path. This was done and a year later a party of more than twenty from the Phil, plus

two couples from Münster, returned for a service to bless the bench. The Kobern-Gondorf choir then added a plaque and behind it planted a wild white rose. Given the emotional connection with both the place and the people made during that two day visit in 2000, it is no surprise that the Phil returned in both 2006 and 2013.

On Monday 29th May the choir travelled across the border to Strasbourg, with a free day on the Tuesday. The first tenor section included the choir's own specialist tour guide in Fred Luther, an architectural draughtsman with a deep love of both Church architecture and all things Victorian. Fred conducted two walking tours of Strasbourg on the Wednesday morning. He recruited Mary Cox to help in this by handing her a Yorkshire flag and inviting her to hold it high and walk in front whilst he carried his other props. These included a cardboard mock up of the cathedral front which he used to explain the unique features of the construction.

Later the choir made the short journey back into Germany to perform a one hour concert – not a joint concert – in an attractive concert hall in Bad Krozingen.

During the short stay in Strasbourg, music director Jill Wild announced her engagement to Jon Henderson, who had travelled with her.

On Thursday the party travelled to Münster where the group was joined by Keith Wood – President of the Phil – with his wife June and their daughter. There followed the now familiar pattern of social events, private parties, a reception in the Peace Hall with the city authorities, and a joint concert.

For once the Münster concert was not sold out; many of the citizens were on a long week-end break marking Ascension Day. Bass soloist Mark Coles joined with the MM, and the Phil also introduced a new style when deputy music director, Berenice Hopkins, joined Eileen Grey at the piano to give a four-handed accompaniment to *The Rhythm of Life*.

Jill Wild is introduced to the tradition of the Kiepenkerl.

With the visits all done the journey home via Rotterdam and North Sea Ferries began at 11am on the Saturday with arrival back in York on the Sunday morning.

Also used on this tour were individual booklets giving the full itinerary and essential contacts etc. Shown here is a booklet from a later tour. Small enough to fit a pocket or a handbag, these guides have given invaluable service over the years and thanks must be offered to Mary Cox who has spent many hours compiling them.

2003 – York

Soon after the choir returned to York, Jill Wild resigned her position as music director, as she had moved from the area in preparation for her wedding. Berry (Berenice) Hopkins – Jill's deputy – immediately stepped up to the role and so led the choir in April 2003 when the MM returned for a sixth visit.

By now the exchanges ran like a well-oiled machine. The joint concert was held in the Tempest Anderson Hall where the two choirs were joined by German soloist Mark Coles and the Salonorchester Münster. During the concert Honorary Membership of YPMVC was awarded to Josef Niehues and Ferdinand aan der Stegge for their work in both establishing and developing the friendship between the choirs. In the partnership history as written by the MM, compliments were paid to Berry Hopkins – the first time the MM had seen her at work. The reviewer noted how impressive it was that the choir of 50 men responded instantly to every movement of her finger, made easier, he noted, by the fact that the whole programme was sung from memory.

On this occasion the concert was on the Sunday evening and a Dinner Dance was held at the racecourse on the Saturday evening.

2004(May) – France

The Millenium European Tour had been a success and sowed the seeds for a second trip. Ideas for choir events can come out of rehearsals, committee meetings, a post rehearsal pint or, as in this case, a round of golf. A focal point was the fact that the cities of York and Dijon in Burgundy, France, had been twinned since 1953, and yet there had been no contact between the Phil and any French choir. No specialist tour company, as in 2000, was engaged to help in this tour – all the planning was done by the choir – primarily by Gerard White the chairman at the time. Many hours were given to the task and many miles covered, but Gerard did benefit by being able to successfully reinvigorate his schoolboy French. Another contributor was Derek Twigg, a choir member, who was, at the time, living both in England and France. By the time the tour took place, Derek had relocated to France; but as early as 2001 he had contacted the tourist board in Dijon to start the planning.

As crows might fly the journeys from York to Münster or York to Dijon are not vastly different, but by coach and ferry they do differ. On the journey to Münster, North Sea Ferries does the bulk of the work; a trip to Dijon, via Dover-Calais requires many more hours of coach travel.

So the tour was planned to break up the journey, and to offer our 80 holidaymakers both a taste of ancient cities and rural France. Reflecting the confidence and success of the Millenium tour there was another commemorative sweater commissioned, this time, appropriately, in light blue.

The journey down included a two night stay in Reims, north east of Paris, an ancient city badly damaged by the 1914-18 war; then two nights in Dijon, the ancient capital of Burgundy. The return leg headed west into the picturesque Loire valley to spend two nights in rural Anger in the Anjou region. Although not so apparent to a modern day traveller, Anjou and the land to the north is that part of France with close historical links with England; having endured medieval dynastic squabbles, whilst enjoying good trading links. The tour then stopped two nights in Rouen, the ancient capital of Normandy, with its particularly close, and contested historical connections. The musical content comprised a concert in Dijon, shared with le Chorum de Dijon, the local male voice choir; and participation in a male voice festival in Anger – Festival d'Choeur d'Hommes d'Anjou. In addition it was hoped to perform short informal concerts in Reims and Rouen Cathedrals.

This was the first time that Berry Lewis (now married) had led the choir on a continental visit and we, and our audiences, appreciated her very good language skills (both French and German). Her first short, informal concert in Reims' Cathedral went to plan, and the stay was once more enlightened by walking tours arranged by Fred Luther.

Most of the people on the tour had not previously visited Dijon and were not disappointed. There is a sense that citizens of one ancient European city easily feel at home when visiting another, and Dijon had that 'comfortable' feel. This was made even more so when our civic reception was held in a vaulted stone hall in the Palais du Duc. The choir was relaxed, with a glass of wine in hand, toasting our hosts in song, in a medieval setting.

The concert was held in the Salon de Flore, an 18th century ballroom in the ornate French Baroque style, within the Palais de Duc. There was one rare sight when the Phil stood on stage holding music folders. It had been agreed that the choir would sing *The Soldiers' Chorus* from Gounod's *Faust* in French. The choir was anxious not to disappoint the audience, and very rarely sings in French; so no chances were taken and copies were used.

Our host choir kindly gave most of the concert over to us, but joined us in a joint item; not as first expected an English piece, but the Russian prayer *Tebe Peom.*

As it transpired, the most memorable part of this male voice concert had nothing to do with the men on stage. With little by way of introduction Berry, an excellent mezzo soprano, turned to the audience, and with Eileen accompanying, began to sing. The words and melody of *When you wish upon a Star* – from Walt Disney's 1940 film *Pinocchio* – floated over the audience, and then moved seamlessly into *La Vie en Rose,* made famous the world over by Edith Piaf. The choir, also hearing this for the first time, was as entranced as the audience which swayed and hummed along. It was one of a number of times in recent years when the Phil has been very proud of its talented director.

The tour moved into rural France and travelled to Anger. Here the local male voice choir had been ambitious enough to hold a week-long regional male voice festival. It was an interesting and ambitious festival with six concerts in a week in various churches in the region. The Choeur Rossica de Saint-Petersbourg, a ten man choir from Russia, sang in five of these concerts. There were three French choirs involved plus one from Osnabruck and us. In the church at Chalonnes on the Loire we shared the Saturday evening with the local choir the Choeur d'Hommes d'Anjou, and the Choeur Rossica de Saint Petersburg. What is most memorable from this evening was not the concert itself but the reception that followed. The three choirs, supporters, and many of the audience, gathered in a large hall where an excellent buffet had been laid out. As is common on such occasions each choir led some impromptu singing. The small group from St Petersburg impressed the most by singing a haunting song led by a young bass soloist – so talented he would have been welcomed in any choir anywhere.

The journey home was broken at Rouen, to the north west of Paris, and once again we were able to sing in the cathedral. Our last Hotel was being refurbished, which meant that some of the public rooms were out of commission. This didn't dampen the mood although there were very few, outside of our party, who heard the informal sing delivered in the, as yet, unfinished foyer. And so back to York!

In a letter of thanks to Gerard White one couple wrote: *Thank-you for a wonderful trip. Not everyone appreciates how difficult it is to put together a near faultless holiday and concert tour, but we do! Thanks to you and your team for a smashing trip, one which we won't forget. You managed to equal, if not surpass, the tour of 2000, and it is moments like this that make the Phil and its supporters such a joy.* A sentiment echoed by many.

A familiar setting for York folk

Berry and choir turn towards Eileen as she receives her bouquet in Anger.

The reception in Anger

2006 – Münster and Dieblich

In June 2006 the Phil visited Münster and made a return visit to Dieblich. This account of the relationship between the choirs has now covered 38 years and yet few pictures of Münster have yet been included. Good prints from the early years are scarce but, by 2006, the age of digital photography was well established, and the choir archive now has a more than adequate supply. A selection is given here showing both Münster and Dieblich. The abundance of digital images now available often show choir members who have died in recent years. This can lead any reviewer to remember and to reflect on both the robustness of life as reflected by the choir, and the fragility of any individual hold upon it.

It was now 38 years since the friendship with Münster began, and so the tried and tested tour planning was as efficient as ever. However, at the last moment, Berry found she was unable to travel, and so Allan Wilkinson, her deputy, stepped out of the tenor section to successfully lead the choir.

The Münster concert was, once more, shared with the Salonorchester and guest soloists; and in Kobern-Gondorf, six years after the first visit, we sang once more with the Kobern-Gondorf choir.

In Münster there was one unexpected yet appreciated presentation. The city council presented Jim Waggott with a certificate of thanks and recognition for his 38 years of commitment, in developing and maintaining the friendship between our choirs and cities. The certificate, which appropriately named him as Jim rather than James, was presented by Oberbürgermeister Dr. Berthold Tillman. The Phil is proud, and indeed very thankful, for all the work that Jim has done over the years, although Jim himself thinks of it as pleasure rather than work; he is, at the moment (February 2016), planning a 2017 exchange which will take his years of dedication to this friendship to 49.

The York tour party included three former Lord Mayors of York: Keith Wood, choir President; David Wilde, a second tenor; and the recently retired Lord Mayor Janet Greenwood, shown here with Oberbürgermeister Dr. Berthold Tillman. This added to the close links between the cities and the choirs.

Sightseeing in Münster

The Little Green Frog sung on the stairs by Neil Wood, Tony Winn, and Duncan Muress led by Richard Kay

The Matthias Kapelle

Eileen Grey and Hazel Hockridge at the bench donated by the Phil

View from the Matthias Kapelle

The late Peter Reid [who took a number of the photographs used in this narrative] with Peter Smith (behind) and 2 members of the Kobern Gondorf choir.

Sunday morning Church service

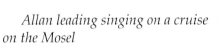

Allan leading singing on a cruise on the Mosel

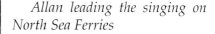

Allan leading the singing on North Sea Ferries

Kath Wilkinson leading the line dancing at the Hotel Pistono in 2006. During the 2013 visit the evening entertainment was an Eileen Soirée – the only time one has been held away from York.

2009 – Let All Men Sing! Celebrating 40 years of Friendship

This was how the Phil titled the April joint concert held in the Chapter House of York Minster. This celebration did emphasise the slight distinction between the choirs in recording dates, with the MM still working a year ahead of the Phil. Ludger Voss of the MM worked hard to produce a book entitled *1968-2008 40 Jahre Partnershaft*, in time for this celebratory week-end. This has proved to be a valuable resource of both facts and photos for this later publication.

Both choirs agreed to mark this anniversary as there were still 14 singers in both choirs who had been part of the very first concert in April 1969. Certificates recognising this achievement were presented by the Lord Mayor at a reception in the Mansion House. Nine of the 14 were present, five from Münster: Constantin Blees; Rudolph Häming; Tono Niemann; Hans-Jürgen Nienhaus; and Rolf Stöppler; and from York: Frank Caine; Peter Evans; Mike Johnson and Tony Sawyer. Rudolph Häming had married Maria the day before the first concert in 1969 and so they were also celebrating their Ruby Wedding, a good indicator that choral singing aids marital bliss.

Mrs. Gladys Price, an accomplished embroiderer, a member of the ladies choir at 'Carols in Kirkgate', and wife to second tenor Derek Price, designed and had made a commemorative banner carrying both city crests and both choir logos. This was presented to the MM at a celebratory dinner held at the racecourse.

The Chapter House was full for the concert, and was a visual as well as an audio spectacle. The two choirs flanked the Salonorchester and once more Mark Coles was the guest soloist with the MM.

To record this significant celebration the Phil had the concert recorded by Gary Skyrme of Just Music and photographed by Kippa Matthews. A double CD was then produced, one a slide show of the week-end, the other being the recording of the concert.

Here are the sleeve notes to that double CD. These record, in the last paragraph, the sadness felt when York singer Bernie Carter, who enjoyed his 62nd birthday at the Celebration Dinner, collapsed and died a few weeks later.

The weekend of 4th and 5th April 2009 will be remembered fondly by many, and we hope that this commemorative pack of photographs and music will add to that enjoyment.

In fine spring weather our guests arrived via North Sea Ferries and Manchester airport. Lunch at the Little Italy Restaurant was followed by a rehearsal in the Chapter House; appreciated by the many visitors to the Minster. It is at this point that our photographic record starts.

At 5.30pm the Lord Mayor of York hosted a reception in the Mansion House – the home of the Lord Mayor since 1730. Guests included the Bürgermeisterin of Münster and the Regional Cultural Attaché from the German Embassy. After greetings from both cities the Lord Mayor was pleased to give scrolls of recognition from the City of York to those 14 singers in both choirs who were there in April 1969 and who are still singing today.

Oliver Haug was able to present the Lord Mayor with the first copy of the history of the twinning of the choirs, copies of which were later given to every member of the Phil. The robed civic party and guests then processed to the Minster upholding another centuries old tradition.

At 7.30pm the music began with both choirs joining in the title song of the evening: 'Let All Men Sing!' At the start of the second half the Lord Mayor presented each choir with a pewter Quaich – a cup of welcome. Jim Waggott – concert manager York, – was delighted to able to use the cup the following evening when proposing the toast to the two choirs at our celebratory dinner. The concert came to a close with choirs, the orchestra and Mark Coles coming together in 'It don't mean a thing/Sing Sing'.

The after concert reception included supper and some more light hearted music.

Sunday was a free day for our guests where old friendships were rekindled and new ones formed.

Later that day, on a fine spring evening, our story moves to York Racecourse where more than 220 met for a celebration dinner. An excellent meal was enhanced by the orchestra who played between courses and by the orchestra, both choirs and Mark afterwards. Toasts and awards included the gift of the celebratory banner to Münster, the conferring of honorary Life Membership of YPMVC on Theo Richter and Gerhard Wild and the presentation of flowers and a card to Rudolf and Maria Häming on their 40th Wedding Anniversary. Colin Hockridge received the second copy of the Twinning History before all copies were distributed. The work done by the team in MM, in particular Ludger Voss in producing this excellent history is appreciated by all in York.

On the Monday afternoon, still in sunshine, the coaches departed for the evening ferry, and our photographic record ends with lunch shortly before arriving back in Münster.

The enjoyable weekend celebrations reflected and enhanced the words used by our President Hon. Alderman Keith Wood in a greeting in the concert programme:

"I would venture to suggest that we have not only achieved the original aims of 'twinning' but have enjoyed ourselves greatly along the way. Long may it continue!"

Ich nehme es mir mal heraus zu behaupten, dass wir nicht nur die ursprünglichen Ziele der Partner-schaft erreicht haben, sondern dass wir in hohem Maße Vergnügen dabei gehabt haben. Lang möge sie weiterleben!

Bernard Carter – Baritone YPMVC: the photo album includes a picture of Bernie Carter celebrating his birthday as part of our celebration dinner on the 5th April. It is with immense sadness that we have to report that Bernie collapsed and died on Tuesday 26th May 2009...

Maintaining the old tradition of processing from the Mansion House to the Minster. The Rt. Hon. Lord Mayor of York Brian Watson with Bürgermeisterin of Münster Beata Vilhjalmsson

Mark Coles and Peter Schwarz singing 'Well did you evah?'

Freya Deitring leads the orchestra

From the heart boys!

Joint item with the commemorative banner on display

Mike and Margaret Johnson with Rudolf Häming

Frank Caine and Peter Evans

Tony Sawyer with Oliver Haug Chairman of the MM and Director of the Salonorchester

Gladys and Derek Price present the commemorative banner to Oliver Haug.

Mike, Rudolf, Frank, Peter and Tony all took part in the 1969 concert.

2009(June) – Lochem & Bruges

The friendship between York and Nijmegen had not flourished. Over time the links between Nijmegen and Münster also faded, and the MM had formed a new bond with the Lochems Mannenkoor. Lochem is an attractive Dutch town close to the German border and a visit by York was planned to take place just a few weeks after the 40th Year Celebrations. By way of introduction, a small group from Lochem had come across to join us in the Minster concert. The proficient York Tour Group arranged a visit which allowed for a two night stay in Lochem and a one night stay in Bruges. On arrival there was a free afternoon in Lochem during which our hosts led walking tours of the town, plus an informal evening in the hotel. The next day (Saturday) there was a joint concert held in a large town centre church – the Grote Kerk. The concert went to plan, and included the joint item *Seventy Six Trombones*. Drawing on the memories of the first visit to Holland in 1969 – 40 years earlier – the Phil relearned *De Zilvervloot*. This was not listed on the programme and was sung, unannounced, to a rapturous response. It was clear to all in the Phil just how important this song is to our Dutch friends. Indeed we believe that both the Lochem and the Nijmegen choirs sang this patriotic song in the streets following liberation in 1945. A new friendship had begun!

The tour moved onto Bruges arriving in the early afternoon on the Sunday and leaving again at 3pm on Monday giving the Phil a full day to explore.

Sightseeing in Lochem- a very attractive town

Chairman Colin Hockridge presents a gift to Gerrit te Rietstap director of the Lochem choir

The post performance party

There were no tours from either side of the North Sea from 2010-2013. It had been hoped that Lochem might come to York during this time, but that visit did not take place until 2015. However, in 2010 there was a change of name in Münster. The Münsterscher Männergesangverein, as the choir had been called for 120 years, merged with the Constantia choir. Both choirs were directed by Gerd Wild and both had declining numbers. With the merger came a new name – MarQant. Though not a recognised German word, we understand it is an expression used to describe 'something special'.

2013 – Münster and Dieblich/Kobern-Gondorf

The Phil was once more on tour, this time, a June visit which included Kobern-Gondorf as well as the scheduled visit to Münster. Nevertheless, despite the familiarity of this route, there were changes made to any previous format. There was no joint concert in Münster. Instead, on the Friday night, there was a dinner to which the Lochems Mannenkoor was also invited. As might be expected during dinner all three choirs took turns to sing, and came together in two joint pieces: the *Huntsmen Chorus,* and *Tebe Peom.*

On Sunday the Phil travelled south to the Hotel Pistono in Dieblich. The joint concert with the Kobern-Gondorf choir and the school Violin orchestra was in aid of a Children's' Cancer Charity.

There was free time on Monday and in the evening the choir held a Soirée. These regular York evenings of 'home-grown' entertainment are described elsewhere in this book. This was the first time one had been held whilst on tour, and it was a very successful evening.

2015

The story comes up to date in 2015 with two distinctive events both linked to a number of significant anniversaries. In April 2015 the Phil reached its 90th Birthday. Lochems Mannenkoor had also asked to visit York in this month. It was decided to invite Lochem to join with us in our birthday celebrations. In addition to our anniversary the date fell within a few weeks of the 70th anniversary of the liberation of Lochem by British troops, and was also close to the 85th birthday of the Lochem choir. This then gave the basis of our April celebrations.

The Phil had also been invited by the Münster city authorities to visit in September to take part in an international concert commemorating the ending of World War ll.

April – York – 90 Years of Song!

It was a pleasure for the Phil to welcome our friends from Lochem, to what was a busy week-end but one graced by some fine spring weather. One advantage of travelling by North Sea Ferries is that the arrival time in York can be no later than 10.30am. This does mean that activities can be scheduled for arrival day. The Lochem men found themselves singing in the small medieval Holy Trinity Church in Goodramgate at 12 noon. The joint concert that evening was held in the De Grey Rooms. This fine 19th century ballroom had been closed for several years until it came under the management of the Theatre Royal and has recently been brought back to life. It was a great success, with some of the audience sat café style around tables. The Lochem choir was conducted by Geritt te Rietstap, who has been its director for 27 years with Gerard Wesselink as accompanist. As has been the case since 2000, the Phil was led by Berry Lewis, with Eileen Grey at the piano. The concert ended with both choirs singing *Nessun Dorma,* a fine way to end the evening, and one which was to evoke fond memories only a few months later.

A 16 page Anniversary week-end Programme was printed which sought to tell the history of the Phil in both words and pictures. [It was the research undertaken to produce that programme which became the catalyst for writing this extended history]. Included in that programme was an article detailing another anniversary, that being the celebration of 50 years of membership of the Phil by Tony Sawyer. This achievement was formally recognised at the gala dinner on the Sunday evening when Tony was presented with a commemorative lapel badge to replace the 25 year service badge he had worn with pride for so many years.

On Sunday afternoon the Lochem men attended a Civic Reception at the Mansion House. These days, fire regulations limit the number that can attend functions in the State room, so it was unfortunate that the Lochem ladies could not be included.

The gala dinner filled the medieval Merchant Adventurers' Hall. The Civic party attended, as did Mr. Steve Kettlewell, Consul for the Netherlands, and two young army captains from the 4th/7th Dragoon Guards. This regiment had been part of the liberating British force in 1945, and had provided the support troop to the town during that summer. When the two officers were introduced the warmth of the applause from our Lochem friends was such as to make us feel both very proud yet very humble. As with the Phil's rendition of *De Zilvervloot* in 2009 we were touched by the depth of emotion that such shared experiences can evoke.

The tour left York on the Monday morning but was able to spend time visiting Beverley before making the short journey to the Hull ferry port.

It was a memorable visit and we were pleased that after having had to postpone an earlier planned visit our new friends had been able to join us at such a significant time. Lochem have in their choir an excellent photographer Mr. Jan Kolkman. Not surprisingly, within a couple of weeks a photographic album of the week-end was made available to all via the internet.

Gerrit leads the choir in the Mansion House

Sitting down to dinner in the Merchant Adventurers' Hall

Post dinner sing in the undercroft

2015(September) – Münster – Music builds Bridges!

The Phil had not hesitated in accepting the invitation from the Münster city authorities to take part in this commemorative week end. The description of it given below was published in the spring 2016 edition of *News and Views* – the publication of the National Association of Choirs. This was the first time since 1969 that the choir had travelled by air rather than ferry. The availability of suitably timed flights between Yeadon airport and Düsseldorf did make the journey swift and comfortable. One memory not recalled in the published article was the response to the Phil singing *Nessun Dorma* during the joint concert with MarQant. Looking down from the stage at two rows filled with friends from Lochem, we were reminded of our concert back in April. It seemed to us, on stage that the Lochem ladies had to hold down their men, who all seemed to be straining to stand and join in. Of such moments are warm memories made!

Music builds Bridges!

York has been twinned with the city of Münster in Germany since 1957. Their two Male Voice Choirs York Philharmonic and MarQant twinned in 1969 and have met regularly since.

Over the years Münster has partnered with many other cities. On the occasion of the 70th anniversary of the ending of World War II choirs were invited from partner cities to come together for a week-end (18-20 September) under the title 'Music builds Bridges - from a disgruntled Europe to a united Europe'. So seven choirs from six cities: Poland (2), Russia, France, Norway, UK and Germany joined with their Münster choral partners to give a total of 14 choirs. There was a wide range of musical styles to enjoy, from madrigals to hip hop; the singers were of all ages, from the under 10s in a children's choir to men in their mid 80s.

It was a busy week-end with street sings on Friday and Saturday, and a full male voice concert with MarQant on Friday evening. The major commemorative concert with all choirs was held on the Saturday evening, followed by singing at a church service on Sunday morning. We didn't appreciate just how busy a time it would be until on the way home we added up the number of different songs we had sung – 41. As a choir we are comfortable giving impromptu sings on the streets [thankfully it didn't rain] and we were looking forward to the concert with MarQant. We were not sure, however, as to the tone and style of the Saturday night combined concert. Was it to be just a celebration of different musical styles, or was the commemorative significance to be included? We knew that, as the first city to be twinned with Münster, we would open the show. With a 12 minute allocation our director Berenice Lewis picked four pieces which were both entertaining and commemorative: 'The Impossible Dream', 'For the Fallen', 'He ain't heavy, he's my brother', and the upbeat spiritual 'I'm Gonna Walk'. This was a good choice well received. A review published in the local paper was complimentary, describing 'a seasoned choir showing great skill in contrasting styles from the calm 'For the Fallen' to the lively lilting 'I'm Gonna Walk'. Of greater interest, however, was the reviewer's need to tell the readers that we were 'directed by a Lady'. It would seem that a female director of a male voice choir is still unusual in Germany. Berry has been our director since 2000 and is the third woman to hold that role.

One interesting aspect of the evening was that the combined shanty choirs from Norway and Germany sang six songs – four in English; 'The Wild Rover', 'Strike the Bell',

'Liverpool Girls', and 'My Bonny lies over the ocean'.

We were looking forward to the Friday evening concert with MarQant as this would be the 16th time our two choirs had shared a concert platform. The venue – the Friedenskapelle – had been chosen with care by our hosts. It had been built, post-war, as the garrison church for British troops but had fallen into disrepair and was refurbished as a concert hall in 2003. Seating about 250 people it had intimate feel, good acoustics and an excellent piano. We were made to feel even more at home with the arrival of more than 30 members of the Lochems Mannenkoor who had specifically made the journey from Holland to join us. This Lochem choir has links with both MarQant and the York 'phil' and visited York in April 2015.

The concert began and almost instantly became one of those memorable occasions when the emotional links between the choir, the music, the conductor and the audience are so heightened as to give a performance which releases the full beauty and power of music. Under the impassioned direction of Berry the choir responded, and that 'intangible essence – the spirit of a piece' which we know is always there, but which we cannot always find, filled the hall. Such moments are hard to describe and need to be experienced to be fully appreciated. We were fortunate to have such a performance on that Friday evening. According to many long-serving singers the choir gave its best performance for many years, and the standing ovation received was the greatest in living memory. It was a proud choir which left the stage that evening.

The remaining engagement was on Sunday morning when we had been invited to sing at a Mass in a large Roman Catholic Church. The liturgical music was to be given by an excellent youth choir and we were asked to provide four items including a piece at the close of the service, to send the worshippers on their way. What should we sing? It was a large building with a big congregation. Berry chose; 'My Lord what a Morning', 'Calm is the Sea' and 'Let there be peace on Earth'. The decision as to the final item was left to the last moment, and the congregation was sent on its way to that glorious Welsh Hymn 'Tydi a Roddaist'. The Mass concluded and we began [with two Welsh speakers in our choir we do sing verse 1 in Welsh) but no one moved. As the last of the four great 'Amens' soared and faded the church erupted in applause – a spine -tingling moment and a wonderful way to end our formal appearances.

A week-end such as this takes a lot of organising and both the city authorities and our friends in MarQant did an excellent job, the social aspects of the week-end being as successful as the music. Even the weather was 'mostly' kind. As singers we men stayed dry but during two rehearsals it did rain and some of our ladies did get wet. En route to a restaurant one group sought cover in a bus shelter. Pity the poor bus driver who on stopping found his shelter full of English women giving a hearty rendition of 'Singing in the Rain'!

The city authorities remembered that, in the years following 1945, it was the work of creative artists reaching out to one another which had helped Germany reintegrate with the rest of Europe. This week-end, 70 years on, served to refresh those links and add to them a cross generational dimension. If the other visiting choirs had the same experience as us then the citizens of Münster can be assured that Music does indeed build Bridges.

Friday night – Graham Kay directs the 'Rhythm of Life' with both Eileen and Berry at the piano

On stage for the International concert with Linda Samwell assisting Eileen.

One of the massed street-sings

Another street performance – thankfully it didn't rain

Lunchtime

Sunday morning church

Back in 1968 the Münsterscher Männergesangverein was, in a spirit of reconciliation and restoration, looking to make choral friends outside Germany. At the same time the York Phil was in a confident mood, growing in success and size, and looking to expand its horizons; it had a spirit of adventure. Nevertheless both choirs put a lot of work into the first meetings – they strove to get the friendship off to a good start – but it is unlikely that anyone, at that time, had a vision of the close alliance that was to evolve and which has thrived now for 47 years. The unstinting and long term dedication of a few, allied to the willing support of the many, has ensured an enjoyable and valued success. This will continue, a visit to York by MarQant is already scheduled for 2017, and by then plans will be in place for the 50th Jubilee celebrations in 2019.

Part 3
The Third Generation
1994-today

Hey, Look me over, Lend me an ear;
Fresh out of clover, mortgaged up to here.
But don't pass the plate, folks, don't pass the cup
I figure whenever you're down and out, the only way is up...
Wildcat: Leigh/Coleman – an upbeat popular 'encore'

Chapter 11
Elisabeth Jill Wild
Fresh Ideas

With Ian Colling's resignation the choir was once more in turmoil. Since 1980 the appointment of musical directors had *not* been 100% successful. Three directors in three years were too many, so the next appointment needed to succeed. Adverts were placed and at least four applied – on paper all well qualified. The interview process, which included the candidates taking part of a rehearsal, suggested a winner. This decision was reinforced by an excellent recommendation from Roy Firth the director of Gledholt MVC. Elisabeth Jill Wild – who liked to be known as Jill – was appointed. This proved to be one time when the recruitment system worked properly.

She had been a choral scholar at Cambridge and after graduation had studied choral and orchestral conducting at the Conservatoire in Geneva for two years. At 28 years of age Jill was the youngest conductor of the Phil to date, and yet had already conducted choirs in France, Switzerland, Canada, Belgium and Portugal. Fortunately her home in West Yorkshire was close enough for her to be able to commute.

Jill's first York engagement was the autumn concert at the Guildhall. Guest soloists were Kate Hudis and Louisa Creed together with Eileen Grey. The first photo we have of Jill with the choir was taken a month later at the Festival of

Remembrance held in the Barbican. This shows Jill stood with the choir joining with the community singing of war-time favourites.

Jill had good support in the musical team. Eileen Grey was accompanist and soloist, and Simon Waggott was deputy musical director. Simon, youngest son of Jim, had joined the choir at the age of 16. A professional musician, Simon is a keyboard player and vocalist with jazz/blues groups. Also on the team was Matheson (Matt) Dowdy – cathedral organist and Bass Lay Clerk at Ripon Cathedral. Matt was assistant musical director and occasional accompanist. The choir was still numerically strong with seventy four members.

Jill did vary her way of teaching. She arrived one evening with copies of a Russian prayer written out phonetically but with no notation. She had heard this piece and wanted the Phil to learn it. With no music available, she took each section through their part and it was learned by rote. That prayer, *Tebe Poem*, has been a favourite with the choir and audiences ever since its first performance in the summer concert of 1995.

Held at the Sir Jack Lyons Concert Hall at the University this was a celebratory event marking the choir's 70th anniversary. The copy of the programme for that night shows just how 'up to date' (a relative term in male voice circles) was Jill's selection.

PROGRAMME

29TH JULY 1995

MUSICAL DIRECTOR - ELISABETH JILL WILD

A Cole Porter Medley	*Arr. Alan Simmons*
Let There Be Peace on Earth	*Arr. Jack Haigh*
Voice of the Child	*Sarah McNeill & Goff Richards*
Eileen Grey - Soprano	
Sing Joyous Bird	*Montague Phillips*
La Belle est au Jardin d'amour	*Britten*
Brown Bird	*Haydn Wood*
Tebe Poem	*Trad. Russian*
Marching Song	*Matyas Seiber & A.L. Lloyd*
Graham Hudson - Bass	
Softly as I Leave You	*A. de Vita & H. Shaper* (Arr. Alan Simmons)
Alexander's Ragtime Band	*Irving Berlin (Arr. Denys Hood)*

INTERVAL

Matheson Dowdy- Organ	
Toccata	*Widor*
Entrance & March of the Peers	*Gilbert & Sullivan ("Iolanthe")*
Love Could I Only Tell Thee	*J.M. Capel & C. Bingham (Arr. Doris Arnold)*
Portrait of my Love	*Ornadel/West (Arr. A. Simmons)*
Ivor Novello Medley	*Arr. Thom Meredith*
Eileen Grey & Matheson Dowdy - Piano Duet	
Arrival of the Queen of Sheba	*Handel*
Jamaican Rumba	*A. Benjamin*
Yellow Bird	*Norman Luboff/M. Keith/ A. Bergman. (Arr. M.C. Frank)*
The Gospel Train	*Spiritual - Arr. Gwyn Arch*
Rhythm of Life	*Coleman (Arr. Richard Barnes)*

THE END

The York Philharmonic Male Voice Choir wishes to thank our sponsors,
Kall Kwik Printing and Smith Bros. (York) Ltd.
for their continuing support during our 70th Anniversary Year

Jill took advantage of the resources available to her, with Eileen and Matt both giving solo and duet performances.

This programme also thanked two sponsoring companies, Kall Kwik and Smith Bros. This fortunate position lasted for some years until Kall Kwik stepped back.

The Phil was grateful for all the financial support received but also for the friendship shared; for with both companies the relationship was more than just a marketing exercise. Some years later the Phil also enjoyed discreet, but much welcomed, financial support from a married couple who enjoyed our performances.

Unfortunately there is no portrait photograph of Jill available to accompany this story, so shown here is a formal shot taken in 1995. Eileen Grey is clearly identifiable in the second row; Simon Waggott is sat on front row far left with Matt Dowdy at his shoulder, second in on the second row. This photo also illustrates another benefit of our long term home at St. William's College; its medieval splendour enhanced many a photograph. There are 42 choristers pictured here, a more normal turn out despite their being 74 listed members.

Jill introduced *Tebe Poem* to the choir in an innovative way; she also sought to increase confidence and raise standards by scrambled singing. She would mix up the four sections of the choir so that each singer had to be more self reliant. This had some interesting outcomes but was a very useful rehearsal tool. Taking the concept further, however, and using it in competition did not find favour with some adjudicators.

There was nothing 'remarkable' about choir life during these years and the corporate extravagance of the 1980s was already past. There were, nevertheless, a number of new experiences for the choir and the high musical standards were maintained.

York was becoming ever more popular with visitors and the Phil received invitations to sing with visiting groups. In 1995 the platform was shared with the Roussland Soglasie Male Voice Choir – a 20 strong group reviving much traditional Russian church music. In March 1996 we welcomed The Chancel Choir of the Chapelwood United Methodist Church from Houston Texas, and in the May performed with The Southern College Symphony Orchestra from Tennessee. This concert was held in the Bootham School Concert Hall. Also used in these years was St Peter's School Chapel further along Bootham; so the Phil was experimenting with new venues.

March 1997 saw the fifth visit to York of the Münsterscher Männergesangverein. There were 127 people in this party so it was a hectic week-end with the joint concert in the Sir Jack Lyons Hall.

The summer concert that year returned to Bootham School and included a special piece of music. Here is the front cover of the programme:

ANNUAL SUMMER CONCERT NIGHT
The York Philharmonic Male Voice Choir
Directed by Jill Wild
proudly presents
ALL IN A SUMMER EVENING CONCERT
featuring
The World Premiere of
'NIGHTMAIL'
Words by W.H. Auden
Music by Alan J. Woods
Bootham School Concert Hall
at 7.30pm
on Saturday 19th July
Sponsored by Kall Kwik Printing and Smith Bros. (York) Ltd.

Henry Brough, a founder member, died in 1990 having sung with the choir for 65 years. His family made a bequest to the choir, and after lengthy consideration the Phil decided to use this money to commission a piece of music. Henry had been a steam engine driver with the LNER and so a setting of the poem *Nightmail* – written by York poet W.H.Auden – was selected. This required the permission of the Post Office, the holders of the copyright, which was freely given. The music was composed by Alan J. Woods, a contemporary of Jill Wild. He had trained at Bretton Hall College Wakefield under James Wild (Jill's father). This first performance was at Bootham School just across the street from the house in which Auden had lived.

It was a challenging piece to learn and sing, particularly as the basses had to simulate the rhythm of a train on the rails. Thankfully there was no derailment.

This concert also saw another innovation – three pianists one piano.

The choir continued to enjoy success at regional competitions and travelled to new events.

In 1996 at the Derwentside Music Festival in Stanley Co. Durham the Phil gained:

Light Opera Class: 1st
Male Voice Class: 2nd
Opera Choral Class: 1st
In 1997 at Biddulph & District Music Festival in Staffordshire the result was:
Choral Recital: 1st (Copeland Trophy)
The Phil returned in 1998 and took 1st prize in the Open Class
In 1998 at the Eskdale Festival of Arts at Whitby the Phil gained:
Sacred Music: 1st
Male Voice: 1st
Choir Recital: 2nd

In 1998 a key appointment was made when Berenice (Berry) Hopkins was appointed as Deputy Director.

This 'comparatively' uneventful period of years was about to change as the choir planned a major European tour (as described in an earlier chapter) to celebrate The Millenium – the year 2000 – which also marked the 75th Anniversary of the choir.

Our turn boys! Jill, Eileen and Berry entertain on the 2000 tour

Not long after returning from this tour Jill announced her resignation. For the first time in its 75 year history this did not cause panic within the choir. As Jill's natural successor, Berry Hopkins, was already in post, the succession was seamless. [Female readers may note that this was also the first time in 75 years that women had been so involved in the planning].

Chapter 12
Eileen Grey (née Henderson)
Life Member – a remarkable contribution

Eileen studied music at the Kesteven College of Education in Lincolnshire, specialising in piano and treble recorder, and she later took up singing with the late Joan Whitworth. Her performing career started as a teenage member of York Youth Opera. She then moved on to York Opera where she played a number of lead roles for many years. She also performed with Yorkshire Chamber Opera and East Yorkshire Opera. As a young singer she was a member of the York Madrigal Group, and it was as a member of this group that she first performed with the Phil in October 1968. She returned as a soloist at 'Carols in Kirkgate' in 1974, and was asked by Brian Lister to help set up the Kirkgate Ladies choir in 1975.

In December 1991, after a break of a few years, and now as Mrs Grey, she was asked by Margaret Martin to return and accompany 'Carols in Kirkgate' – a single week booking which has lasted 24 years.

Eileen has been the principal accompanist to the Phil ever since that 'one week booking'; she also sang both solos and duets until 2005, and plays piano duets and even trios. She also coaches prospective choir members, who may be uncertain of their vocal range or ability, and guides them through the audition.

In 1993 Eileen sought to revive another choir tradition – a choir singing evening, a social evening gathered around a piano, reminiscent of the 'Smokers Reunions' held before the war but without the smoke. The first of these was held in her front room on 28th July 1993 and 14 people turned up. This was followed by another which reflected an interest and enthusiasm within the choir, and also, made it clear that Eileen and Roger's front room was too small to host such an event. Other choir pressures led to a gap of a few years and the next one was held in 2005. Planned on a bigger scale, the evening was held in the Poppleton Community Centre and the chairman that year – the late Jim Rayne – gave it the title: 'Eileen's Soirée'. They have been held every year since with, ideally, two events a year in spring and autumn.

Eileen started the evenings in order to give ordinary singing members a chance to perform solos or in small groups, in front of friendly and familiar faces, without the stress of a 'real' audience. She knew only too well most singers only sing solo at an audition and never again. The soirées allow people to gain confidence, and, hopefully, provide the choir with more potential concert soloists. In this respect the soirées have the same objective as the Inter-Choir Competition of the 1930s, but without the element of competition.

These evenings do not just include vocal items, as members are encouraged to show their skills on a variety of instruments. It also gives a chance for the ladies of the 'Phillies' to show what they can do. Within this group are members of the Kirkgate Ladies and other choirs, as well as current/former members of musical theatre groups. There are also some with no performing experience at all, so once more it is a way of gaining confidence in front of an audience.

In a 'normal' soirée some 25-30 people will take part and the biggest ever turnout was 66, a number which filled the room on what, ironically, was a very warm evening in May.

Eileen is particularly pleased with the formation and success of 'The Three Tenors'. Started one evening as a comic tribute to the highly successful concerts by the great tenors Domingo, Carreras and Pavarotti, it was thought that our version 'wasn't that bad' and so it has grown into a group which has performed in concerts. To date five of our tenor sections have taken part. What is not widely known is that the musical choices e.g. *Vienna City of Dreams, Come back to Sorrento, You are my Heart's delight* are all chosen and arranged for three voices by Eileen.

Yellow Bird

Lily the Pink – James Elliot and Robin McDermott

In 2008 Eileen became an Honorary Life Member of the Phil. Given her dedication to the choir over so many years it was only right that she has been recognised in this way, being only the fourth woman ever to be given this honour.

As accompanist, Eileen is assisted by a page turner. For a number of years this task was undertaken by Mrs Janet Close; but for the last ten years has been done, on a rota basis, by members of the 'Phillies'. Even this job has grown over the years and does, sometimes, include adding percussion to a performance. In this respect prior experience as a primary school teacher is an asset. The contribution of these willing volunteers which includes attendance at rehearsals as well as concerts, is much appreciated.

The Phil is also fortunate in having other accomplished accompanists willing to work with it sharing the heavy Christmas programme with Eileen and covering for any absences. Malcolm Maddock does most of this work, with David Hammond, a talented former student at York University, also being an excellent choice.

Chapter 13

Berenice (Berry) Lewis (née Hopkins)
Long term stability and success

Berry grew up in Leicester where she studied piano and organ with Howard Gregory and sang with the Leicestershire Youth Choir. She came to York in 1989 to study Linguistics and German at York University. Taking full advantage of the rich and diverse musical community there, Berry became involved in various groups as pianist, conductor, singer and violinist. As Music Director of the university's Gilbert and Sullivan Society [following in the footsteps of David Keeffe 20 years earlier] she directed large scale productions of Princess Ida and Ruddigore, and performed in other shows.

Whilst working for her degree, Berry also made time to coach singers, teach the piano and act as regular répétiteur for the York Musical Theatre Company and York Opera. During her student years she was organist at St. Denys' Church Walmgate. She was appointed Director of Music at York's Central Methodist Church in 1998, the same year that she became Deputy Music Director of the Phil. When she accepted the post of Director of the Phil in 2000, she joined Jill Wild in sharing the distinction of being the youngest directors in the Phil's history. She has one other distinction, that of being the best singer ever to lead the choir. In 2003 Berry married and moved to Beverley, East Yorkshire. She resigned her post at Central Methodist but retained leadership of the Phil. Berry now teaches piano and singing and is active in the musical life of Beverley.

In 1980, when David Keeffe was appointed director, there was a wish that the choir would benefit in some way from his links with the university. Nothing happened at that time; the choir had to wait twenty years to truly benefit from this student body. The Phil has now enjoyed 15 good years under Berry's leadership. Other York graduates, known to Berry, have also served the choir in recent years, including Gary Skyrme of 'Just Music', who recorded and produced the last three CDs, and David Hammond, accompanist.

In the last 15 years the choir has celebrated a number of key anniversaries and travelled more than ever before. The European tour of 2000 brought a rather uneventful decade to a close and gave the choir a zest for adventure. Berry's tenure began with a visit to the Sheffield Arena in November 2000, to take part in another massed choir event on behalf of Yorkshire Cancer Research. Since then, travel has been a regular feature in the choir's life, with visits to Scotland, Wales, Northern Ireland, France, Belgium, Holland and Germany. There was, as well, disappointment in 2002 when a planned visit to Norway had to be cancelled, a visit which remains on the 'wish list'. The anniversaries have included: 40 years of twinning with MarQant (Münsterscher Männergesangverein) in Münster; 50 years of 'Carols in Kirkgate'; and 90 years in the life of the choir. In addition, three CDs have been produced for public sale, plus a private commemorative audio recording and photograph album of the 40th Year celebrations with MarQant. Technology has also been embraced, with the choir now using its third electric stage piano. Always having our own piano available wherever we sing ensures consistency, but takes away the quirkiness of earlier years and the variations in performance that resulted from an out of tune piano with occasional missing keys.

Berry's first competition was in March 2001 at the Eskdale Festival of Arts at Whitby. This was the centenary year for the Festival and entries were up 24% on the previous year, so there were a number of good choirs present. It must have been a frustrating day for Berry. In the afternoon Male Voice Class, the Phil came joint third, also getting third in the Sacred Class. Clearly not disheartened Berry led the choir into the prestigious Recital Class in the evening gaining first place beating the Rodillian Singers by three marks. The following year the results were: Male Voice: third; Sacred Music: first; Recital: second. But by 2003 hard work brought results, as reported in the YEP:

FRIDAY 20th JUNE 2003.

Choir chalks up three titles

by Richard Edwards

richard.edwards@ycp.co.uk

THE York Philharmonic Male Voice Choir swept the board in a prestigious choir contest.

The successful singers competed in the Eskdale Festival, at Whitby Pavilion, and scooped first prize in the Sacred Music Class, the Male Voice Choir Class and the Recital Class.

Neil Wood, choir stage manager and baritone singer, said: "It all came right on the day.

"A lot of work has been put in by the chaps this year, it has been a busy one, and the day itself was especially busy, but the performance came up to the right level.

"The atmosphere on the way home was electric, everyone was buzzing."

Members of the choir are preparing for a concert at the Central Methodist Church, in St Saviourgate, York, on Saturday, July 5.

Berenice Lewis, the choir's musical director, is pictured clutching the three trophies watched by members of the choir.

● Picture: Garry Atkinson

The Phil did not enter Eskdale in 2005 and 2006 but has been back every year since. A number of members have taken to staying in Whitby for the week-end or longer and the choir's track record has been good; for example in both 2009 and 2010 the choir won four classes. Other regional competitions entered included a disappointing day at Wharfedale in 2006 and a winning visit in March 2013 to the Don Valley Music Festival in South Yorkshire. That prize included a barrel of beer which, due to logistical issues, has never been claimed [given the references to pubs and some photographs in this narrative this may seem to be abnormal behaviour].

The choir had not issued a recording since 'Music for Pleasure' in 1990. That was a tape cassette, and we were now in the age of the compact disc. Bringing the choir's recorded library up to date was one of the first major tasks of Berry and team and 'In Harmony' was issued in 2002. It was recorded in the rehearsal venue St.Williams College, by John Mills, so it was appropriate that a photograph of the college appeared on the sleeve. It was an eclectic mix of 22 tracks which showed the breadth of the repertoire. The Russian prayer *Tebe Peom* by Bortiansky is between *Psalm 23* by Schubert and *Tom the Piper's Son* by Edmund Walters. *Yesterday* by Lennon and McCartney is between a spiritual *Little Innocent Lamb* and *Voice of the Child* by Goff Richards. There were also four Christmas Carols on the disc including two with the Kirkgate Ladies.

ON SONG: Members of the York Philharmonic Male Voice Choir present Oswald Gillery, 89, who sang in the very first Carols In Kirkgate a copy of their CD, from left, Richard Kay, Tony Suckling, Terry Yates, and Colin Hockridge *Picture: Garry Atkinson*

In 2007 the CD 'Let All Men Sing' was recorded and produced by Gary Skyrme. This was completed in two sessions at St Chad's Church in York, and on both days the 'Phillies' did an excellent job in preparing refreshments to keep the choir going. There are 19 tracks on this CD, once more showing a wide range of repertoire, including *Autumn Leaves* in an arrangement by Gerd Wild the director of the Münsterscher Männergesangverein (MM).

There was a live recording of the 40th Anniversary concert with the MM and Salonorchester in 2009 made into a commemorative double CD with a photo album of the celebrations. A copy was given to all who had taken part. The last recording during these years was in 2011 celebrating the 50th Year of 'Carols in Kirkgate' – the first full recording of carols since 1976.

CDs produced since 2000 plus earlier tape cassettes

The European tours enjoyed since 2000 have been described in an earlier chapter; France 2004, Germany 2006, 2013, 2015, and Holland and Belgium 2009. In between these tours the choir has also explored more of the British Isles with trips to Northern Ireland, Scotland and Wales.

In March 2005 the Phil entered the Coleraine International Choral Festival. We sang in two classes coming second out of four in the male voice class and third from nine in the Light Entertainment class. The winners of the male voice class, Boyan from Ukraine, bemused us somewhat by ignoring the set time allowed for competition and giving a 'short concert'. This did not, however, detract from a most enjoyable week-end spent in spring sunshine in a most attractive part of the British Isles. The most evocative photograph of the trip is shown below, an impromptu sing on the Giants Causeway, the second world heritage site (the other being Fountains Abbey) to be used as a concert platform in six months. This sing was followed a short time later with another at the Bushmills Distillery.

Giant's Causeway

Bushmills Distillery

In July 2005 the choir was in Ayr in Scotland to take part in Ayr 800 – celebrating 800 years of the town. This too was a most pleasant trip which included a Civic Reception and a full concert by the Phil in the Town Hall. The invitation had been issued by the Ayr Arts Guild prompted by family links – Berry's husband Rob is a son of Ayr. This was such an enjoyable visit that the Phil was delighted to be asked to return in July 2008.

Civic reception at Ayr

The only country left to visit was Wales and this came in 2011 when the choir fulfilled an ambition which had been held since the 1930s – to take part in the Llangollen Eisteddfod. The Phil passed the audition, and in July fulfilled this ambition, but not with the hoped for results. The choir had not expected to win but had hoped to avoid last place. Unfortunately that was the outcome seventh out of seven.

True to form and tradition, the Phil was the smallest choir competing with only 32 singers; one choir from South Wales had almost 100 on stage. Neither did our musical choice find favour with the adjudicators, but this was difficult to determine as time constraints meant that almost no feedback was given. Not too disheartened, we entertained the crowd outside one of the beer tents and enjoyed the rest of our stay in what is a beautiful part of the world. These photos show the choir on arrival, and visiting the Pontcysyllte viaduct. We gave short performances at both ends adding a third world heritage site to our list of venues.

The choir has also sung in a number of new local venues, which shows that despite performing in the region for decades, fresh spaces and audiences can still be found: Alanbrooke Barracks, Topcliffe, in honour of the Queens's Golden Jubilee; the Tom Stoppard Centre at Pocklington School, with the Kirkgate Ladies as guests – a rare opportunity for our Christmas Ladies to sing a wider range of music – Selby Abbey; Brigg and Beverley.

Other locations have become favourites and have been revisited. In July 2002 the choir revived the tradition of a 'Dales Day Out' with a trip to Gunnerside. This was organised by top tenor Graham Edwards and included singing to a packed out audience in the Methodist chapel. This has become a bi-annual event in the choir's diary. The adjacent dale, Arkengarthdale, has also been visited, with both villages providing enthusiastic audiences and excellent village teas. In September of the same year, at the invitation of the National Trust, the Phil gave an evening concert at Fountains Abbey 'Fountains by Floodlight'. A night-time setting in the ruins of the Cistercian Abbey creates an atmosphere unlike any other. The concert was a success and the Phil is pleased to have been able to make return visits. In December 2007, the choir accepted a booking which could have been a 'one off' but has proved to be quite the opposite. A small choir of 12-16 singers was asked to entertain diners at Betty's Restaurant York in an evening known as 'Carols by Candlelight'. Two performances were given, and the small choir felt a little outside of its comfort zone. The diners and Betty's thought otherwise. In 2008, we gave four performances, in 2009 five, then six the next year. We have been back every year since, with the choir now feeling fully at home. Christmas Carols were also needed in December 2010 when the Phil sang in the foyer of York Hospital, and on that occasion moved onto one of the wards where the wife of a member was being treated. A concert of this style had not been done for a long time, and like so much else, has become a regular feature.

It is a sad reality, given a choir of this size and with an average age of membership 65 plus, that the Phil will occasionally attend funerals. What is less common is to attend weddings of younger singers. In 2003 we sang for Berry and Rob in Beverley, and in 2005 for Richard Kay and Ruth in York. Even rarer is an invitation to sing at a Baptism, but one the choir was delighted to accept on behalf of Berry and Rob.

In 2006, in the midst of these busy years, the choir was given a severe shock. The Dean and Chapter of York Minster handed the management of St William's College to a professional events company, and an unsustainable increase in the room hire charge forced a move to the Central Methodist Church. After a 35 year residency, it took some time to adjust to the change, but the choir settled and still uses the Central Methodist Hall. Six years later in 2012 came another wrench, with the last performance of 'Carols in Kirkgate' in the Castle Museum. After 51 years a chapter came to an end but the show carried on. There was a great sense of relief and satisfaction when this Christmas show successfully transferred from the Castle Museum to the Merchant Adventurers' Hall.

Anniversaries continued to be celebrated. In May 2005 the 80th anniversary concert was held in the Guildhall with guest soloist Wendy Goodson, and on the 29th July there was a celebration Dinner Dance at the racecourse. It is not possible to know how much the food may have changed since earlier dinners, but the menu descriptions certainly had. What might have been called 'Roast Pork' in an earlier age was now; 'Eye of Pork Loin carved onto a Rich Apple Risotto offered with Wild Mushrooms & Red Onion Confit, Balsamic and Redcurrant Jus'.

On the weekend of the 3rd – 5th April 2009, the Münsterscher Männergesangverein and the Salonorchester Münster visited York to celebrate forty years of friendship between the two choirs. This was the biggest event the Phil had organised in many years and was a memorable occasion. The Chapter House in York Minster has a sensitive and evocative acoustic. Despite its grandeur, its circular shape, together with a full audience fanned out around the choirs and orchestra, gave the evening a sense of intimacy.

Chapter House 2009

There was a different feel in 2012 when the Phil took part in two community events. In June the Olympic torch passed through the city and the Phil gathered by the city walls to sing it on its way. In July the city celebrated the 800th Anniversary of the granting of its charter. As part of this there was a grand community choral celebration. A flyer for the event said: *...as hundreds of voices come together to sing 'This York' a new choral piece by award winning composer Benjamin Till using words from the resident of York....a choral procession will create a pageant of joyful song and dance culminating in the premiere of 'This York' at Clifford's Tower.*

Intermixed with the big events, throughout this time, the choir continued with what might historically be called its 'normal' work; local concerts supporting local causes helping to raise thousands of pounds each year. When requested, time would be found to give occasional concerts in retirement homes as in this press article from January 2010 showing the choir helping Mrs Sally Cartwright celebrate her 104th birthday. We had sung for Sally a year earlier on her 103rd and had a diary entry to be there for the 105th. Sadly Sally passed away shortly before that concert was due.

Concerts have been shared with other local choirs: the Rodillian Singers from Wakefield; Driffield Male Voice; and Harmonia from Malton; and the Phil shares the platform on the annual visits of Norwegian choirs who meet to compete in 'Yorvik'. The choir also seeks to give performing opportunities to young singers and instrumentalists. All these activities are not unique to the Phil but are embedded in its DNA, and help it to play a full part in the cultural life of the city.

In addition to Berry and Eileen, the musical team is strengthened by Graham Kay as Deputy Director, and Richard Kay as Assistant Director. Together this father and son team, a baritone and tenor, bring a wealth of performing experience and musical skill to the choir.

MANY HAPPY RETURNS: Sally Cartwright celebrates her 104th birthday in style as she is serenaded by the York Philharmonic Male Voice Choir at Field Court Heworth

Picture: Nigel Holland

Sally celebrates 104th birthday

by RICHARD HARRIS
richard.harris@thepress.co.uk

ONE of York's oldest people has celebrated her 104th birthday with a visit from York Philharmonic Male Voice Choir.

Sally Cartwright, nee Todd, who celebrated the milestone yesterday, was born in 1906, in Thornton, near Pocklington, and was one of 12 children although only her youngest sister survives, 91-year-old Nora.

Like last year, she was serenaded on her big day by members of the York Philharmonic Male Voice Choir.

Her niece, Doreen Simey, said that apart from her hearing, for which she must wear hearing aids, her aunt was in good health.

She said: "She is wonderful, she was one of 12, but there is only her baby sister left.

"She has looked after herself all these years and her brain is better than yours or mine, she has a wonderful memory."

Mrs Cartwright continues to live on her own in York, althouth there is a warden nearby.

When she was born the two world wars were still to happen and the Titanic was yet to be

EDWARDIAN DAYS: This photograph, taken in about 1911, shows Sally (dark dress) standing next to her father, William Todd

port and the moon landings were purely science fiction.

As a child she taught herself to play the piano on a tiny pedal organ in the village chapel, and still entertains friends with recitals at the home.

She married her husband, Herbert, in 1928. He died in 1991.

The couple had two sons, Stanley and Norman, and a host

"The world is a very different place, but I've had a wonderful life – I've really enjoyed it."

Asked if there was a secret to long life, she said: "I haven't really got a secret – it is all natural. I just try and keep myself active, and also I was brought up in the country on the farm so I had lots of fresh air."

Mrs Cartwright continues to enjoy the fresh air; her hobbies

Events of 1906

· Prime Minister Henry Campbell-Bannerman, the Liberal candidate, won the 1906 General Election
· The San Francisco earthquake, which recorded 7.8 on the Richter scale, caused the deaths of more than 3,000 people.
· The world's first feature film, The Story Of The Kelly Gang which documented the life of Australian bushranger Ned Kelly, was released
· Mount Vesuvius in Naples, Italy, the only active volcano in mainland Europe, erupts killing more than 100 people
· Charles Stewart Rolls and Henry Royce founded Rolls Royce Limited.
· On Christmas Eve, Canadian Reginald Fessenden makes the first radio broadcast which consisted of a poetry reading, violin solo and a speech.

Births in 1906
· English poet John Betjeman, Soviet leader Leonid Brezhnev, American actress and writer Mary Astor and Italian film director Roberto

LIKE FATHER...
...LIKE SON
An Evening of Song with
Graham and Richard Kay
With accompanist Malcolm Maddock
Joseph Rowntree Theatre
Sunday 28th April 2013, 7.30pm
Tickets £8 from YTR: 01904 623568 or www.yorktheatreroyal.co.uk
Helping to raise money for York Against Cancer

Given the large number of Christmas engagements, the choir has to know a full programme of suitable music. Therefore two complete programmes need to be known from memory each year. With only one rehearsal a week and frequent concerts, this gives little time for learning, so training tracks are recorded by Berry and are made available through the choir's website. In addition there is a monthly rehearsal for each section led by Graham or Richard. These start 45 minutes before a full rehearsal. The choir is truly fortunate to have such strength in depth in the musical team; and is never without a conductor. [These days Richard, being the one most likely to be leading the songs in the Snickleway Inn, is the one most likely to be seen on social media].

Richard conducting without spilling his beer

Richard led this small team to victory at Eskdale 2016

The timeline has reached 2015: 90th anniversary year, and the catalyst for this narrative. The two truly memorable events of this year: the April celebratory week-end shared with Lochems Mannenkoor; and the September visit to Münster, have been described in an earlier chapter. But not reproduced there was the article by Tony Sawyer which appeared in the concert programme in April – the month in which Tony was congratulated on his 50 year membership of the Phil. Here is that article.

Tony Sawyer reflects on his life of 50 years in our choir

Given the DNA of the choir, its focus, the commitment and long service of its members it is no surprise that the 'phil' has reached its 90th anniversary. So let us celebrate with honour and respect, looking back with pride, enjoying the present day and looking forward to continued success.

The thought that 50 years have passed since I joined takes some digesting yet when compared with my family life at home, and my family life in the choir maybe time passing quickly is not surprising.

I grew up on a farm in Heslington Village, now part of the University and growing another crop. As my adult voice began to develop Frank Morton – the Heslington Church Choirmaster and a long serving member of the bass section of the Phil – suggested I come to rehearsals and consider joining the choir. I know he wanted me to join but I smile to remember that I had a van and Frank only had a bike so I could also give him lifts into York. That was in 1963 – yes 52 years ago! I served a two year apprenticeship as my voice and ability developed and became a member in 1965.

In a rehearsal in the Railway Institute Dining Hall I received official membership into the top tenors and recall a feeling of pride which has underpinned my support of the 'phil' over all these years. In the second half of that rehearsal Brian Lister took the choir outside and we gathered around a locomotive turntable so that we could practice singing outside in preparation for our Dales Tour the following Saturday. We sang in the Great Hall at Castle Bolton [great acoustic] at midday and at Grassington in the evening. In my first concert I had the honour of singing a solo [a two year apprenticeship does work].

Music helped develop my relationship with Hazel and in 1967 we married at Stamford Bridge so will be celebrating our Golden Wedding in two years time. The choir came to the wedding and at our request sang 'Deep Harmony'.

Both 'marriages' have provided the same 'constant' and a lifetime of enjoyment throughout the years. The support and understanding of Hazel has always been important, particularly in those early days when I joined the first choir visit to Holland and Germany in 1969, leaving Hazel and our first child Helen (as a new born baby) at home. We visited Nijmegen then Münster and received heartfelt, delightfully warm receptions in each city.

These days as I watch our younger men fitting into the choir itinerary whilst keeping all their other plates spinning aloft, I am reminded of a personal brush with the Law.

The police pulled me over inviting me to explain my excessive speed (75mph in a van restricted by law to 50mph). Listening to my intention to be on time at choir rehearsal; whilst including a call at the farm in Heslington to check on a pig due to farrow must have sounded unusual; yet humour prevailed. I won a reprieve, and arrived at rehearsal rather late.

Single events or high points of the choir's history are perceived somewhat personally and for me are many, but not to say varied, as they were invariably musical achievements giving that great 'buzz' factor. Inviting Lochem choir to share our anniversary week-end will, I am sure, prove to be one such high, building on the extremely warm reception we were given during our stay in Lochem in 2009.

At an early age I was fortunate to engage with the bedrock of comradeship which is the essence of the York Philharmonic Male Voice Choir. From that day to this it has given me a profound sense of 'being' and has fulfilled life's aspirations.

The 'phil' over the years continues to receive many accolades to greatness musical and otherwise

Long may we continue!

Tony and Hazel Sawyer

These sentiments are shared by many long serving members of the choir.

There were two other notable events in the year. The Phil invited the York Priory Choir to take part in the autumn concert. This ladies choir is the surviving section of the York Old Priory Choir, and is, therefore, the only York choir older than the Phil. It was also the one which influenced the young Phil the most, and so it was a suitable occasion to acknowledge this debt.

The year ended with another encouraging first. We took the Christmas show to the Galtres Centre in Easingwold, the first time the event had ever been outside York, and attracted an audience of 180.

The story of 90 years in the ongoing life of the Phil has now been told. It has described choir life without explaining 'why' the Phil has survived and thrived when so many other choirs have failed; yet it gives some clues, and suggests that reaching a long life is not a complicated process. All societies start with the coming together of a few enthusiastic, like minded, individuals. A set of objectives is agreed and put into practice; a culture is formed and more people are attracted to join. The culture of the Phil was established early on, and was summed up in a letter sent to the choir by Jack Forster on the occasion of the Phil's 10th Birthday:

You have achieved success in the competitive field of which you have very reason to be proud, but to me, of far greater importance and more worthy of commendation is your service to the community. Your willingness to help any good cause and your desire to give pleasure to your fellows is more to be admired than prizes won.

Written in 1935 those words still ring true today; the culture of our choir has not altered over many years. There is great pleasure to be had in singing well together, and that pleasure is heightened by an appreciative audience. It is the bond between choir, the musical director, and the audience which gives life to any song. The Phil performs as often as it sensibly can and would surely fail if it spent its time in the rehearsal room and not on stage. The confidence and ability to sing a wide range of music, on street corners, in village halls and the Royal Albert Hall, from retirement homes to stately homes, and from rural chapels to York Minster, attracts both singers and listeners. There is 'something for everyone' in a typical male voice concert. The track listings for the CDs 'Let all men sing' and 'In Harmony' are a reminder of the scope of the repertoire.

1 **Let all men sing** *Keith Christopher*
2 **Soldiers' chorus** from 'Faust' *words: Henry Chorley; music: Charles Gounod*
3 **My luve is like a red, red rose** *traditional, arr. Hugh S. Roberton*
4 **Ma belle Marguerite** *words and music: A.P. Herbert and Vivian Ellis, arr. R.B. Lister'; solo:* ***David Pike***
5 **George Jones** *words: Henry P. Becton; solo:* ***Colin Hockridge***
6 **Hello, Dolly!** *Jerry Herman, arr. Clay Warnick*
7 **Just a closer walk with thee** *traditional, arr. Ed Lojeski*
8 **Calm is the sea** *words: John Guard; music: Heinrich Pfeil*
9 **God's choir** *Ray Overholt, arr. Howard Benton*
10 **Gloria** from Mass in C *words adapted by J.S. Stallybrass; music: W.A. Mozart, arr Percy E. Fletcher; quartet:* ***Steve Cox, Richard Kay, Neil Wood and Graham Hudson***
11 **Shall we gather at the river** *R. Lowry, arr.Alwyn Humphreys*
12 **The ghosts' high noon** from 'Ruddigore' *words: W.S. Gilbert; music: Sir Arthur Sullivan, arr. Denys Hood*
13 **With cat-like tread** from 'The Pirates of Penzance' *words: W.S. Gilbert; music: Sir Arthur Sullivan; solo:* ***Richard Kay***
14 **Sweet lass of Richmond Hill** *traditional, arr. Edmund Walters*
15 **Sweet and low** *words: Alfred. Lord Tennyson; music: Joseph Barnby; arr. Denys Hood*
16 **Autumn leaves** *words: Johnny Mercer; music: Joseph Kosma, arr. G. Wild*
17 **She** *words: Herbert Kretzmer; music: Charles Aznavour, arr. Alan Simmons*
18 **Do you hear the people sing?** from 'Les Misérables' *words: Herbert Kretzmer; music: Claude-Michel Schönberg, arr. Ed Lojeski; solos:* ***Neil Wood and Richard Kay***
19 **I'm gonna walk** *traditional, arr. Alwyn Humphreys*

Let All Men sing

1	Hey, Look Me Over	CY Coleman (arr. Warnick)
2	The Impossible Dream	Mitch Leigh (arr. Ringwald)
3	Let There Be Peace on Earth	Arr. Jack Haigh
4	Little Innocent Lamb	Spiritual, arr. Bartholomew
5	Yesterday	Lennon & McCartney (arr. Simmons)
6	Voice of the Child	Goff Richards
7	Psalm 23	Schubert
8	Tebe Poem	Bortniansky
9	Tom the Piper's Son	Edmund Walters
10	Eriskay Love Lilt	Scottish Trad, arr. Roberton
11	She's Like the Swallow	Canadian Trad, arr. Simmons
12	Give Me That Old Time Religion	Spiritual, arr. Simmons
13	Ride the Chariot	Spiritual, arr. W. Smith
14	Rhythm of Life	Cy Coleman (arr. Barnes)
15	Alexander's Ragtime Band	Irving Berlin (arr. Hood)
16	Gwahoddiad	Hartshough (arr. Davies)
17	The Boar's Head Carol	Trad, arr. Fitzgerald
18	Coventry Carol	Trad, arr. Gilbert
19	Jesus Christ the Apple Tree*	Elizabeth Poston
20	The Infant King*	Basque Noël, arr. Willcocks
21	Hail, Smiling Morn	R. Spofforth
22	Wandering the King's Highway	Leslie Coward (arr. Stickles)

**With the Kirkgate Ladies.*

In Harmony

These bonds between choir and audience run deep and have given the Phil its powers of endurance. The story of the first 15 years, from birth to the war is one of constant achievement; there was always 'another mountain to be climbed'. Forced into a 'restart' in 1946 this pattern was repeated until 1976 with each summit higher than the one before. The choir has thrived for 50 years since that last high peak was conquered, and has held on to its quality, its popularity, its reputation, and its founding principles. This has been made easier by the trust between its singers and long serving, skilled and committed music directors. The problems caused by a poor match of choir and conductor were seen in the earlier chapter on York Male Voice Choir, and has also been seen in the life of the Phil. Thankfully the Phil has managed to resolve any such issues without damage, and has been particularly fortunate in its three longest serving conductors, Cecil Fletcher, Brian Lister, and our own Berry Lewis. So the answer to a 'long life' is simple; enjoy your music, do it well, share it with others, and then singers will want to join, and many will want to listen.

At the end of 2015 the Phil has 61 members, a typical number in its life; but what is encouraging is the falling age of recruits in the last three years. Of the last seven new members, two are under the age of 30 with the group having an average age of 46.

This narrative was planned to stop at December 2015. However it has been stretched to the 27th February 2016 when the Phil entered the Mrs Sunderland Competition at Huddersfield. The choir had not been on stage in the Huddersfield

Town Hall since 1994. We gained second prize in the Recital Class competing with six other choirs – all female. In the Male Voice Class there were echoes of the past as it was an open competition and we had a choir of only 33 singers. We came second to Colne Valley – a specialist competition choir – which had nearly 60 men on stage. These were two good results, but the memorable comment on the day came after the performance. A thoughtful Berry, addressing no-one in particular said, *"If I were invited to direct Colne Valley, I wouldn't take it – I couldn't leave you. They are good –very good – but what they do, and how they work is different – it's not us!"* She had no way of knowing how her thoughts echoed those of Cecil Fletcher more than 85 years earlier when he declined the invitation to lead York Male Voice Choir.

So the life cycle of the Phil, successfully and confidently rolls on: staying true to its past; enjoying the present and looking to the future. There is, then, only one way to close this narrative – *TO BE CONTINUED.*

List of abbreviations

AWS ....Archie Sargent
Burton Stone Lane...local term to describe the whole neighbourhood either side of Burton Stone Lane
CHF ....Cecil Fletcher
JHF ....Jack Forster
CWM.........................Cocoa Works Magazine
DM ....Deutschmark – German currency pre-euro
Groves ....Local term to denote the district around Lowther Street and Penleys Grove
Leeman Road ....local term to describe the whole neighbourhood through which Leeman Road passes
LNER........................London and North Eastern Railway
LP ....Long playing record
LRAS ....Leeman Road Adult School
MM............................Münsterscher Männergesangverein now known as MarQant
MVC..........................Male Voice Choir
N&V ....Notes and Views
OP ....York Old Priory Choir
PN.............................Philharmonic News
RBL...........................Richard Brian Lister
SPW .........................S.P. Wilson
The Phil or YPMVC .York Philharmonic Male Voice Choir
YEP ....York Evening Press
YMS..........................York Musical Society
YMVC ....York Male Voice Choir
VPP ....Voices Pipes and Pedals
WGB.........................Walter George Birch
WHB ....William Henry Birch

Acknowledgements

Thanks are due to: Barbara Lister; Brian Sargent; Kathy Pickard; Linda Rodgers; Ken Horwell; David Poole; Jules Slingsby; and the staff at York Explore. Many choir members have helped in particular: James Elliot; Jim Waggott; and Eileen Grey; helped by Steve and Mary Cox; Peter Evans; Robin McDermott; David Pike; Linda and Roger Samwell; Tony Sawyer; Jill Swift; Ludger Voss; Allan Wilkinson; Gerard White; and Keith Wood. Special thanks are due to my wife Hazel, for her patience and for her willingness to comment on and correct the text.

The opinions expressed and any errors made are entirely mine

Retired chorister Fred Luther, whose contributions to the success of continental tours have been acknowledged, died in April 2016 aged 82.

Life member Frank Caine, whose memories of recording with Yorkshire TV are included and whose photograph appears on 203 died in June 2016 aged 84.

About the author

The 50th Year Jubilee Concert in 1975 was the first time Colin sang as a member of the Phil. Since then the choir has played a key role in his life and he has served as chairman, treasurer, producer, soloist, but above all else – chorister. He is not York born, nor even a Yorkshireman, but hails from Barnstaple in North Devon. However, like many others over the years, once settled in York he has never left.

Back Cover 2015 Photograph: Reading from the left back row

D.Gulliver, B.Park, S.Watson, R.McDermott, J.Elliot, T.Knowles, A.Houghton, C.Hockridge, S.Boothman, I.Burks
G.Walton-Pratt, P.Evans, J.Williams, T.Green, D.Pike, M.McGrath

A. Suckling, A. Sawyer, R.Kay, H.Revell, C.Hill, R.Samwell, D.Embleton, A.Durham, I.Reavill, G.Hudson, D.King, A.Wells, J.Waggott,
J.Webster, B.Hunter, R.Prendergast, P.Newman. J.Kirk

Seated: G.Tingle; G.Kay; S.Cox; B.Lewis; P.Smith; E.Grey; G.Edwards; C.Samwell; D.Wilde

Those not shown plus new plus new singing members as at Spring 2016: A. Bolton; F.Caine; C.Dryland; M.Ellerker; G.Greenbank; J.Hanks; S.Healy; M.Johnson; D.Lilley; N Lomas; J.Mackenzie; M.Parrott; D.Price; D.Parkinson; I.Pooley; J.Rutherford; R.Sykes; D.Todd; S.Waggott; M.Wash; S. Winston; G.White; T.Yates,